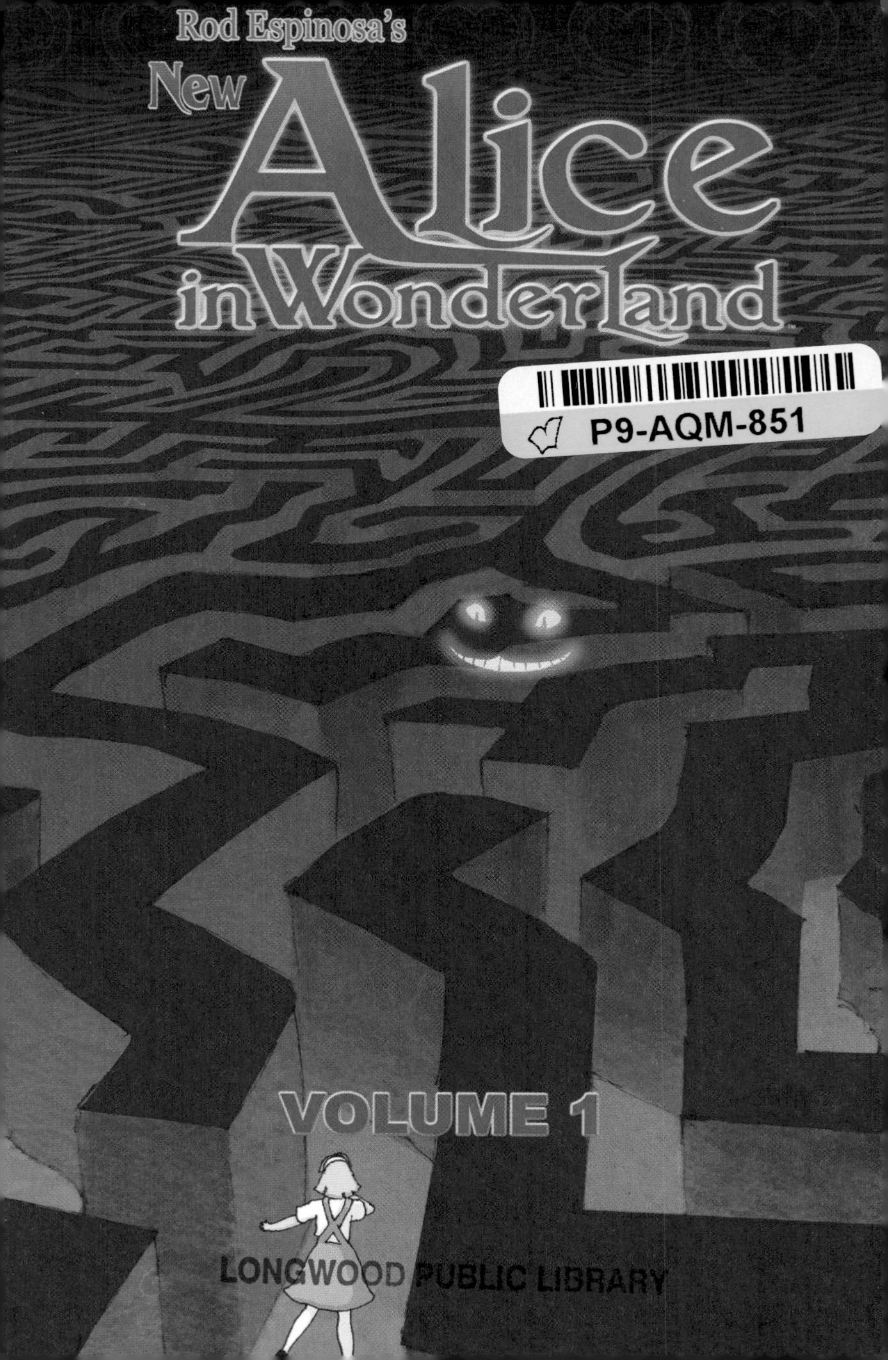
Rod Espinosa's
New
Alice in Wonderland
VOLUME 1

Rod Espinosa's

New Alice in Wonderland ™

Original Story - Lewis Carroll
Adaptation & Art - Rod Espinosa
Graphic Designer - Rod Espinosa
Cover Design - Guru e-FX
Layout - Doug Dlin

Editor in Chief - Jochen Weltjens
President of Sales and Marketing - Lee Duhig
Art Direction - Guru e-FX
VP of Production - Rod Espinosa
Publishing Manager - Chris Aguilar
Publisher - Joe Dunn
Founder - Ben Dunn

Come visit us online at www.antarctic-press.com

New Alice in Wonderland Volume 1 by Rod Espinosa
An Antarctic Press Color Manga

Antarctic Press
7272 Wurzbach Suite 204 San Antonio, TX 78240

Collects *New Alice in Wonderland* issue 1-4
First published in 2005 by Antarctic Press.

New Alice in Wonderland, July 2006.

"'You're not going to say something like "Oh, my paws and whiskers," are
you?' she said quietly."

ISBN-10: 0-9768043-8-7
ISBN-13: 978-0-9768043-8-3

Printed and bound in China.

VOLUME 1

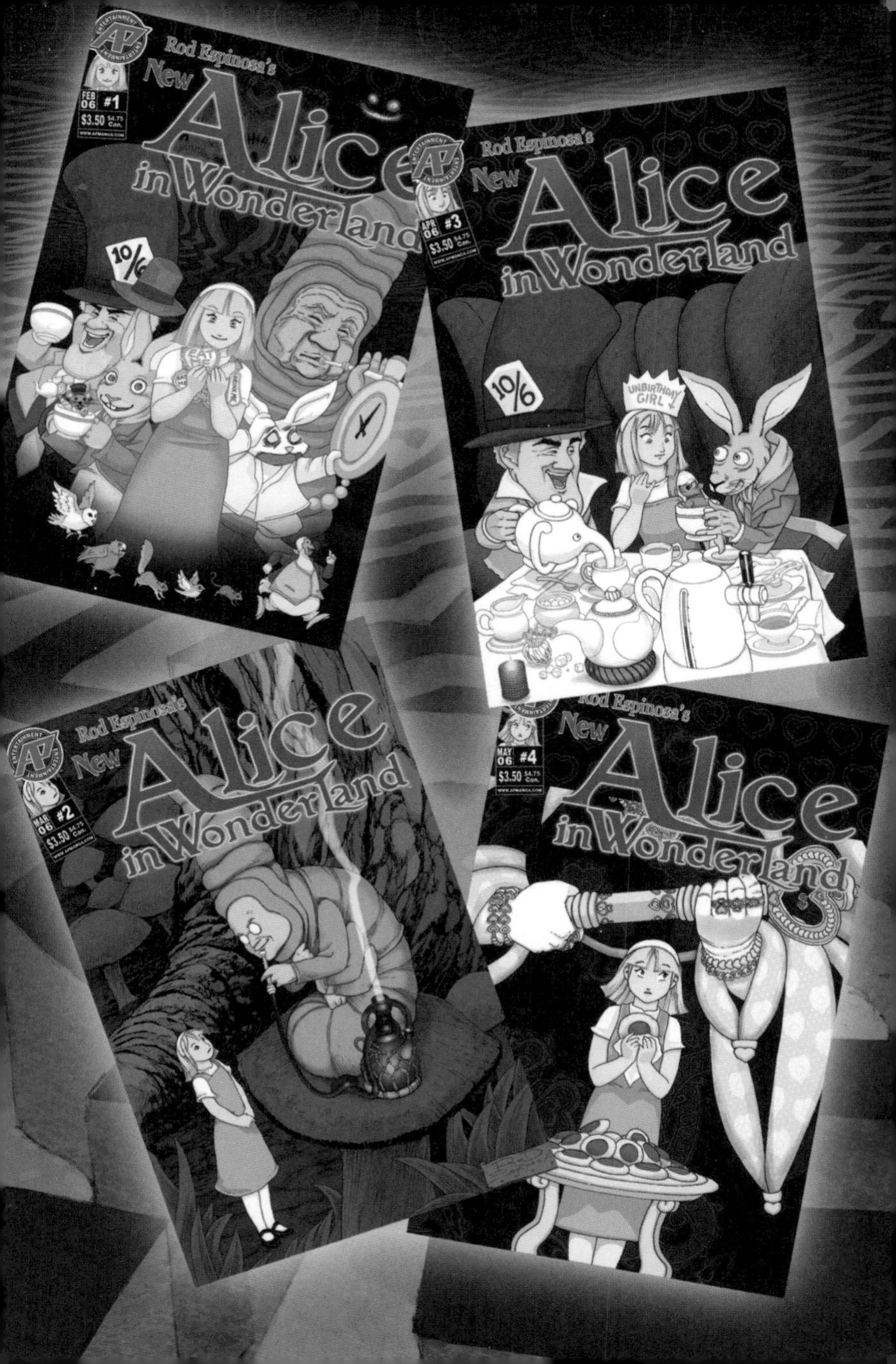
Rod Espinosa's
New
Alice in Wonderland
FEB 06 #1
$3.50 $4.75 Can.
10/6
Rod Espinosa's
New
Alice in Wonderland
APR 06 #3
$3.50 $4.75 Can.
10/6
UNBIRTHDAY GIRL
Rod Espinosa's
New
Alice in Wonderland
MAR 06 #2
$3.50 $4.75 Can.
Rod Espinosa's
New
Alice in Wonderland
MAY 06 #4
$3.50 $4.75 Can.

Introduction

It's a funny story how all this came about. It began during a late-night conversation at a 24-hour restaurant. David Hutchison, author and writer of many manga books in his own right, mentioned to me that he was thinking of doing his own version of The Wizard of Oz. I thought it was a brilliant idea. Then it got me thinking, "I want to do a classic adaptation of my own!" What better title to mirror his choice than Alice in Wonderland?

Working on Lewis Carroll's classic has been a great experience. At first, I had many ideas of what to insert, modernize or change. But as I read the source material and appreciated the beauty of the story for itself, I realized the original story was a very good one and I had to be faithful to the basic narrative. From there, it has been quite an adventure translating this story into comic form. It's been a treat paying homage to John Tenniel, Arthur Rackham, and of course, Walt Disney.

It's been reward enough to be able to travel through a famous author's world, participate in it, and hopefully contribute something positive to it. It has been an honor and a privilege to translate one of the most beloved classics into comic book form for people to read and enjoy. I've had my fun making it. Now it's your turn to have fun! Enjoy the show!

-- Rod Espinosa
May 2006

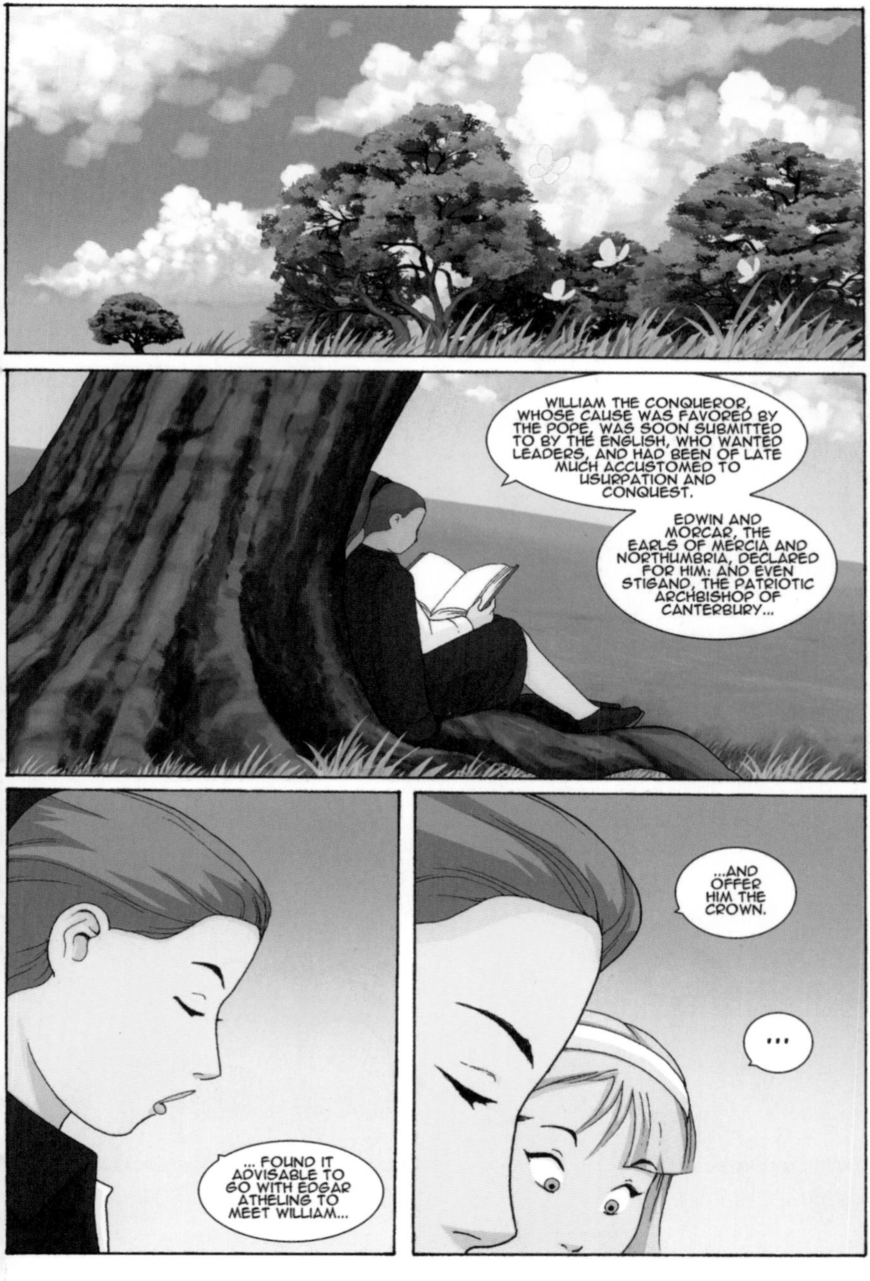
WILLIAM THE CONQUEROR, WHOSE CAUSE WAS FAVORED BY THE POPE, WAS SOON SUBMITTED TO BY THE ENGLISH, WHO WANTED LEADERS, AND HAD BEEN OF LATE MUCH ACCUSTOMED TO USURPATION AND CONQUEST.
EDWIN AND MORCAR, THE EARLS OF MERCIA AND NORTHUMBRIA, DECLARED FOR HIM: AND EVEN STIGAND, THE PATRIOTIC ARCHBISHOP OF CANTERBURY...
... FOUND IT ADVISABLE TO GO WITH EDGAR ATHELING TO MEET WILLIAM...
...AND OFFER HIM THE CROWN.
...

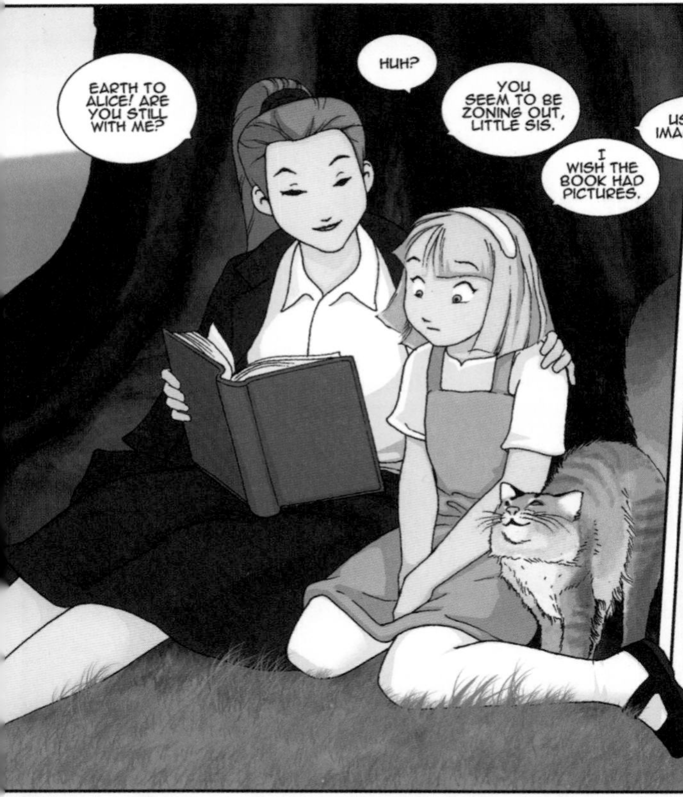
EARTH TO ALICE! ARE YOU STILL WITH ME?
HUH?
YOU SEEM TO BE ZONING OUT, LITTLE SIS.
I WISH THE BOOK HAD PICTURES.
USE YOUR IMAGINATION, DEAR.

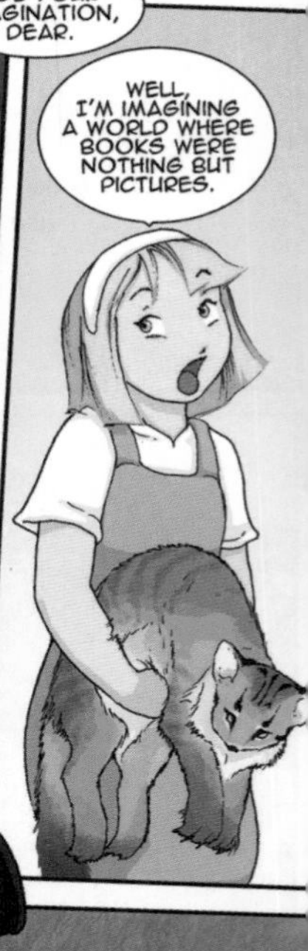
WELL, I'M IMAGINING A WORLD WHERE BOOKS WERE NOTHING BUT PICTURES.

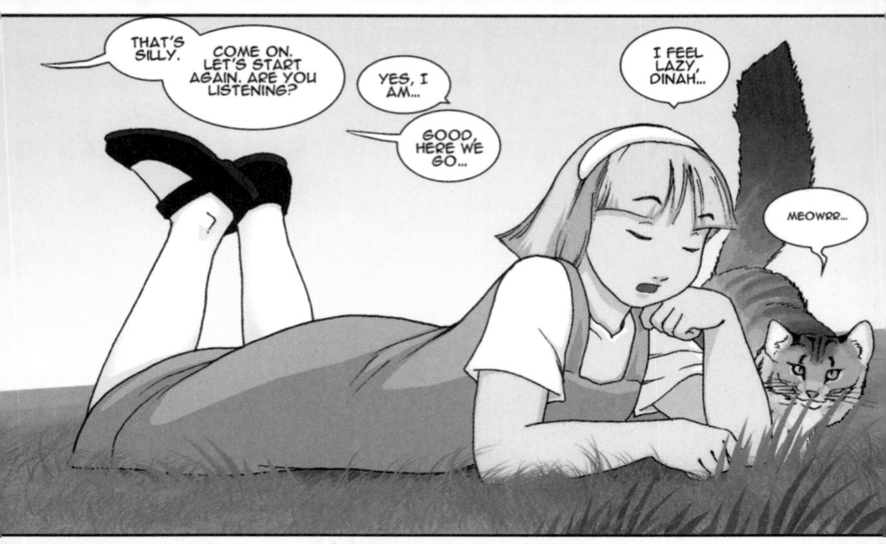
THAT'S SILLY.
COME ON. LET'S START AGAIN. ARE YOU LISTENING?
YES, I AM...
GOOD, HERE WE GO...
I FEEL LAZY, DINAH...
MEOWRR...

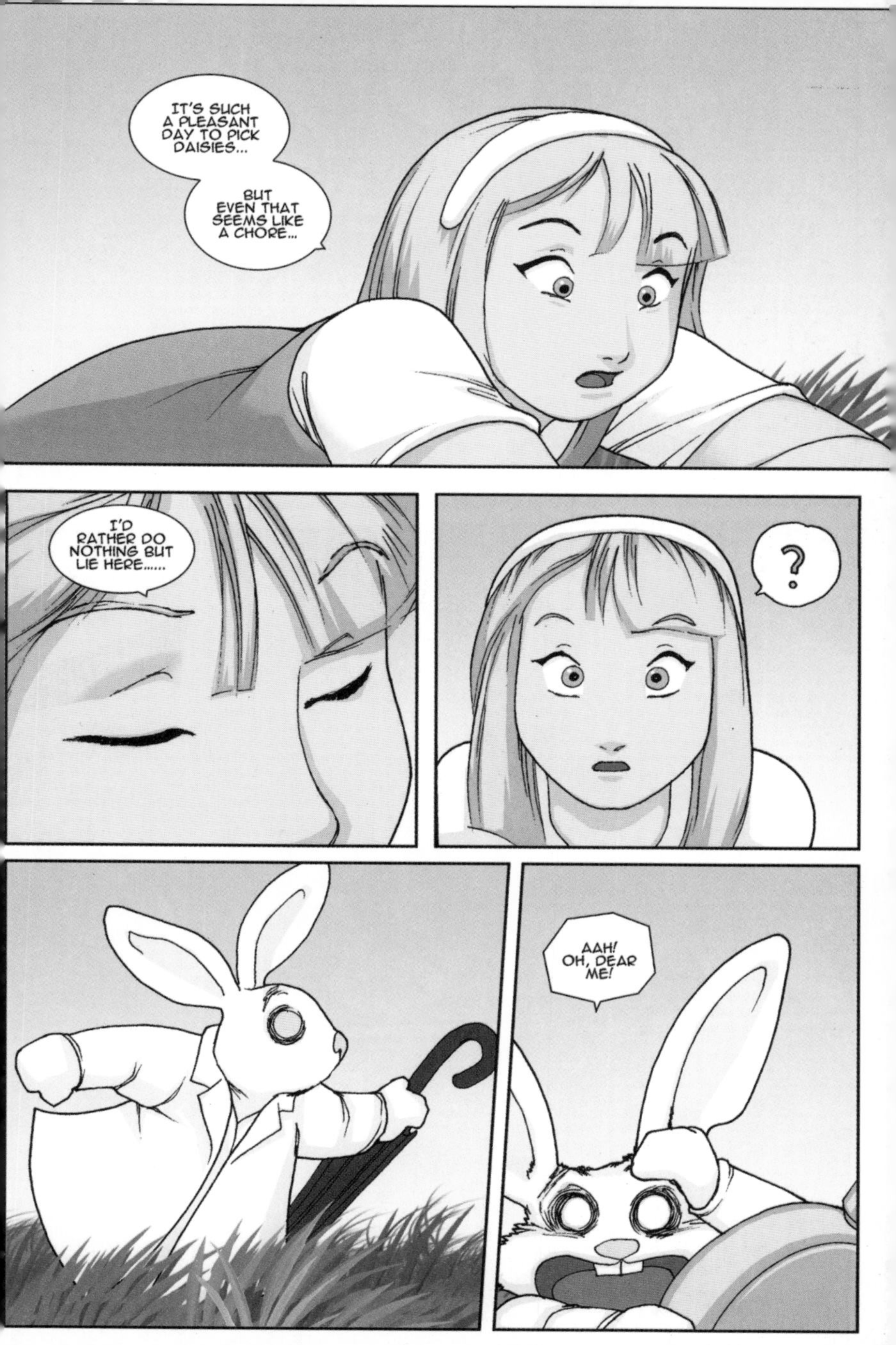
IT'S SUCH A PLEASANT DAY TO PICK DAISIES...
BUT EVEN THAT SEEMS LIKE A CHORE...
I'D RATHER DO NOTHING BUT LIE HERE......
?
AAH! OH, DEAR ME!

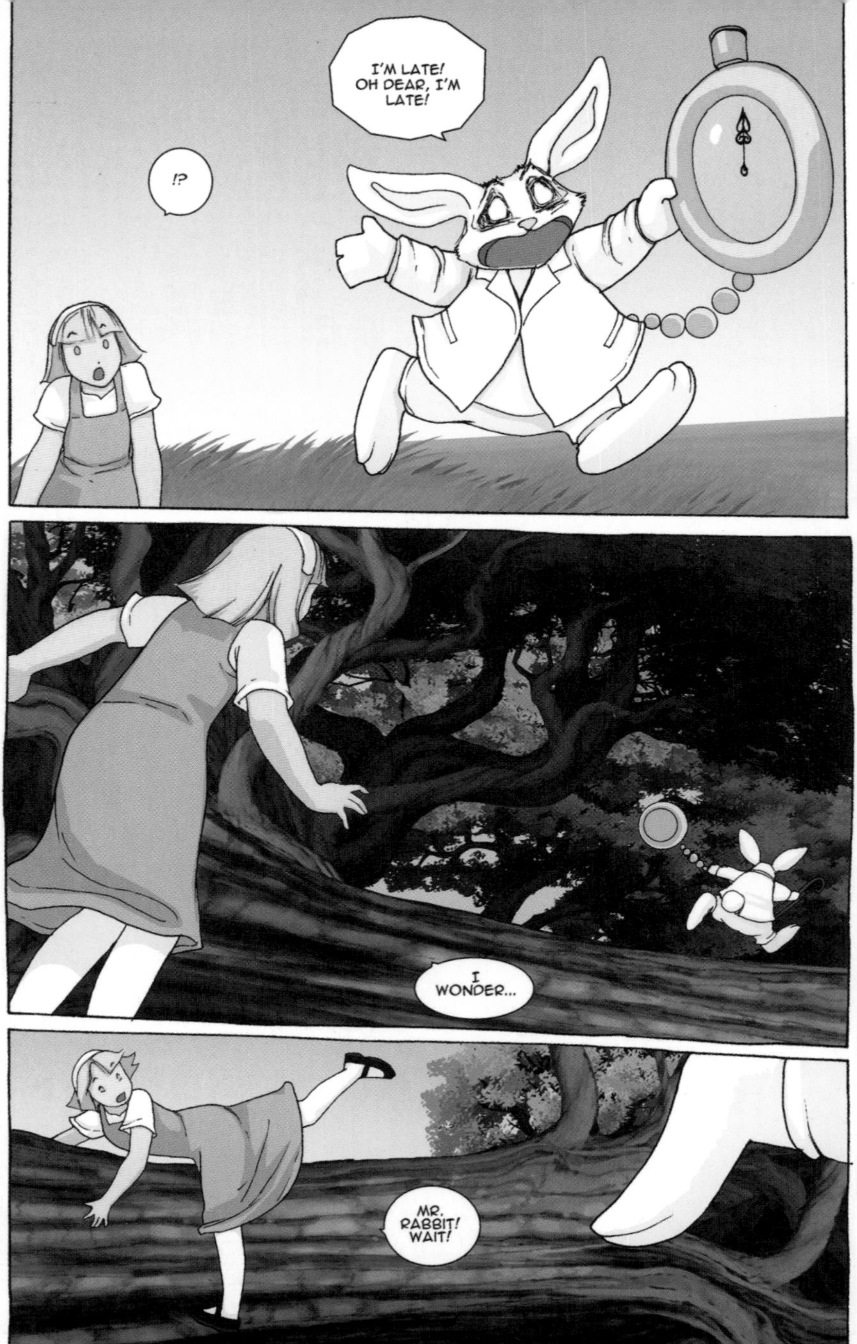
I'M LATE! OH DEAR, I'M LATE!
!?
I WONDER...
MR. RABBIT! WAIT!

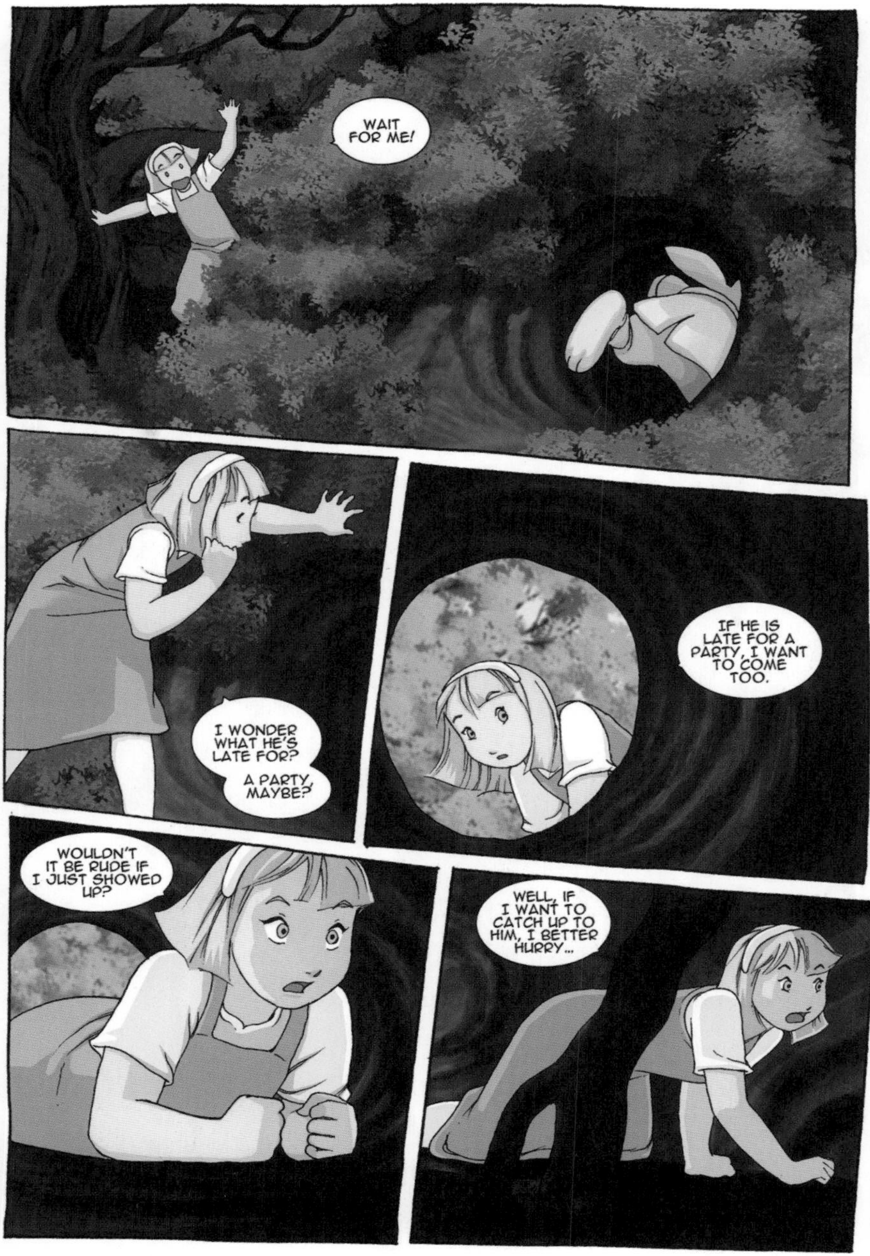
WAIT FOR ME!
I WONDER WHAT HE'S LATE FOR?
A PARTY, MAYBE?
IF HE IS LATE FOR A PARTY, I WANT TO COME TOO.
WOULDN'T IT BE RUDE IF I JUST SHOWED UP?
WELL, IF I WANT TO CATCH UP TO HIM, I BETTER HURRY...

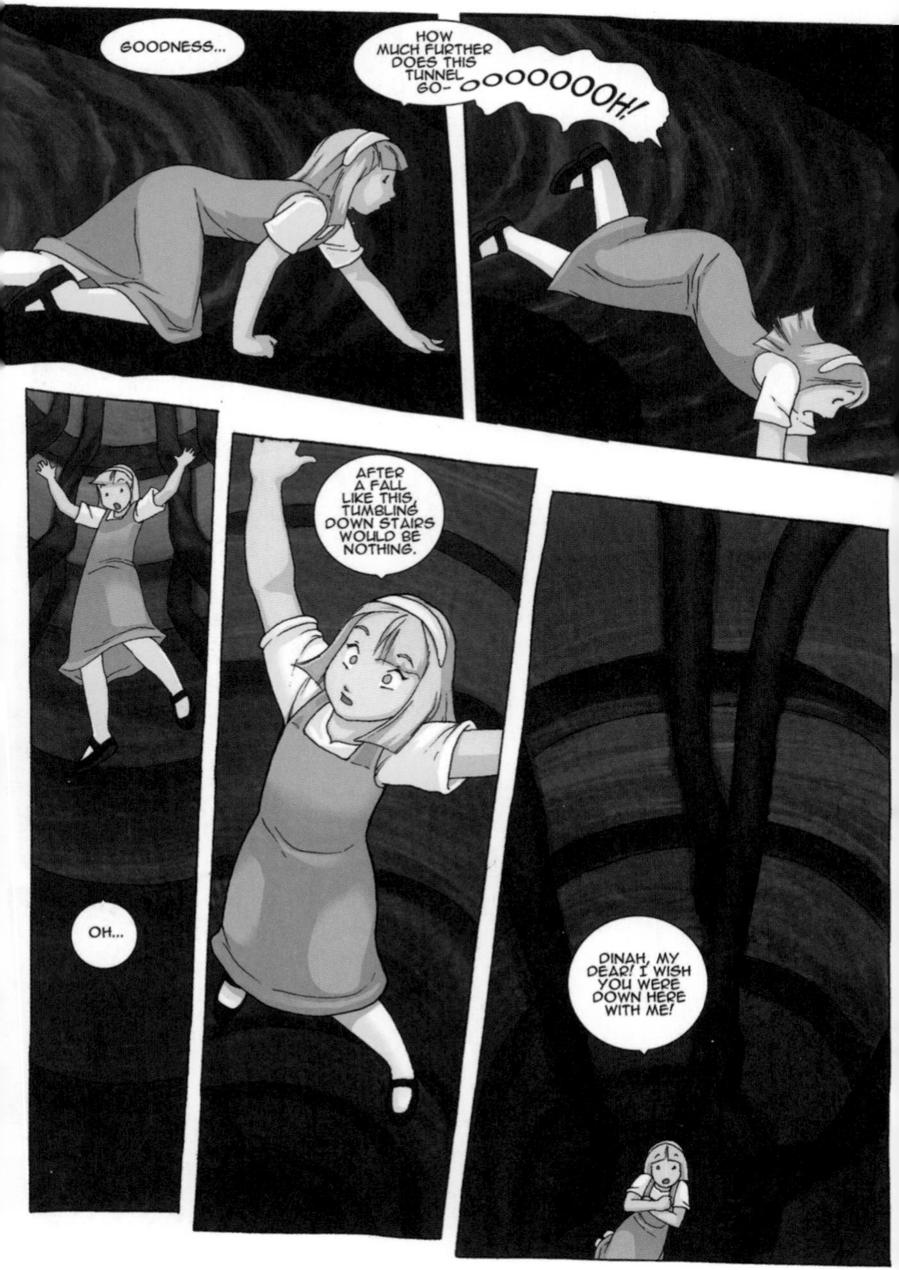
GOODNESS...
HOW MUCH FURTHER DOES THIS TUNNEL GO- OOOOOOOOH!
OH...
AFTER A FALL LIKE THIS, TUMBLING DOWN STAIRS WOULD BE NOTHING.
DINAH, MY DEAR! I WISH YOU WERE DOWN HERE WITH ME!

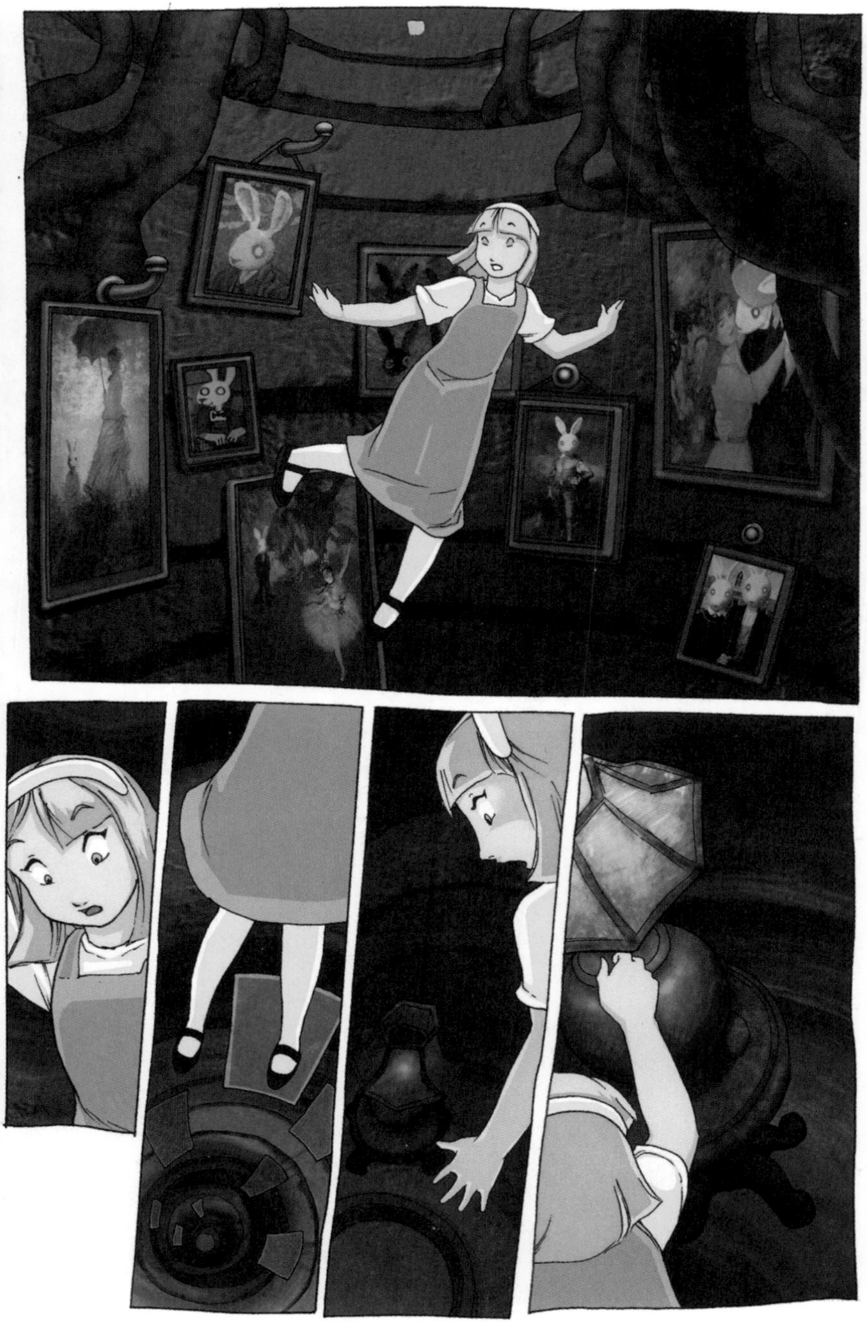

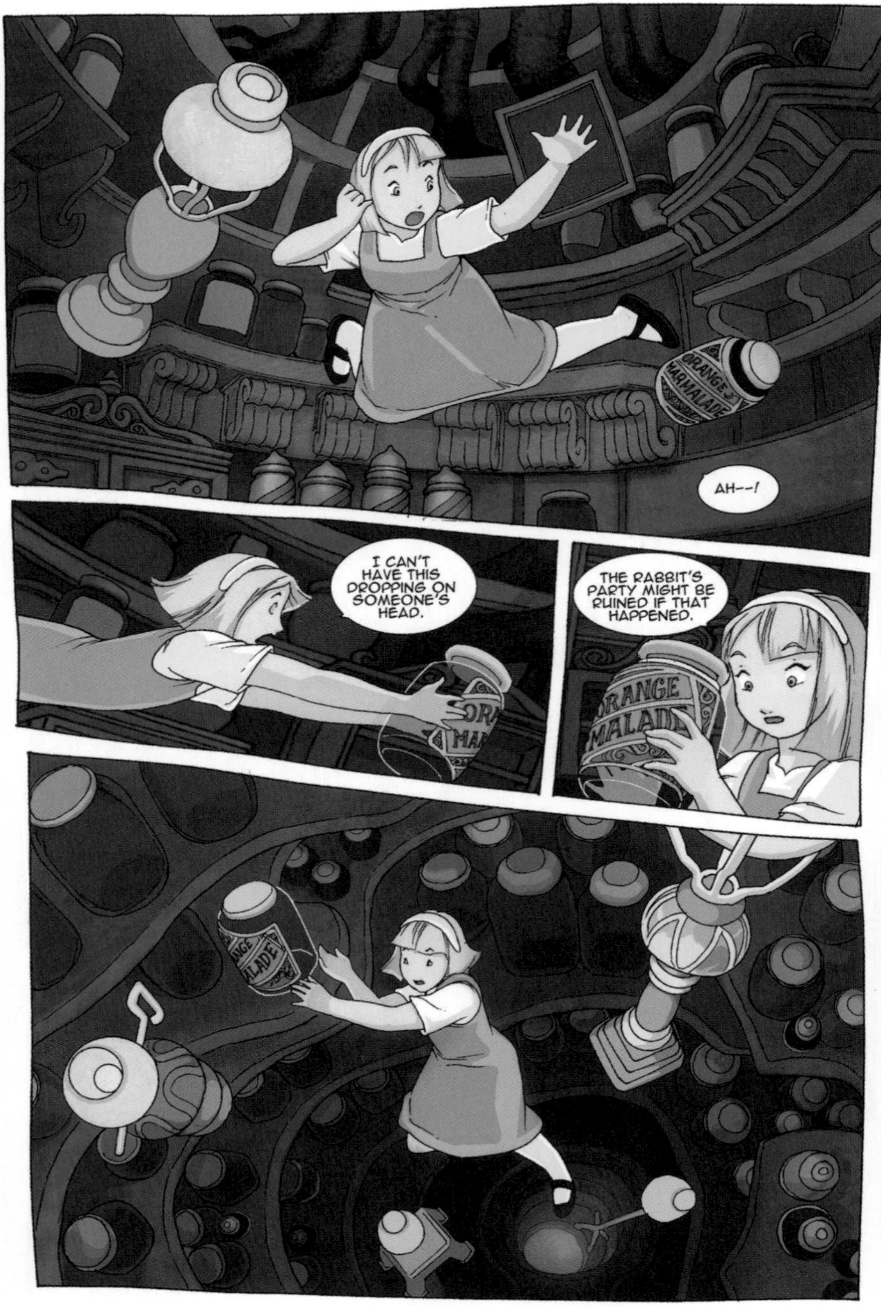
ORANGE MARMALADE
AH--!
I CAN'T HAVE THIS DROPPING ON SOMEONE'S HEAD.
THE RABBIT'S PARTY MIGHT BE RUINED IF THAT HAPPENED.

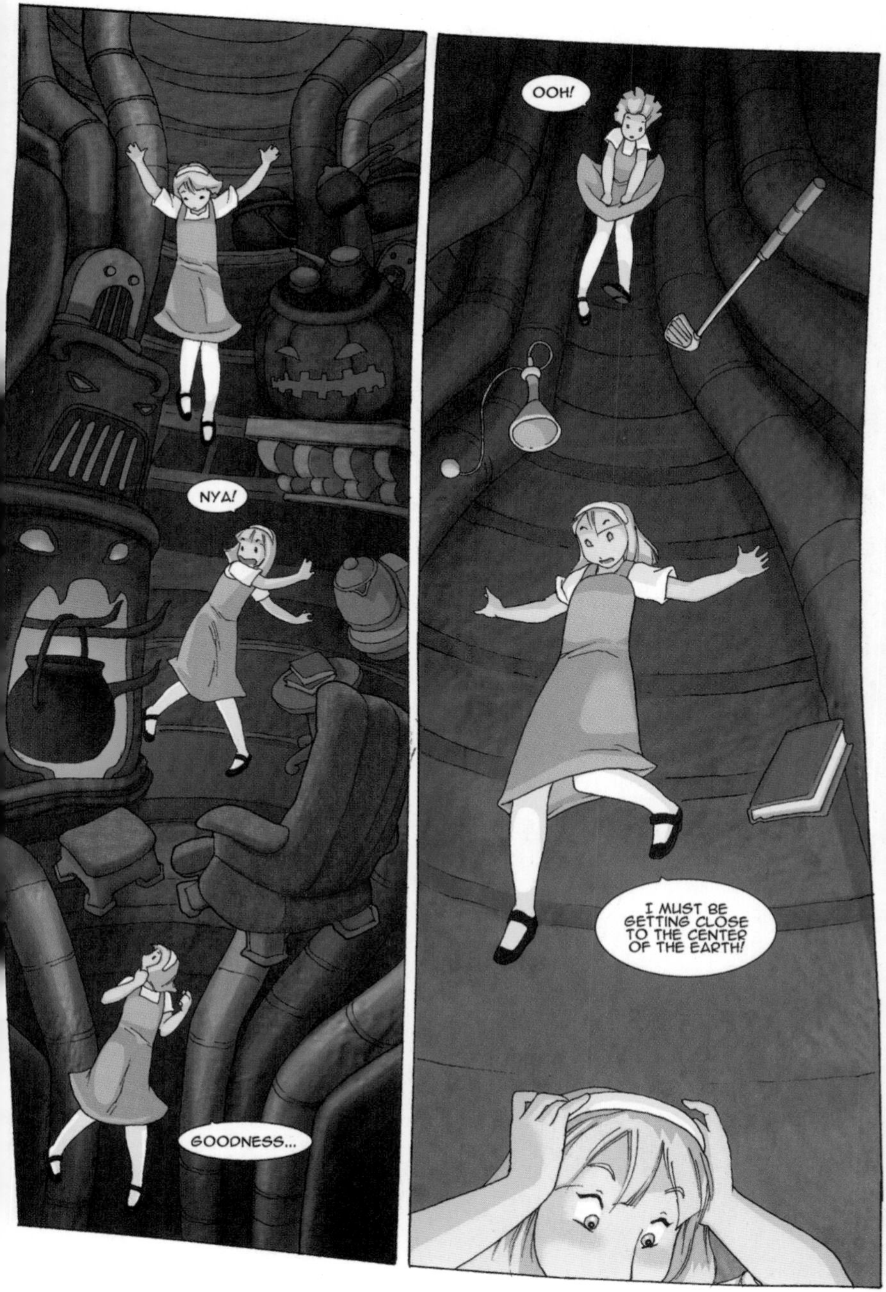
NYA!
GOODNESS...
OOH!
I MUST BE GETTING CLOSE TO THE CENTER OF THE EARTH!

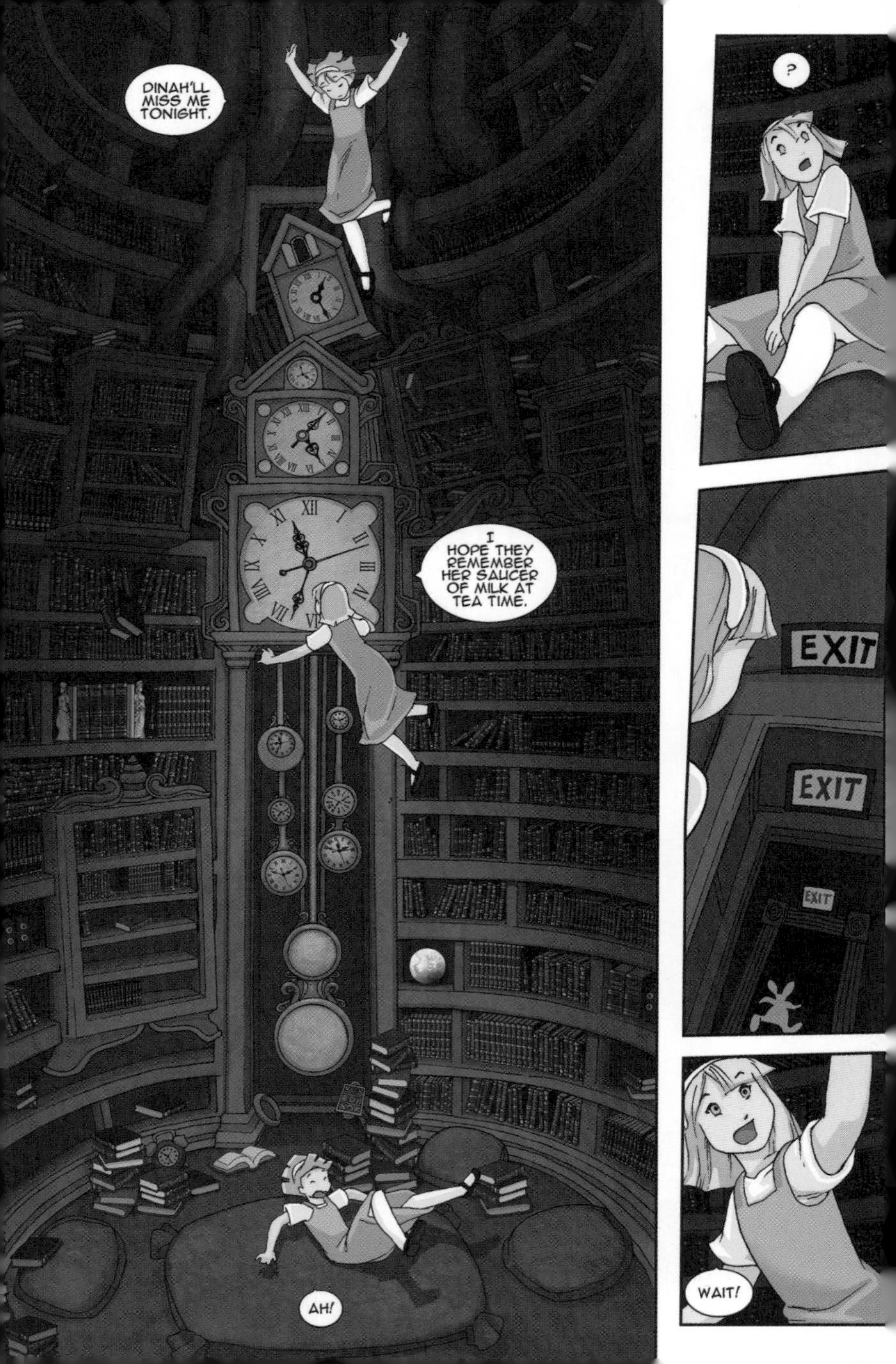
DINAH'LL MISS ME TONIGHT.
I HOPE THEY REMEMBER HER SAUCER OF MILK AT TEA TIME.
AH!
?
EXIT
EXIT
EXIT
WAIT!

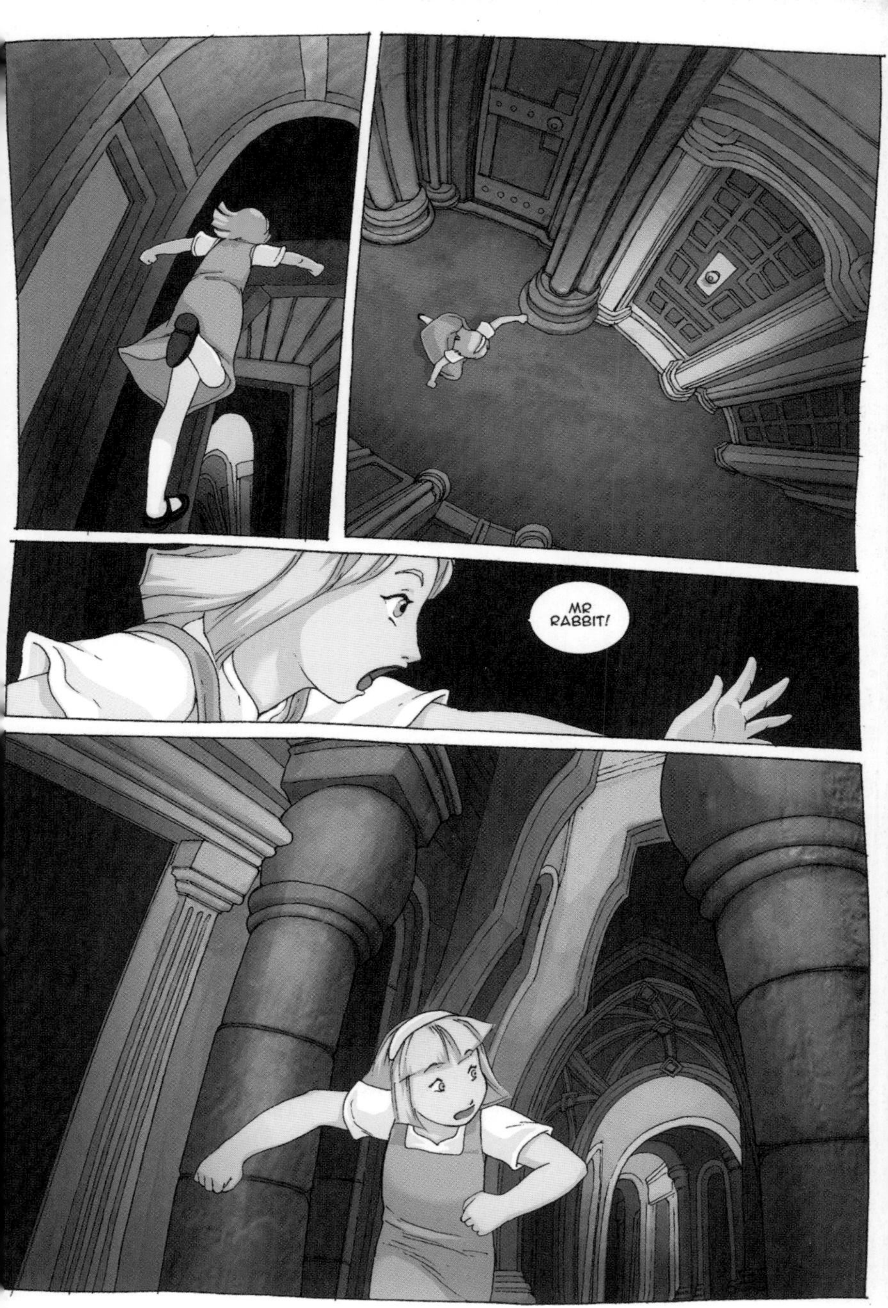
MR RABBIT!

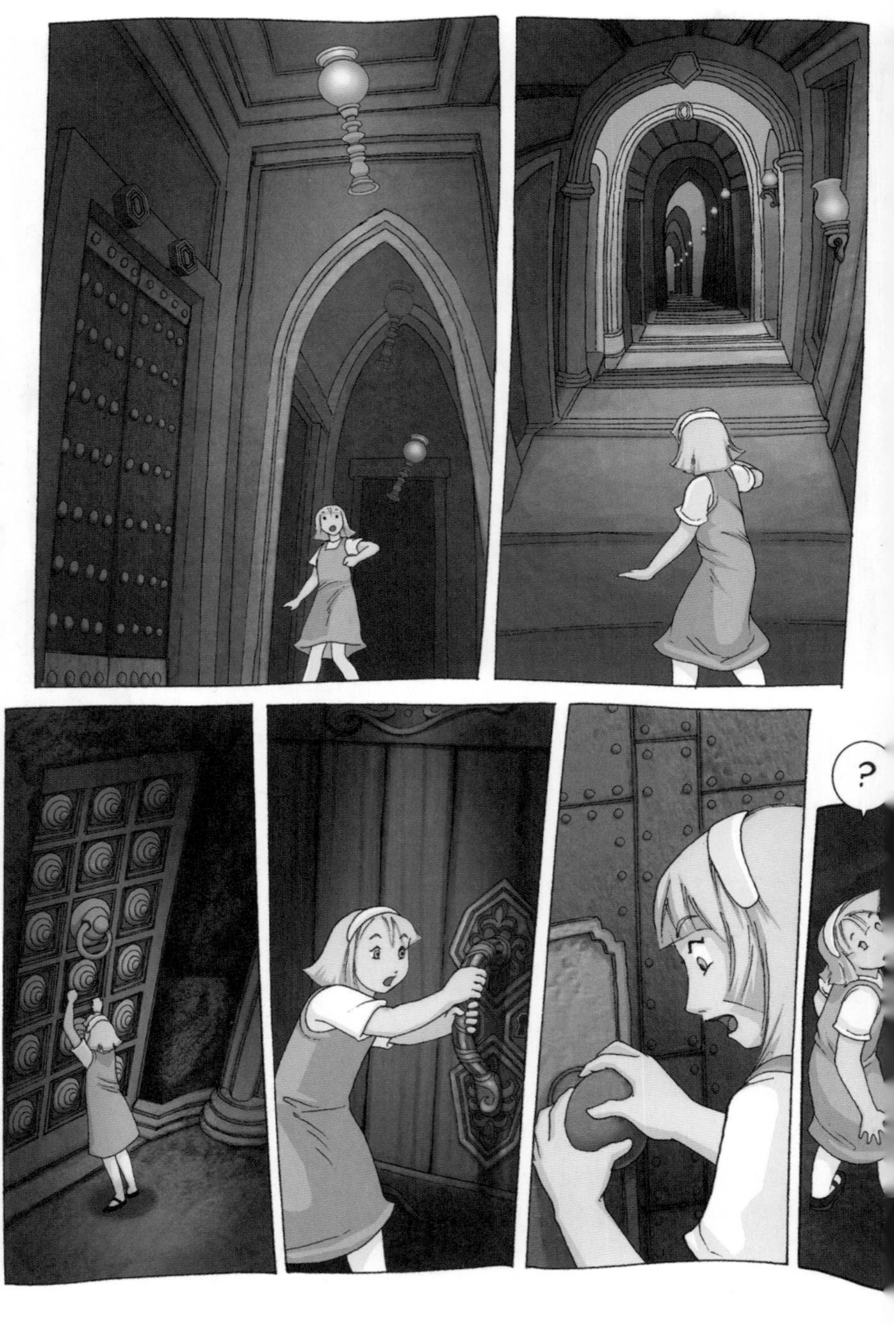
?

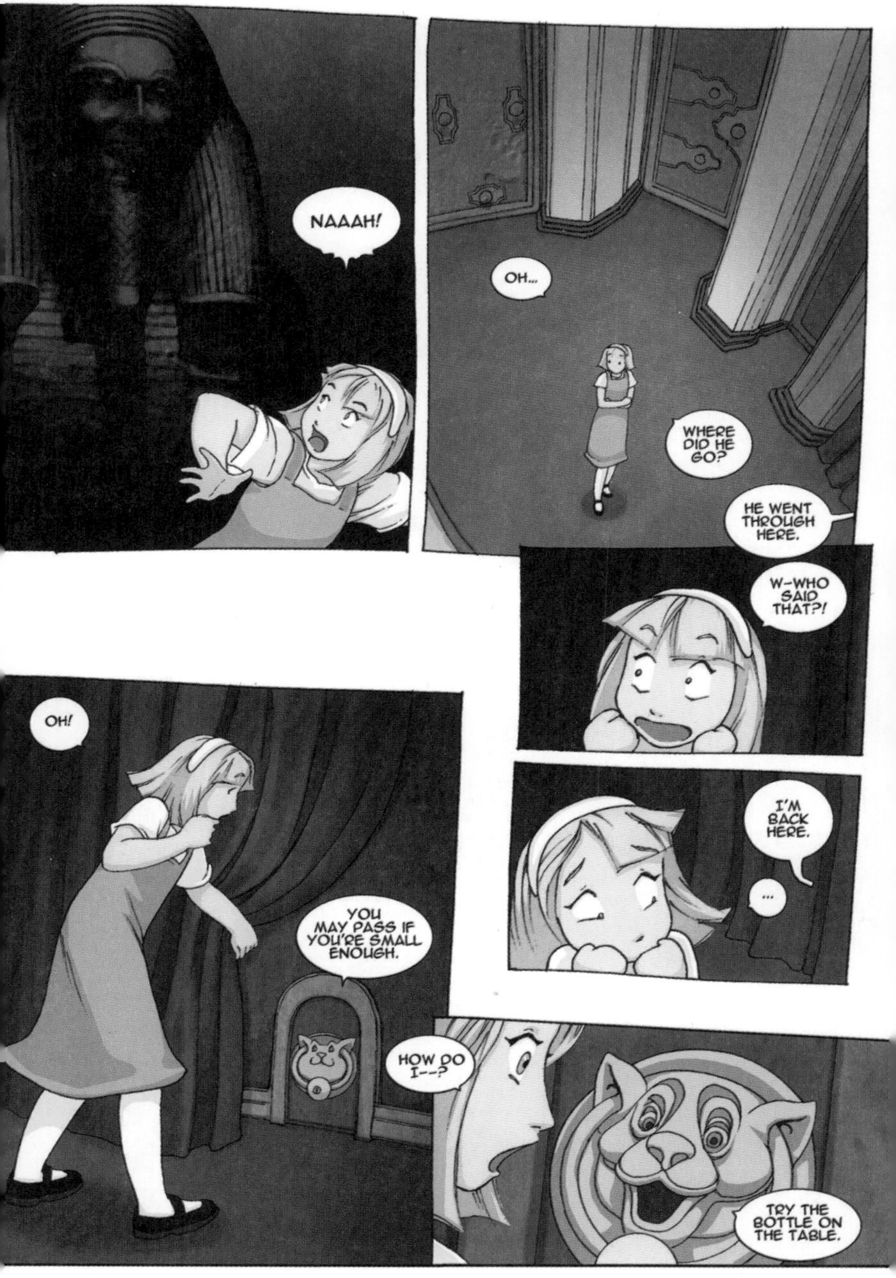
NAAAH!
OH...
WHERE DID HE GO?
HE WENT THROUGH HERE.
W-WHO SAID THAT?!
I'M BACK HERE.
...
OH!
YOU MAY PASS IF YOU'RE SMALL ENOUGH.
HOW DO I--?
TRY THE BOTTLE ON THE TABLE.

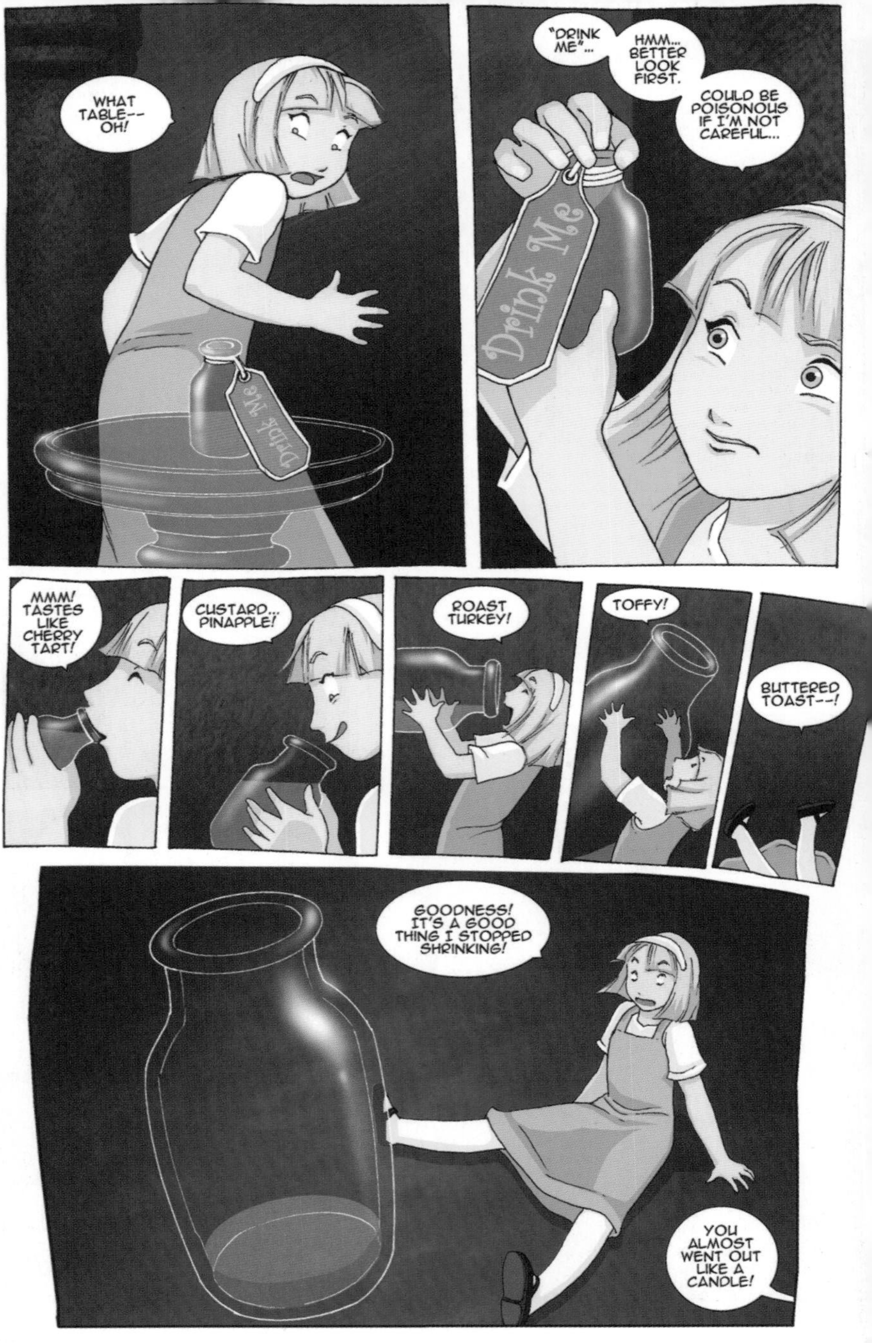
WHAT TABLE--OH!
"DRINK ME"...
HMM... BETTER LOOK FIRST.
COULD BE POISONOUS IF I'M NOT CAREFUL...
Drink Me
MMM! TASTES LIKE CHERRY TART!
CUSTARD... PINAPPLE!
ROAST TURKEY!
TOFFY!
BUTTERED TOAST--!
GOODNESS! IT'S A GOOD THING I STOPPED SHRINKING!
YOU ALMOST WENT OUT LIKE A CANDLE!

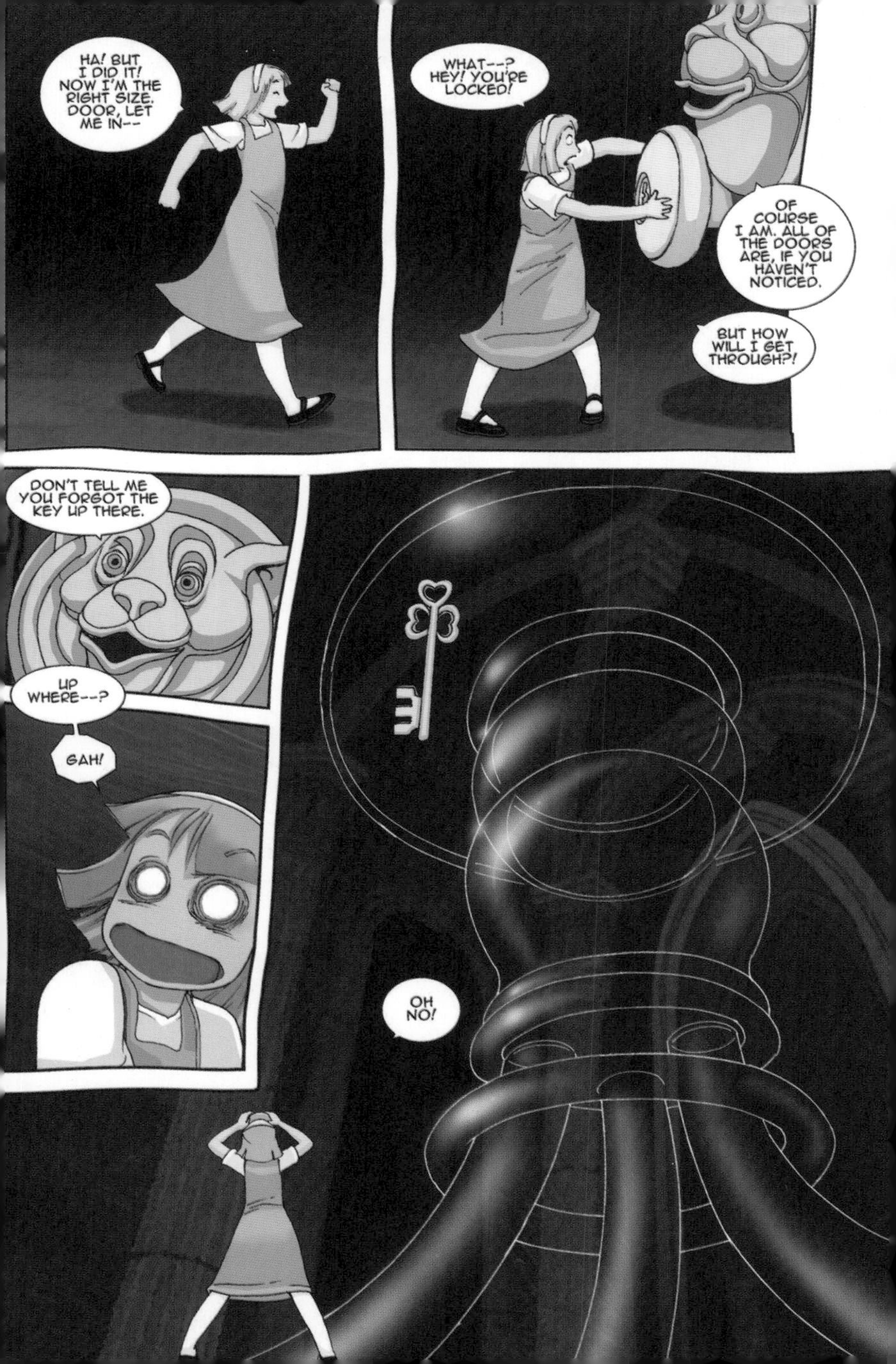
HA! BUT I DID IT! NOW I'M THE RIGHT SIZE. DOOR, LET ME IN--
WHAT--? HEY! YOU'RE LOCKED!
OF COURSE I AM. ALL OF THE DOORS ARE, IF YOU HAVEN'T NOTICED.
BUT HOW WILL I GET THROUGH?!
DON'T TELL ME YOU FORGOT THE KEY UP THERE.
UP WHERE--?
GAH!
OH NO!

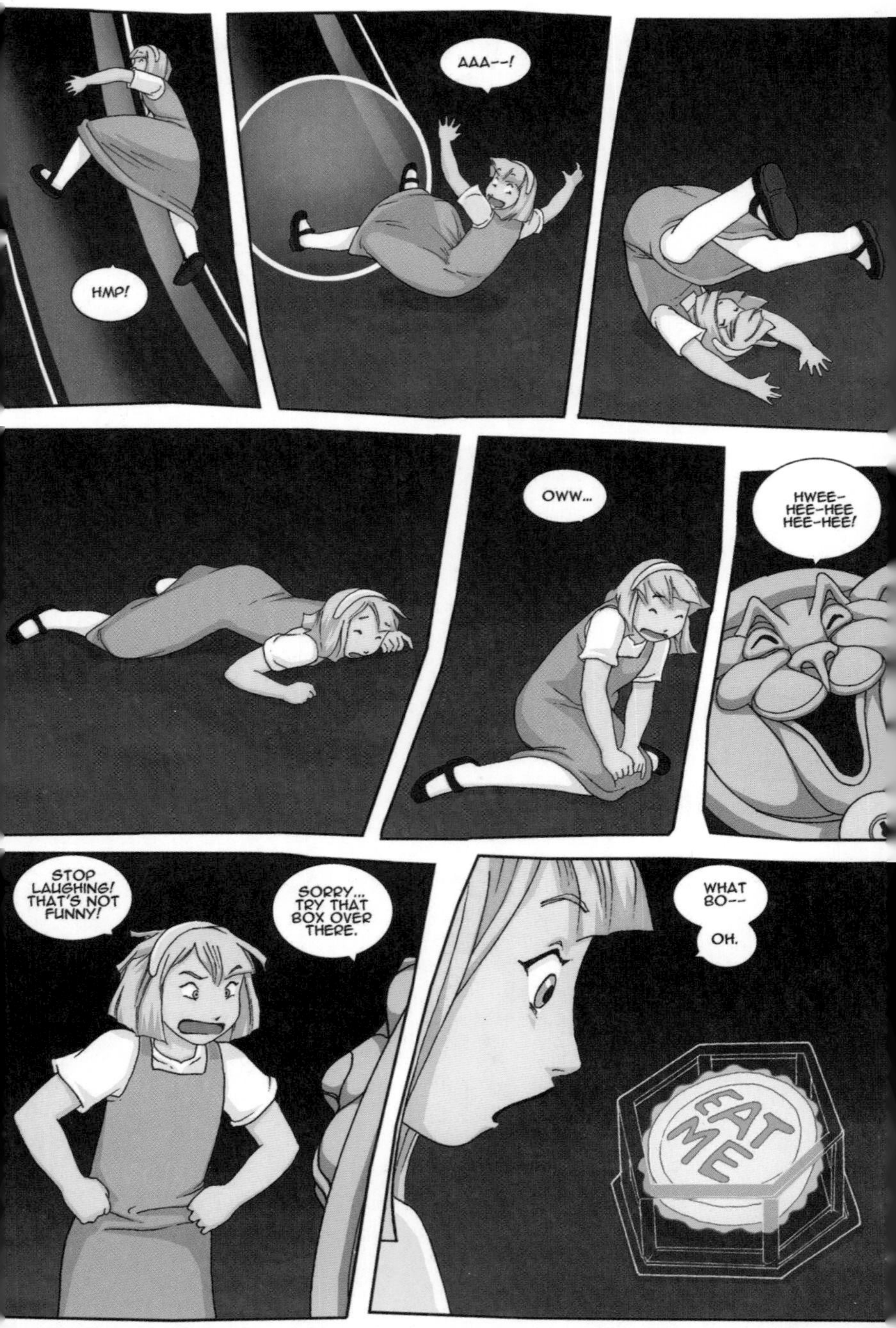
HMP!
AAA--!
OWW...
HWEE-HEE-HEE HEE-HEE!
STOP LAUGHING! THAT'S NOT FUNNY!
SORRY... TRY THAT BOX OVER THERE.
WHAT BO--
OH.
EAT ME

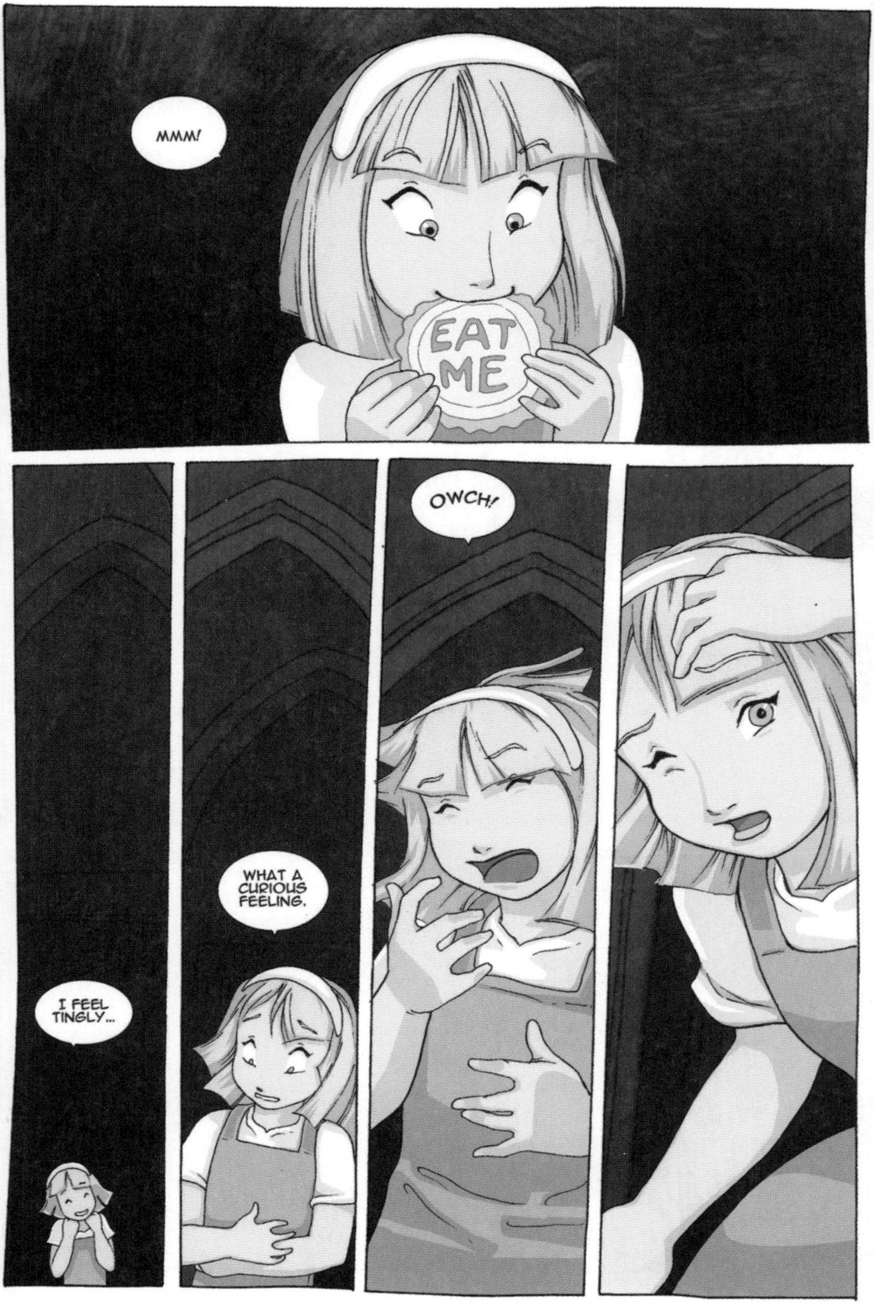
MMM!
EAT ME
I FEEL TINGLY...
WHAT A CURIOUS FEELING.
OWCH!

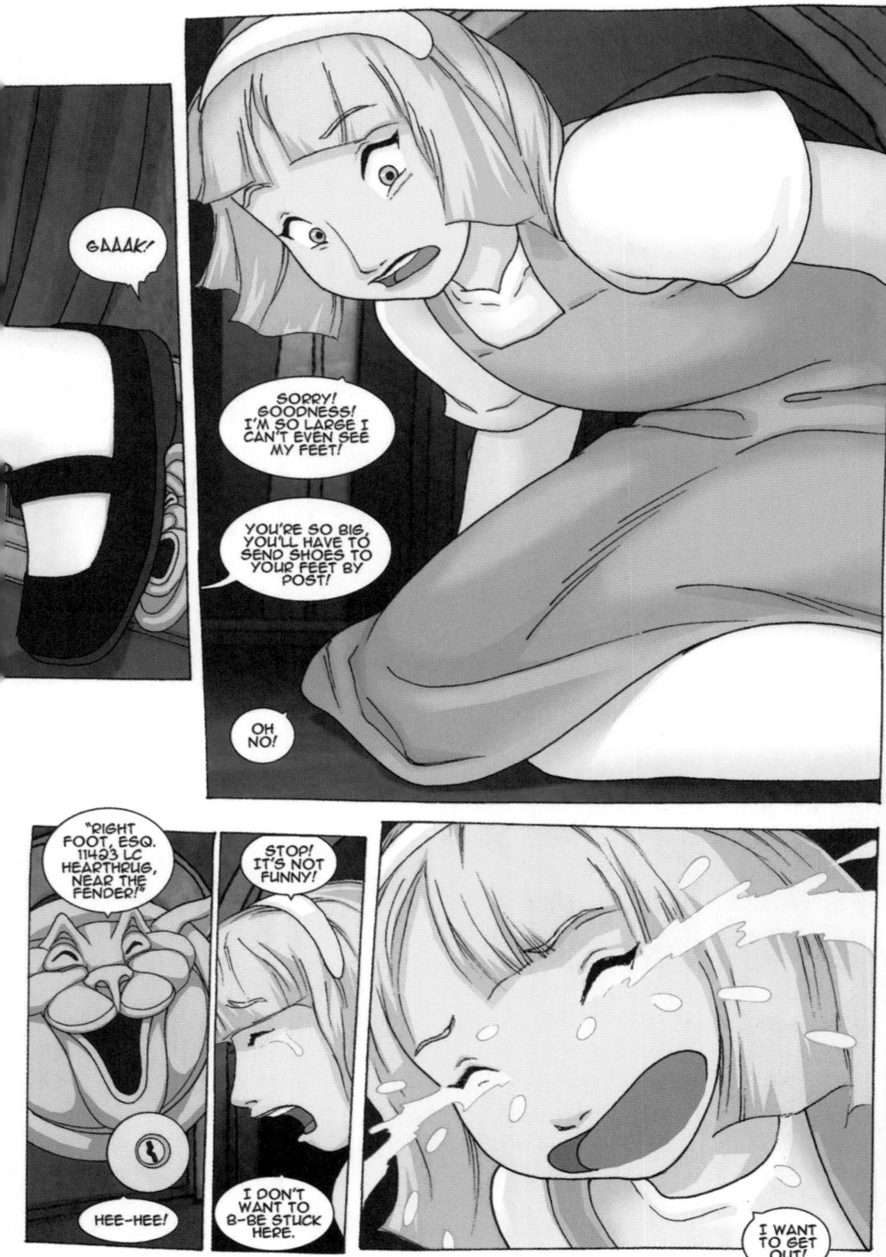
GAAAK!
SORRY! GOODNESS! I'M SO LARGE I CAN'T EVEN SEE MY FEET!
YOU'RE SO BIG, YOU'LL HAVE TO SEND SHOES TO YOUR FEET BY POST!
OH NO!
"RIGHT FOOT, ESQ. 11423 LC HEARTHRUG, NEAR THE FENDER!"
HEE-HEE!
STOP! IT'S NOT FUNNY!
I DON'T WANT TO B-BE STUCK HERE.
I WANT TO GET OUT!

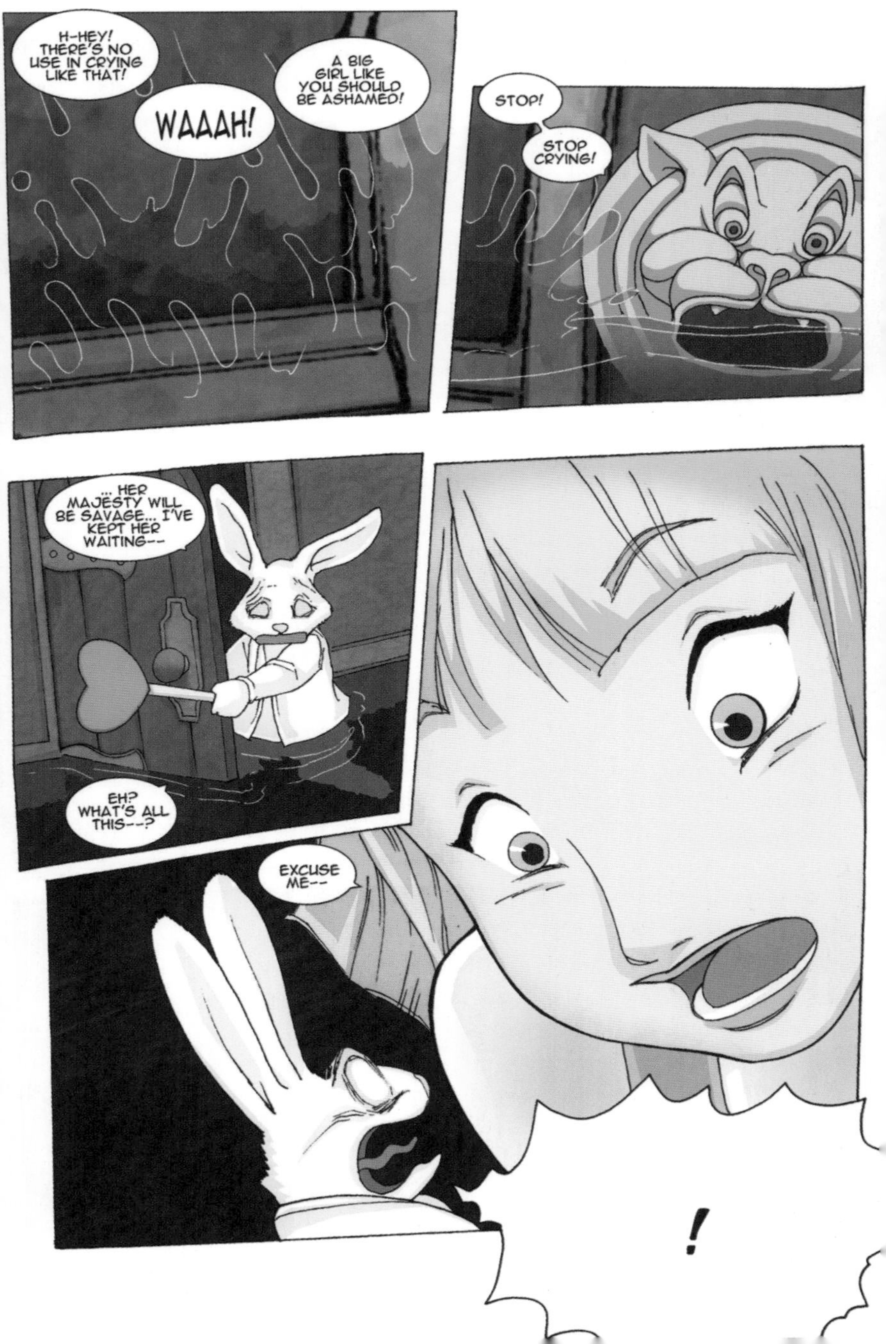
H-HEY! THERE'S NO USE IN CRYING LIKE THAT!
WAAAH!
A BIG GIRL LIKE YOU SHOULD BE ASHAMED!
STOP!
STOP CRYING!
... HER MAJESTY WILL BE SAVAGE... I'VE KEPT HER WAITING--
EH? WHAT'S ALL THIS--?
EXCUSE ME--
!

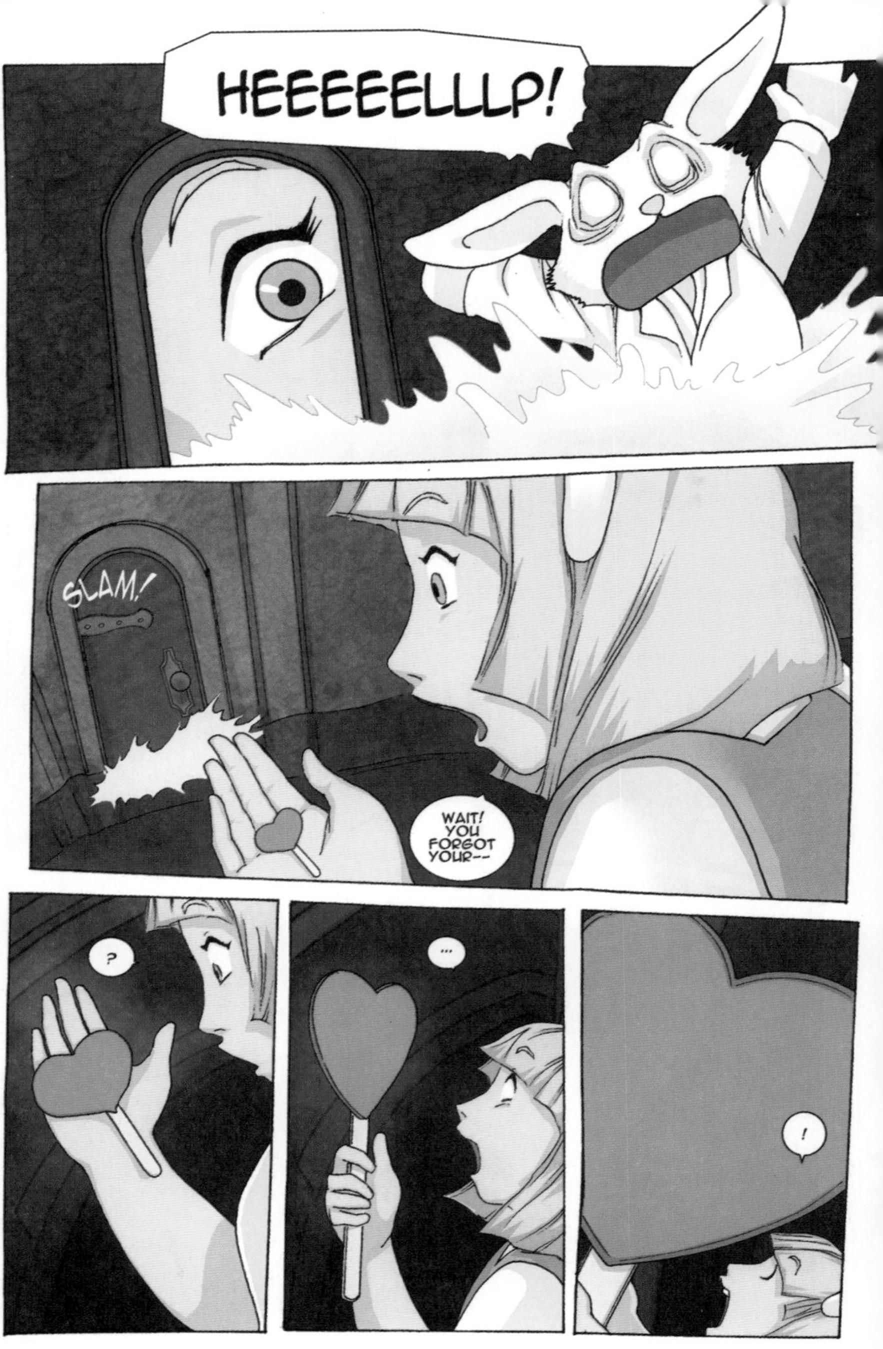
HEEEEEELLLLP!
SLAM!
WAIT! YOU FORGOT YOUR--
?
...
!

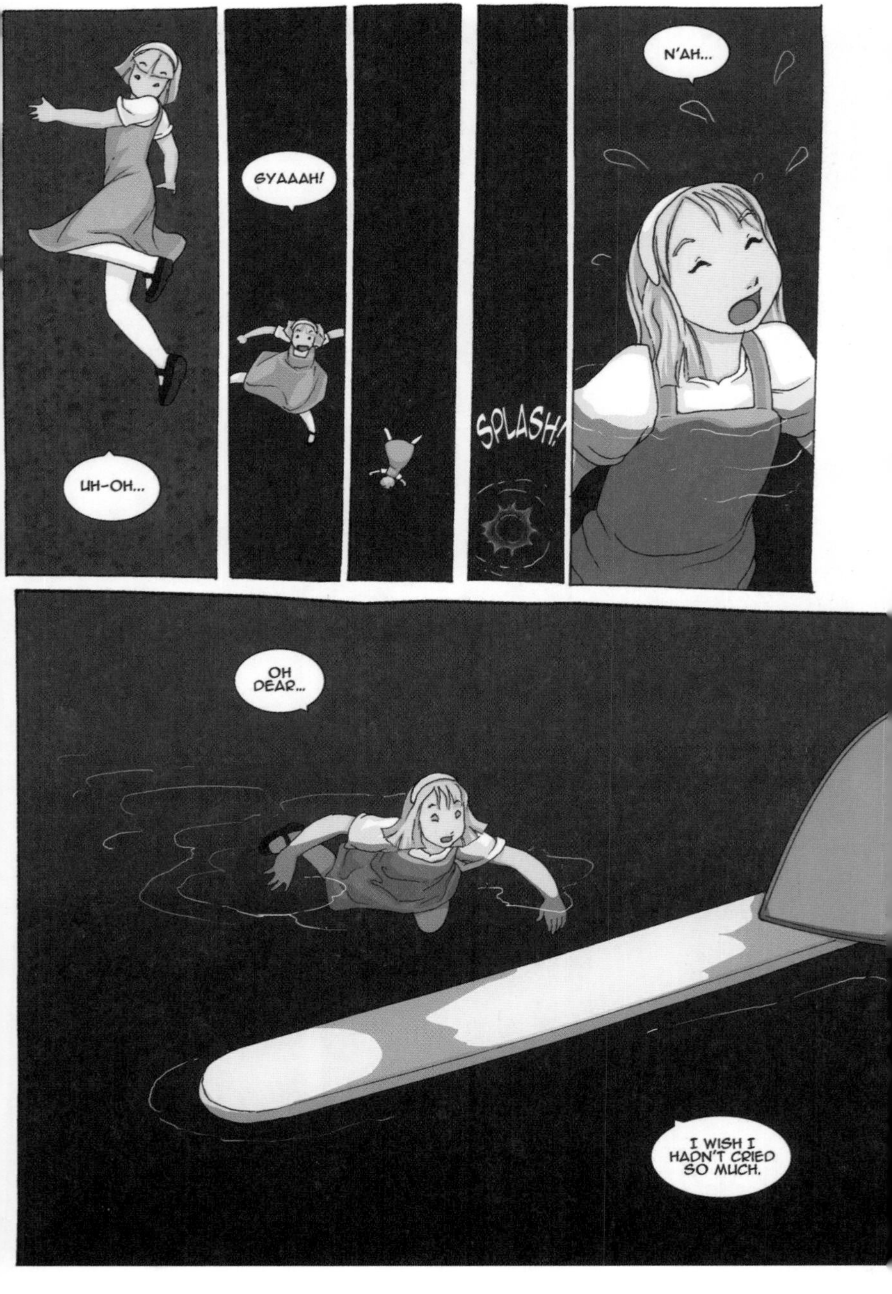
UH-OH...
GYAAAH!
SPLASH!
N'AH...
OH DEAR...
I WISH I HADN'T CRIED SO MUCH.

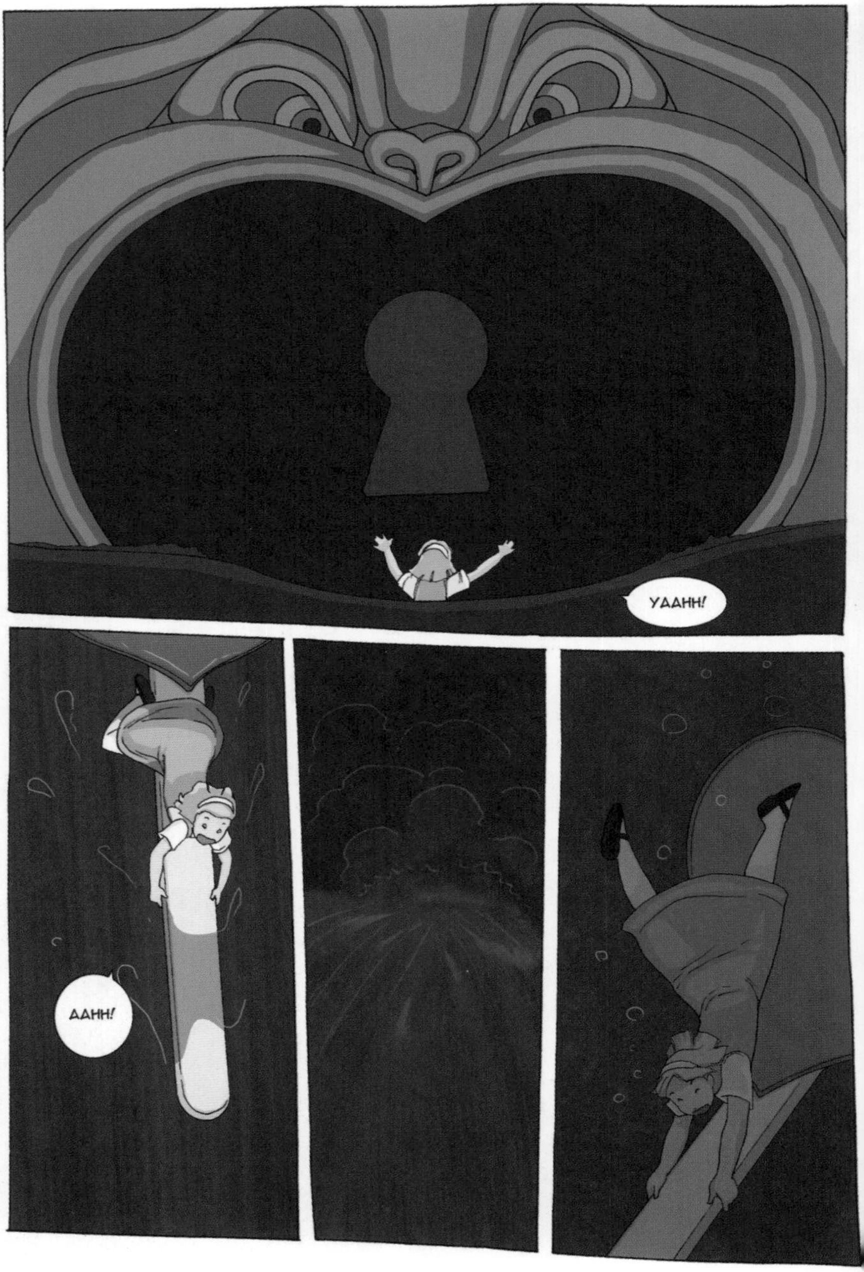
YAAHH!
AAHH!

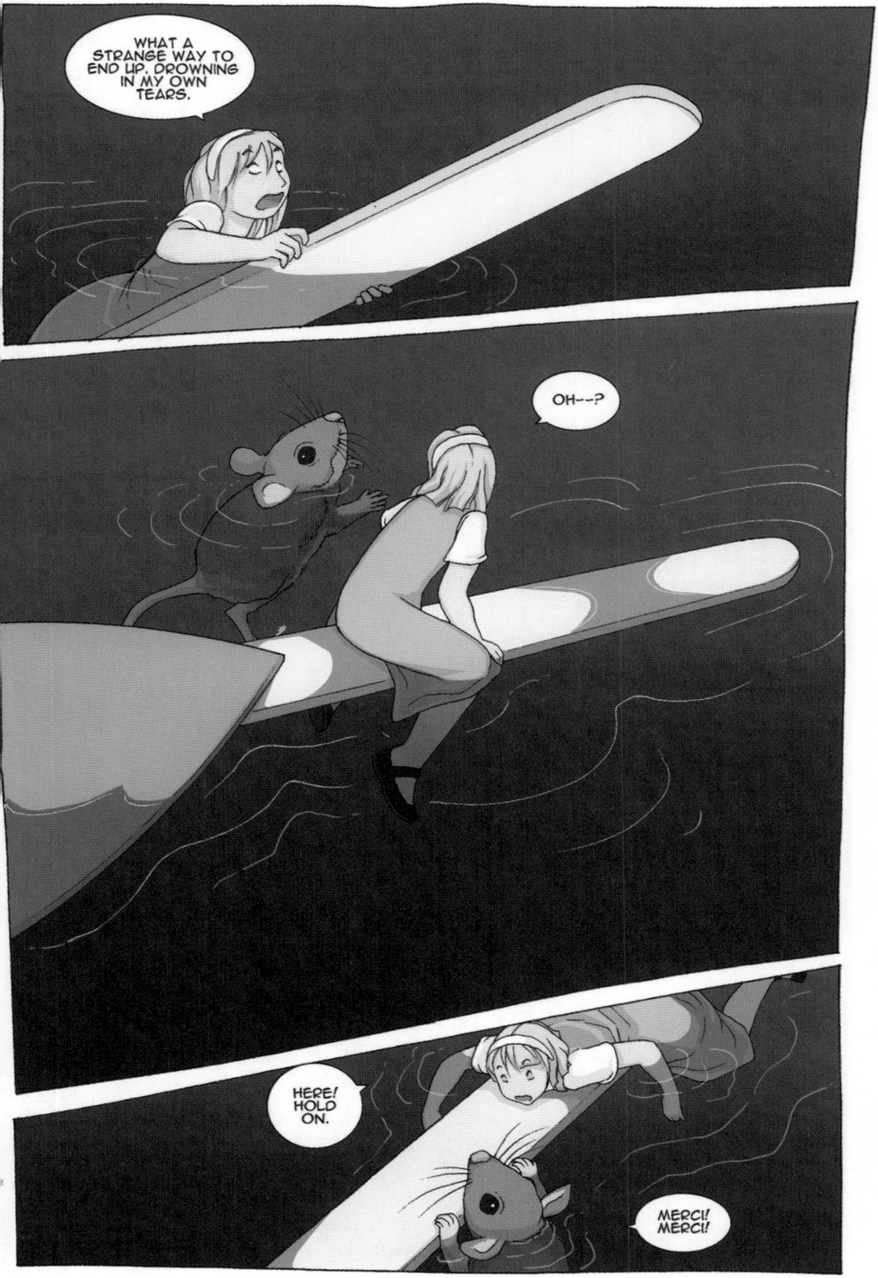
WHAT A STRANGE WAY TO END UP. DROWNING IN MY OWN TEARS.
OH--?
HERE! HOLD ON.
MERCI! MERCI!

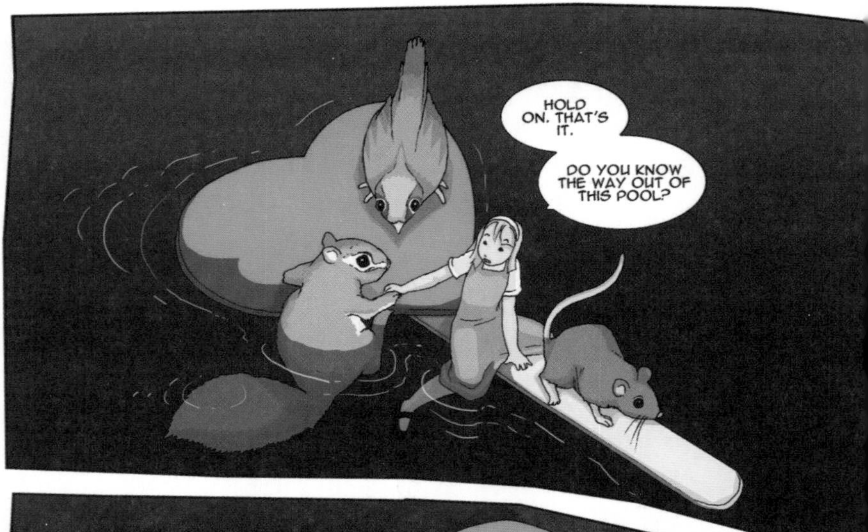
HOLD ON. THAT'S IT.
DO YOU KNOW THE WAY OUT OF THIS POOL?

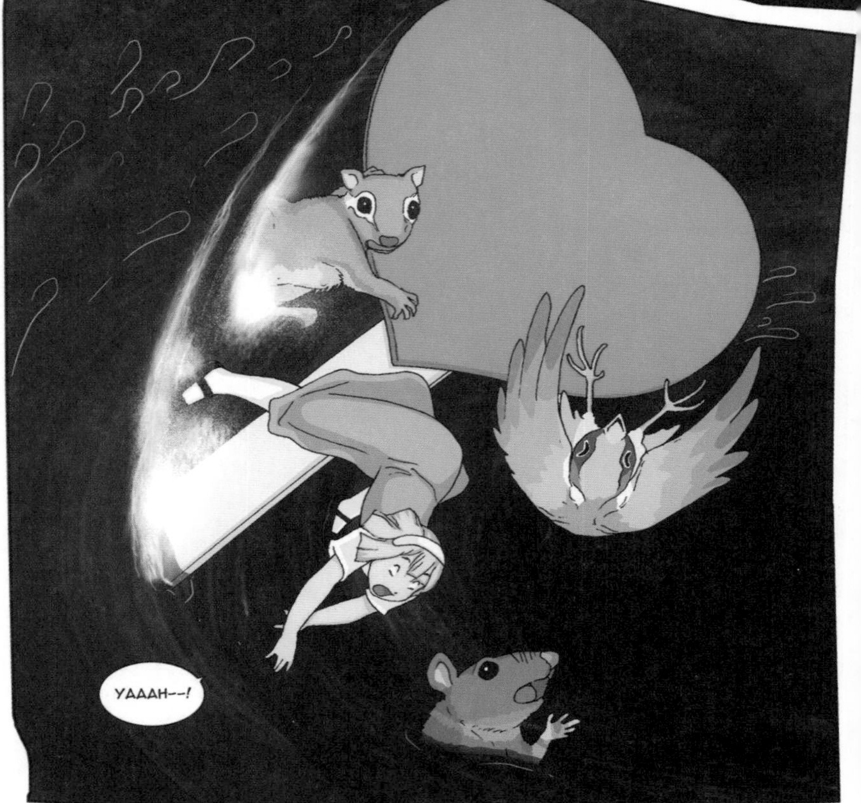
YAAAH--!

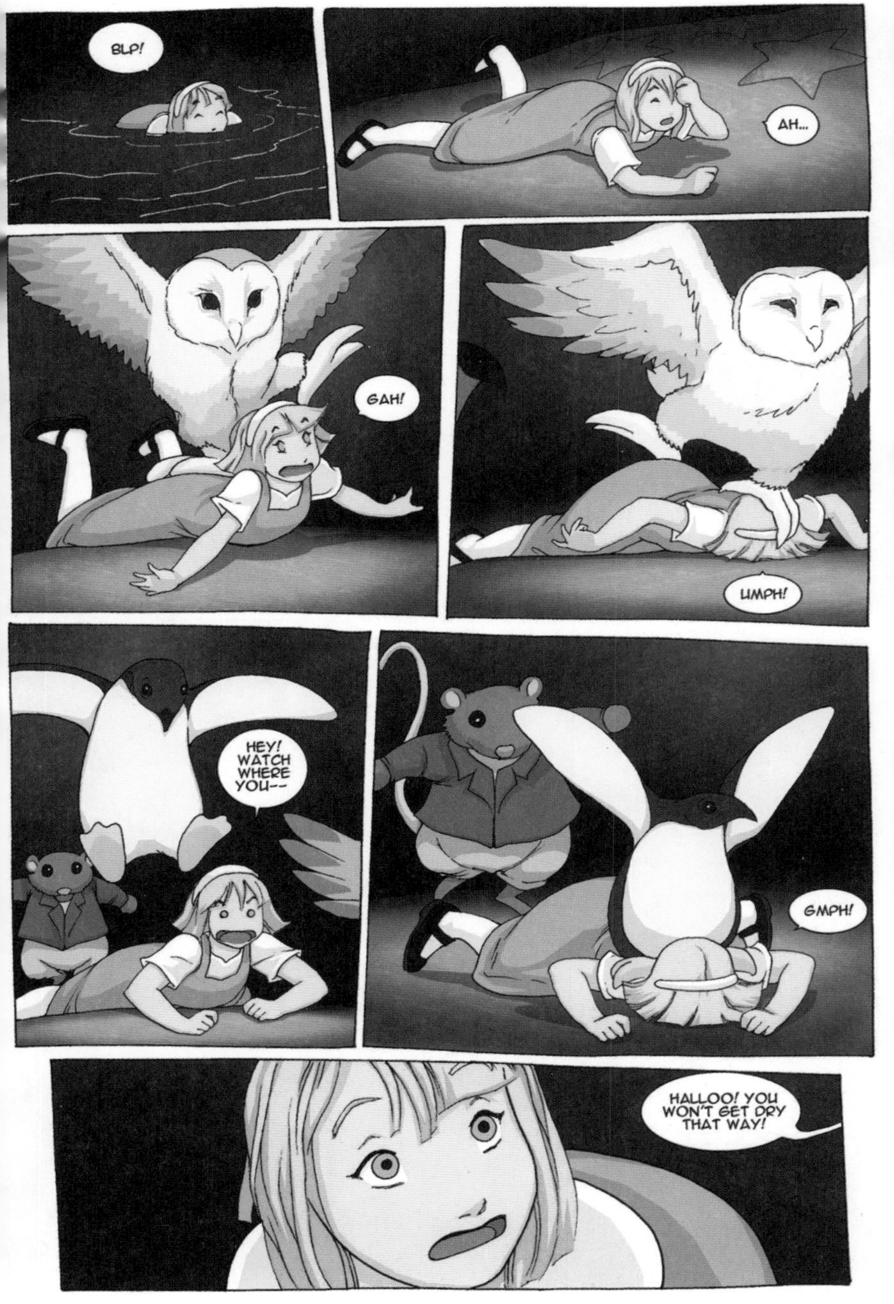
BLP!
AH...
GAH!
UMPH!
HEY! WATCH WHERE YOU--
GMPH!
HALLOO! YOU WON'T GET DRY THAT WAY!

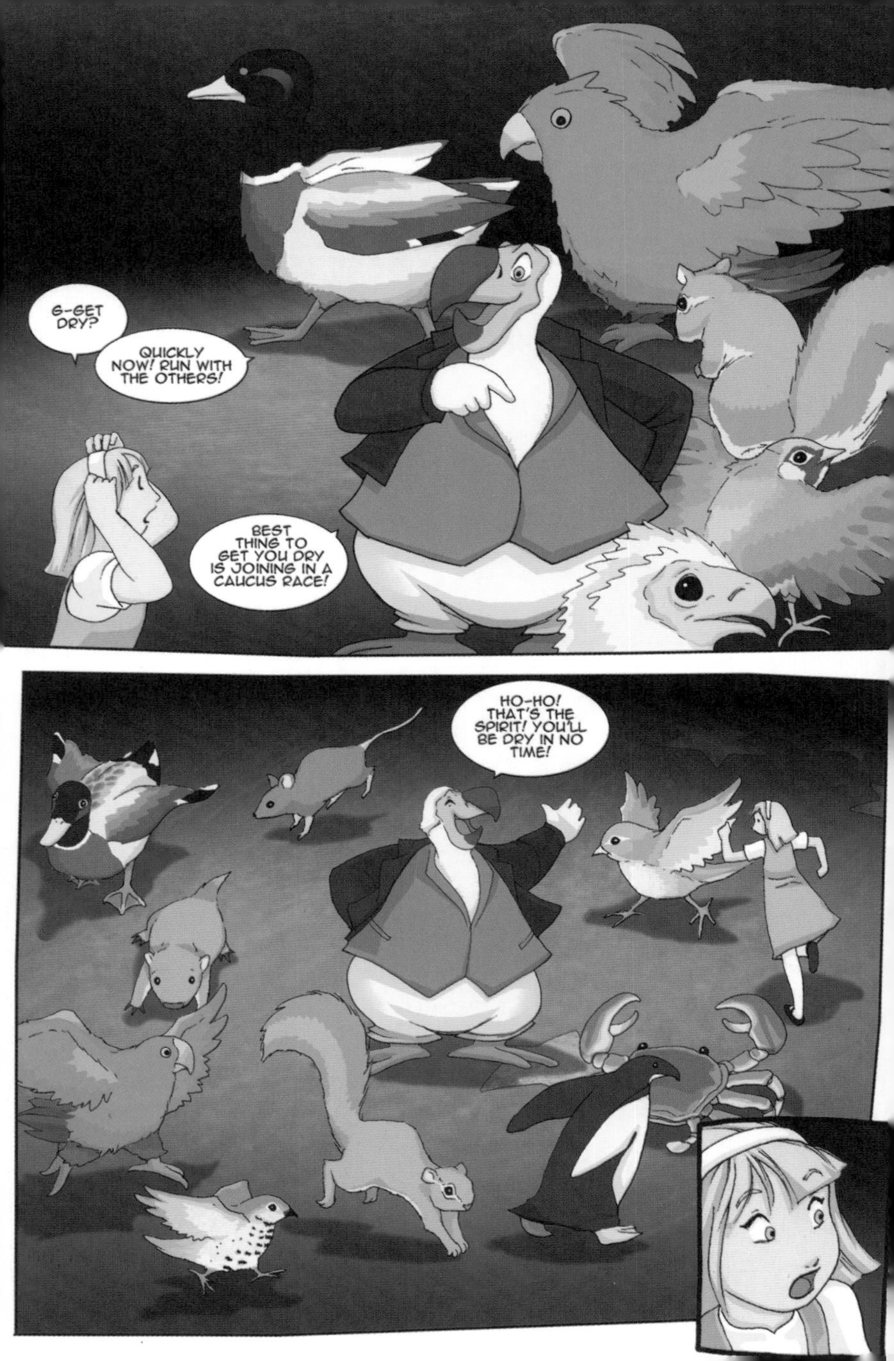
S-GET DRY?
QUICKLY NOW! RUN WITH THE OTHERS!
BEST THING TO GET YOU DRY IS JOINING IN A CAUCUS RACE!
HO-HO! THAT'S THE SPIRIT! YOU'LL BE DRY IN NO TIME!

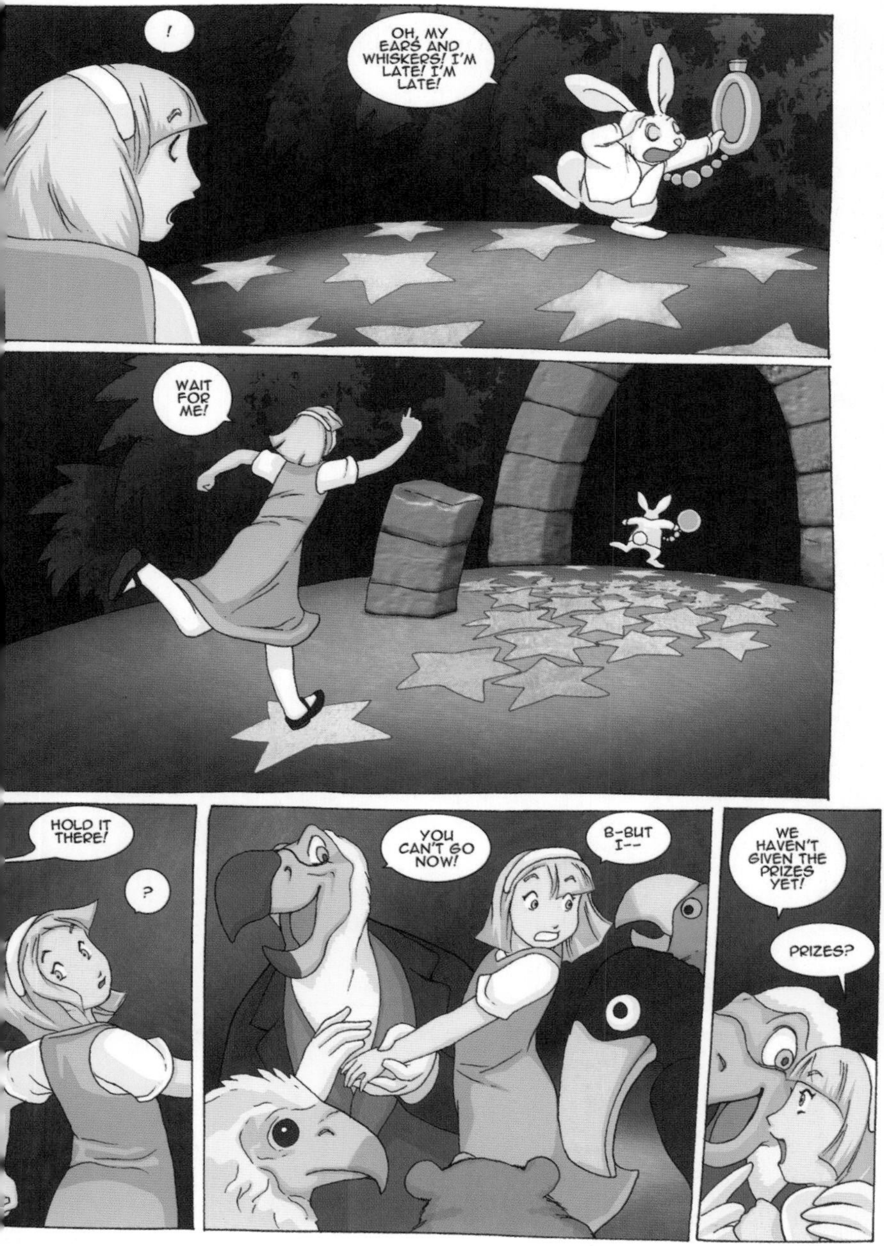
!
OH, MY EARS AND WHISKERS! I'M LATE! I'M LATE!
WAIT FOR ME!
HOLD IT THERE!
?
YOU CAN'T GO NOW!
B-BUT I--
WE HAVEN'T GIVEN THE PRIZES YET!
PRIZES?

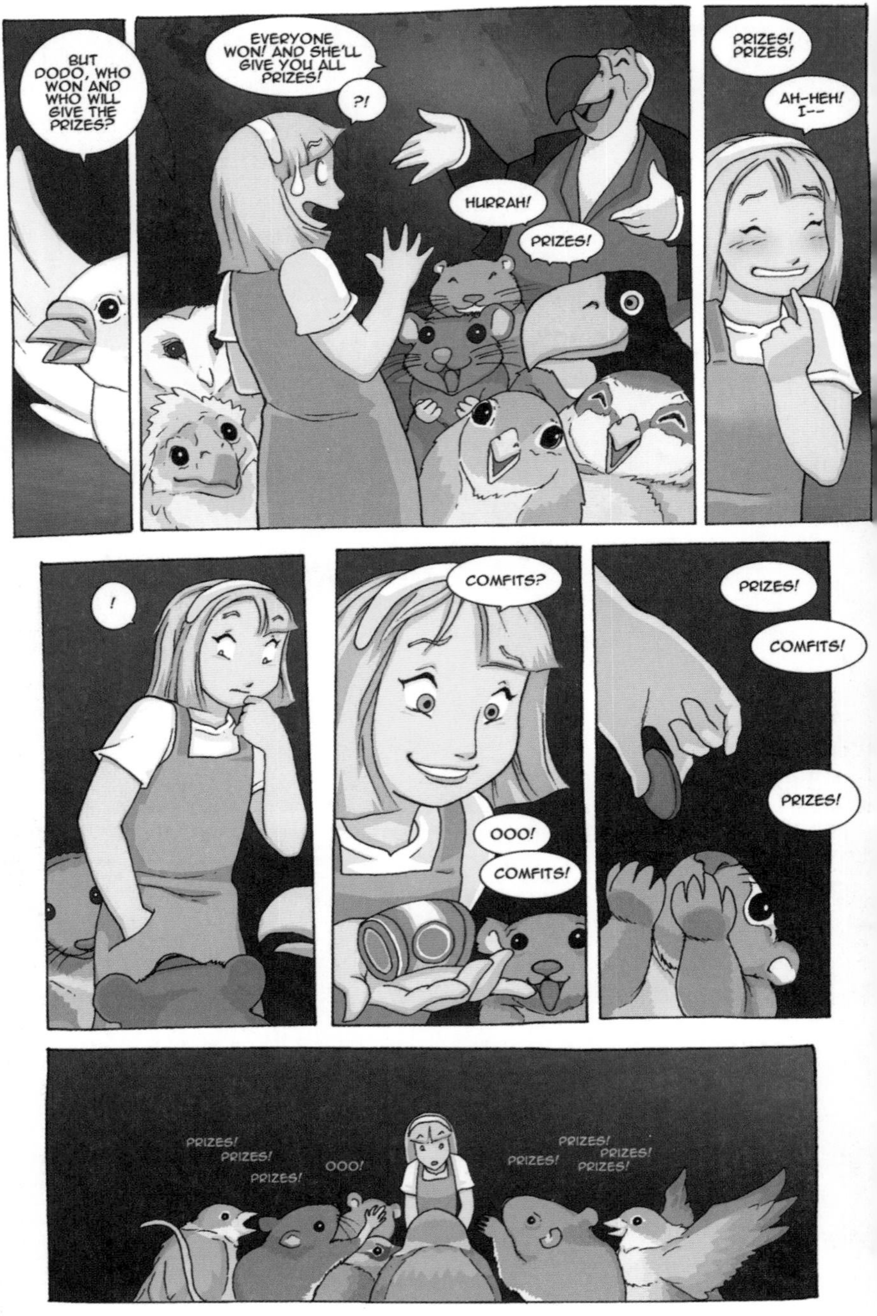
BUT DODO, WHO WON AND WHO WILL GIVE THE PRIZES?
EVERYONE WON! AND SHE'LL GIVE YOU ALL PRIZES!
?!
HURRAH!
PRIZES!
PRIZES! PRIZES!
AH-HEH! I--
!
COMFITS?
OOO!
COMFITS!
PRIZES!
COMFITS!
PRIZES!
PRIZES!
PRIZES!
PRIZES!
OOO!
PRIZES!
PRIZES!
PRIZES!
PRIZES!

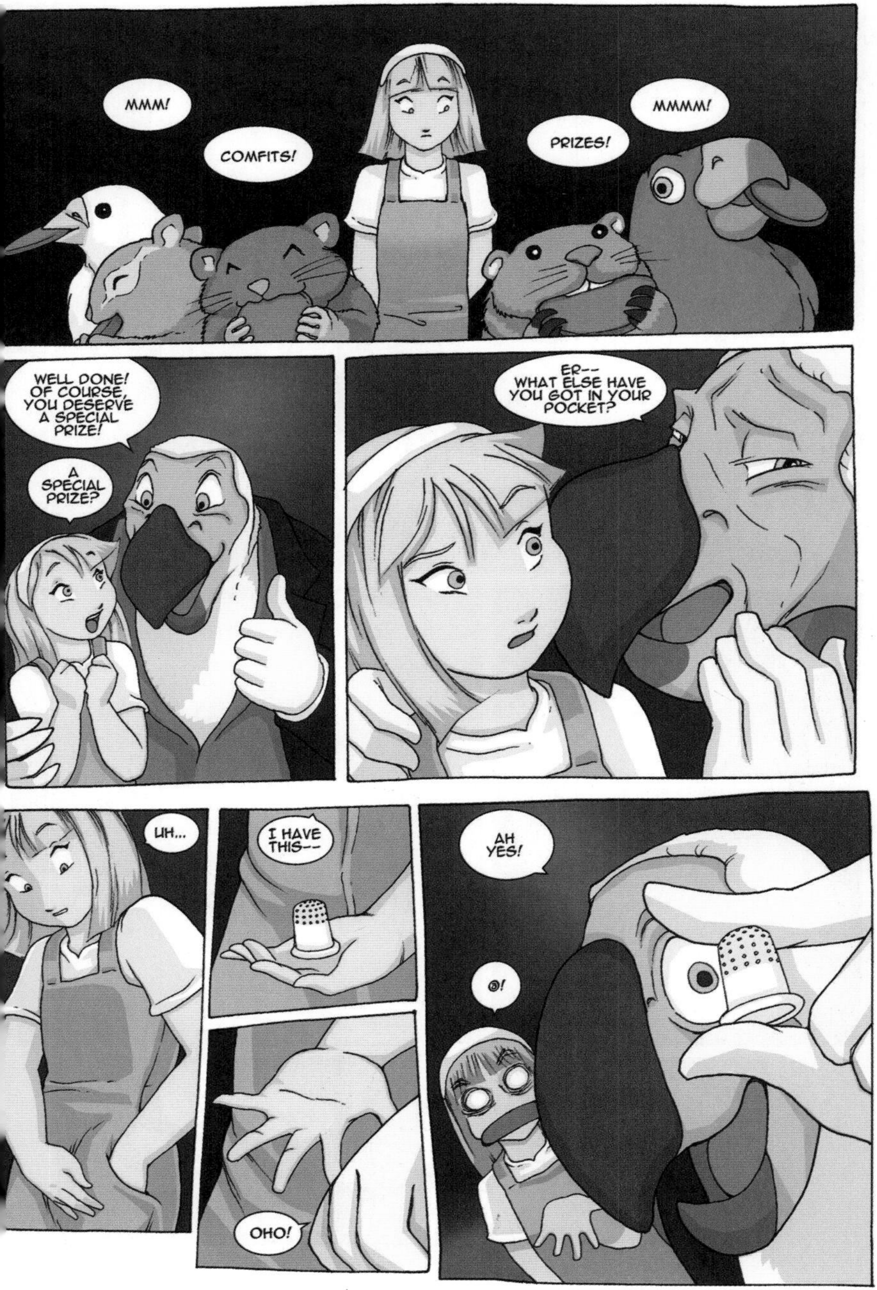
MMM!
COMFITS!
PRIZES!
MMMM!
WELL DONE! OF COURSE, YOU DESERVE A SPECIAL PRIZE!
A SPECIAL PRIZE?
ER-- WHAT ELSE HAVE YOU GOT IN YOUR POCKET?
UH...
I HAVE THIS--
OHO!
AH YES!

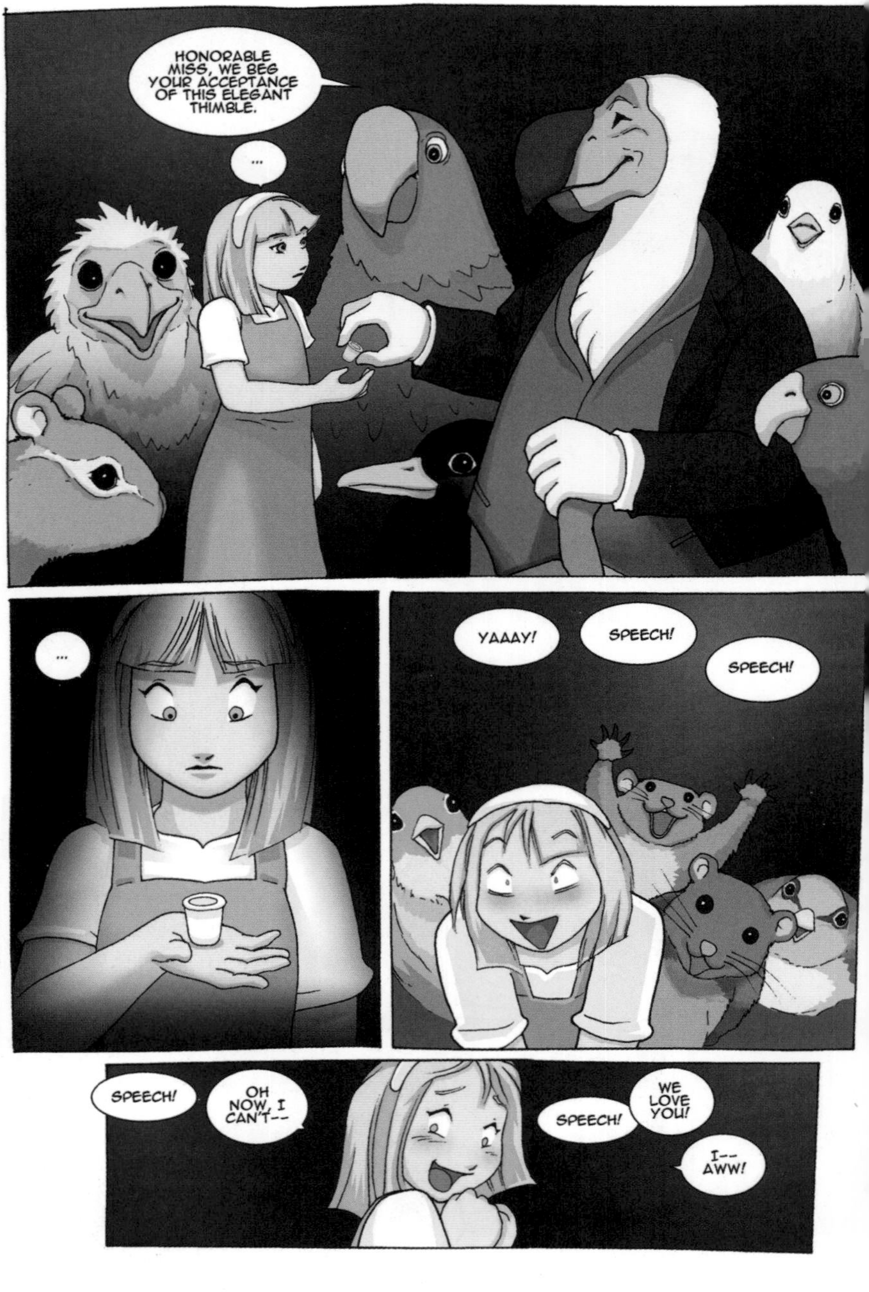
HONORABLE MISS, WE BEG YOUR ACCEPTANCE OF THIS ELEGANT THIMBLE.
...
...
YAAAY!
SPEECH!
SPEECH!
SPEECH!
OH NOW, I CAN'T--
SPEECH!
WE LOVE YOU!
I-- AWW!

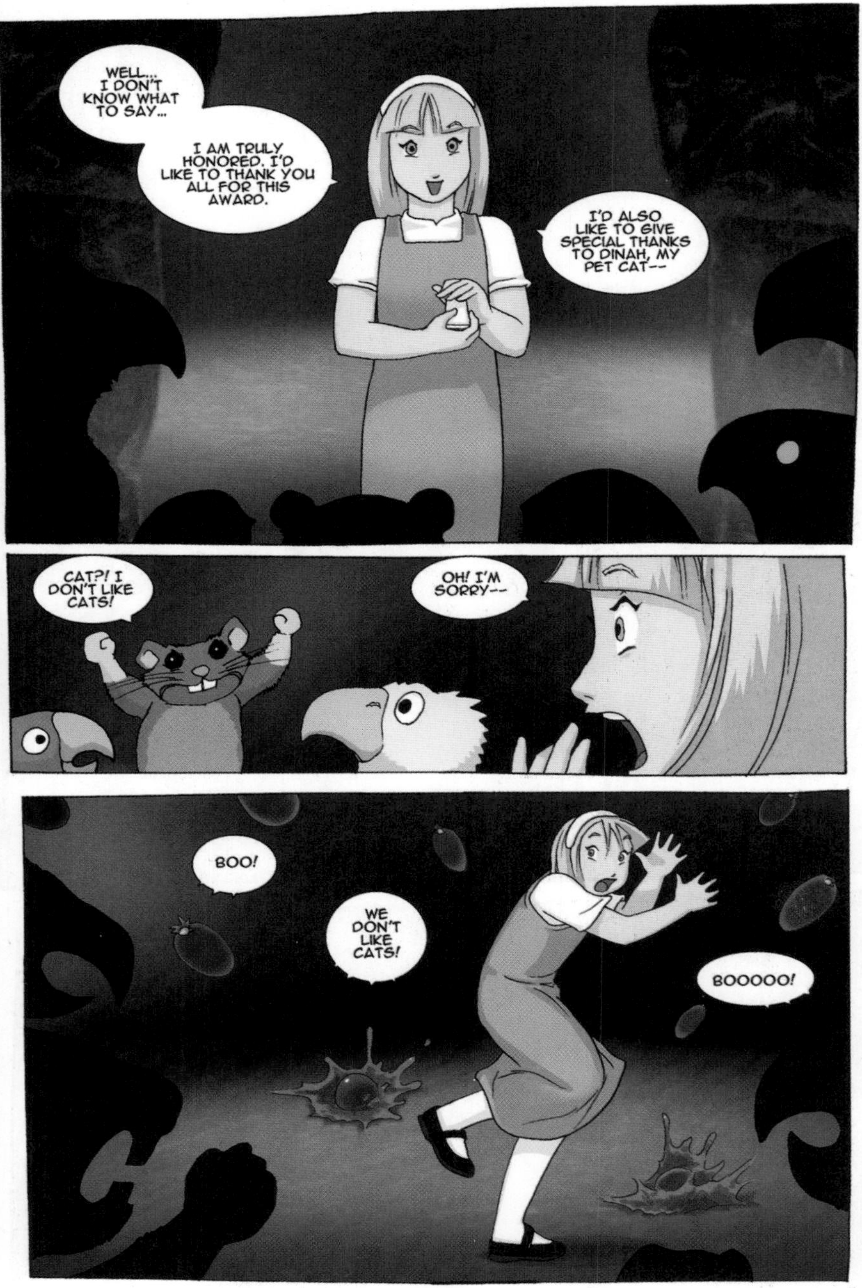
WELL... I DON'T KNOW WHAT TO SAY...
I AM TRULY HONORED. I'D LIKE TO THANK YOU ALL FOR THIS AWARD.
I'D ALSO LIKE TO GIVE SPECIAL THANKS TO DINAH, MY PET CAT--
CAT?! I DON'T LIKE CATS!
OH! I'M SORRY--
BOO!
WE DON'T LIKE CATS!
BOOOOO!

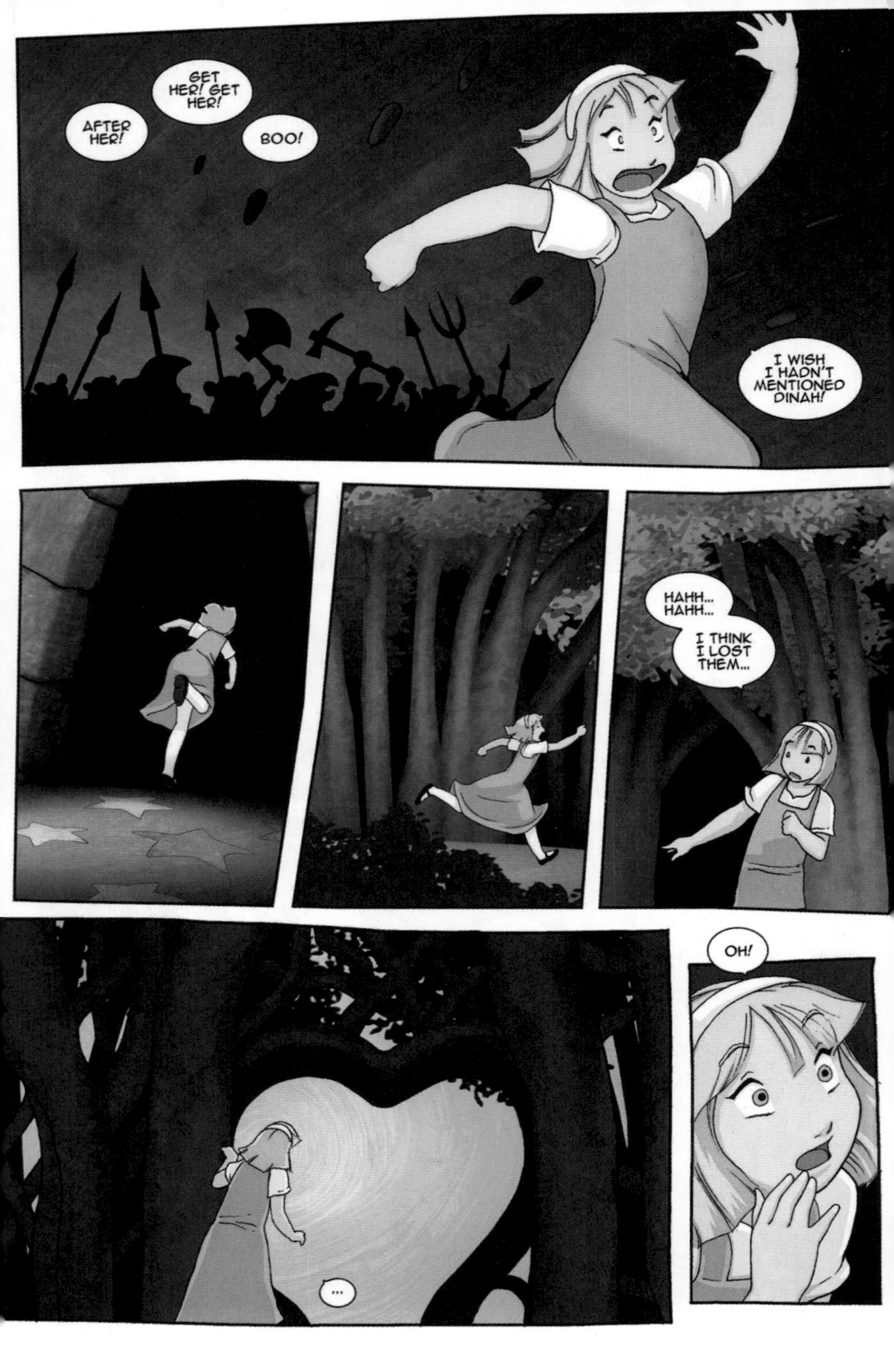
AFTER HER!
GET HER! GET HER!
BOO!
I WISH I HADN'T MENTIONED DINAH!
HAHH... HAHH...
I THINK I LOST THEM...
...
OH!

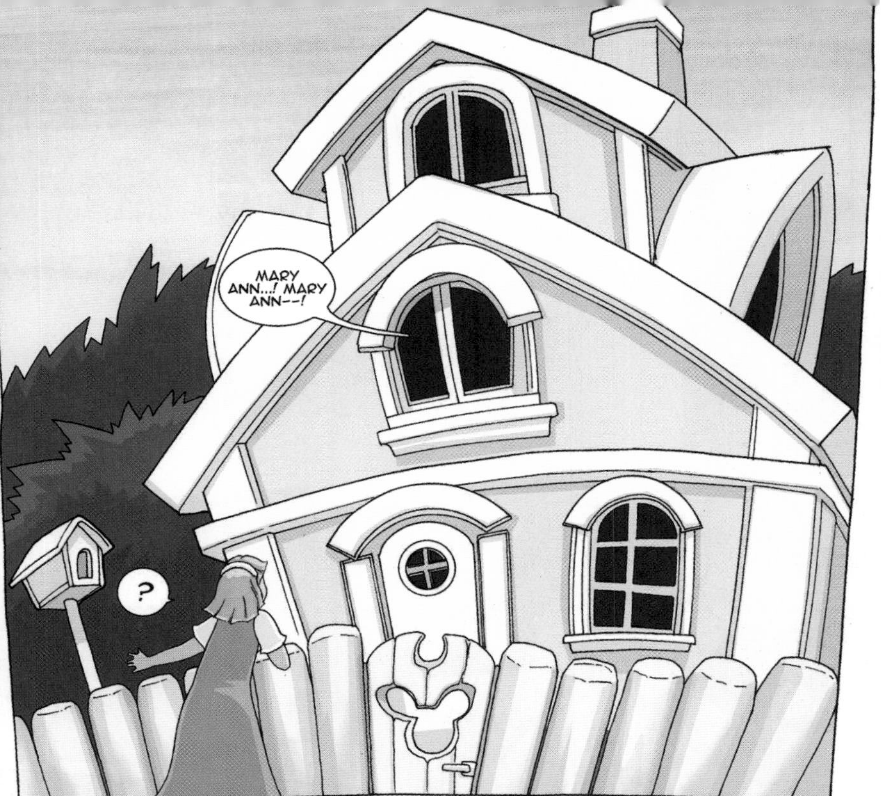
MARY ANN...! MARY ANN--!
?

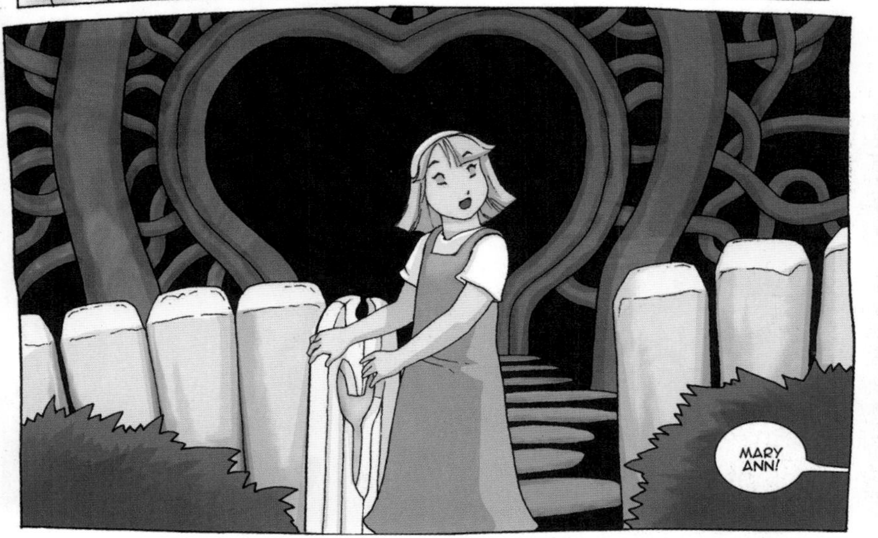
MARY ANN!

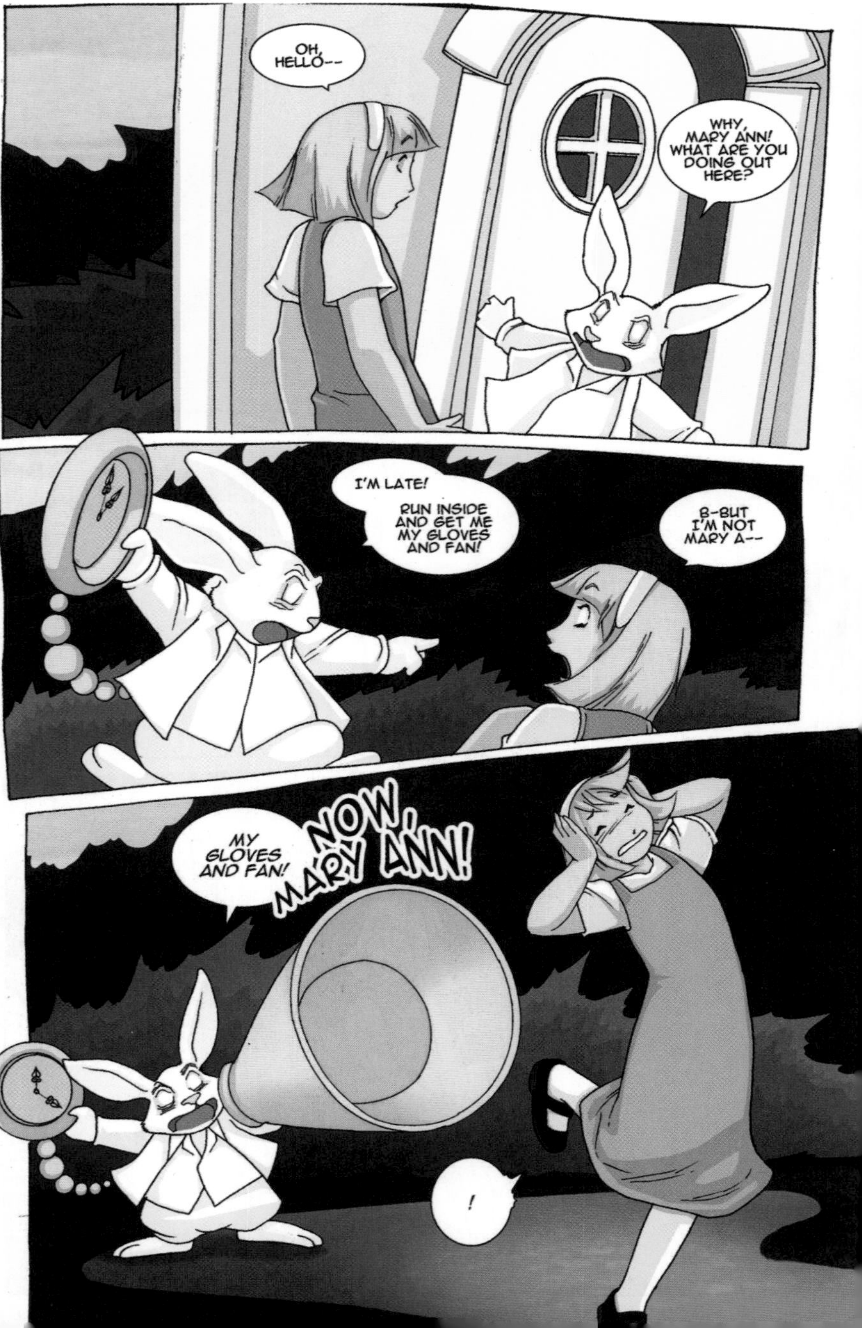
OH, HELLO--
WHY, MARY ANN! WHAT ARE YOU DOING OUT HERE?
I'M LATE!
RUN INSIDE AND GET ME MY GLOVES AND FAN!
B-BUT I'M NOT MARY A--
MY GLOVES AND FAN!
NOW, MARY ANN!
!

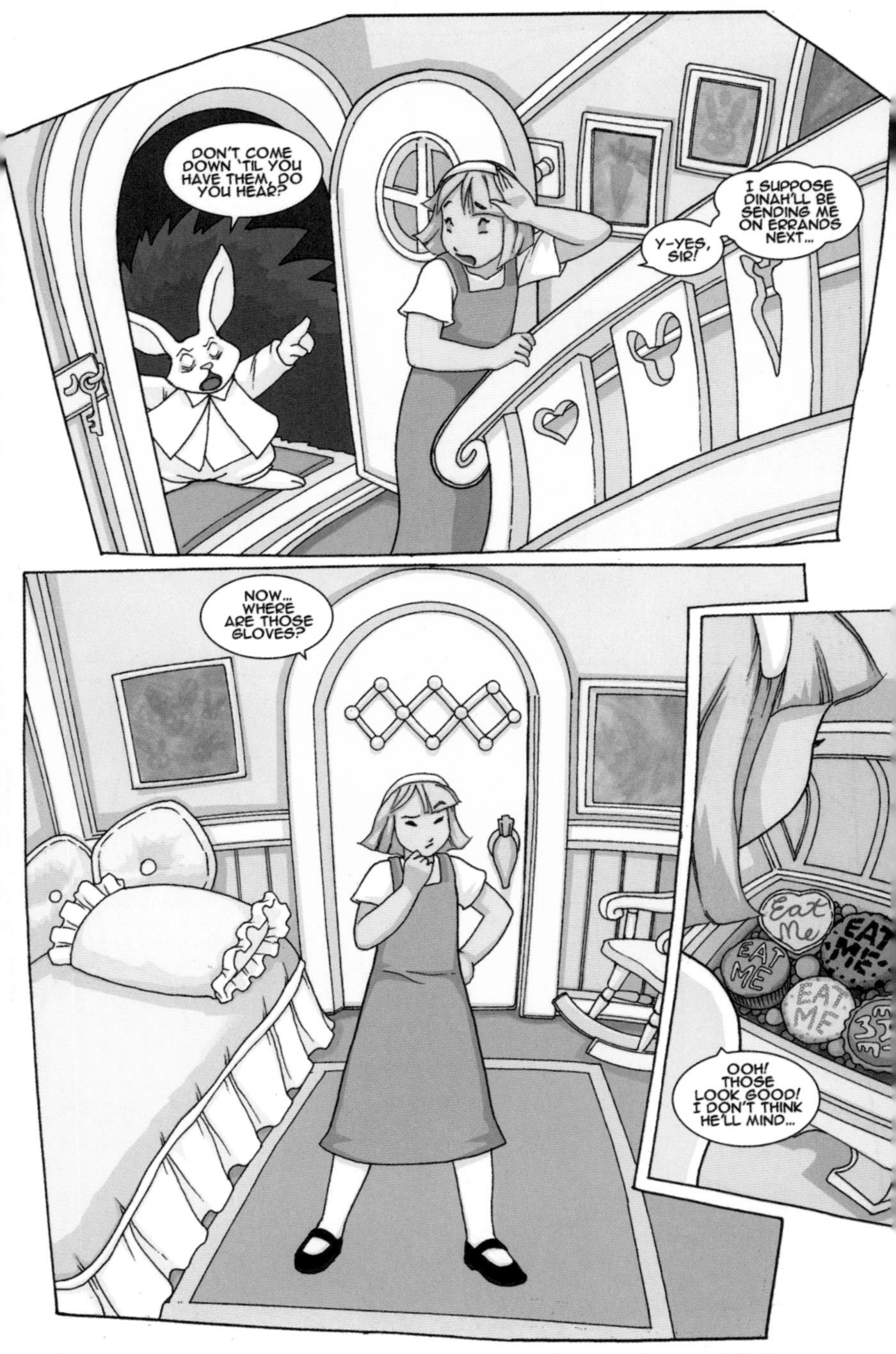
DON'T COME DOWN 'TIL YOU HAVE THEM, DO YOU HEAR?
Y-YES, SIR!
I SUPPOSE DINAH'LL BE SENDING ME ON ERRANDS NEXT...
NOW... WHERE ARE THOSE GLOVES?
Eat Me
EAT ME
EAT ME
OOH! THOSE LOOK GOOD! I DON'T THINK HE'LL MIND...

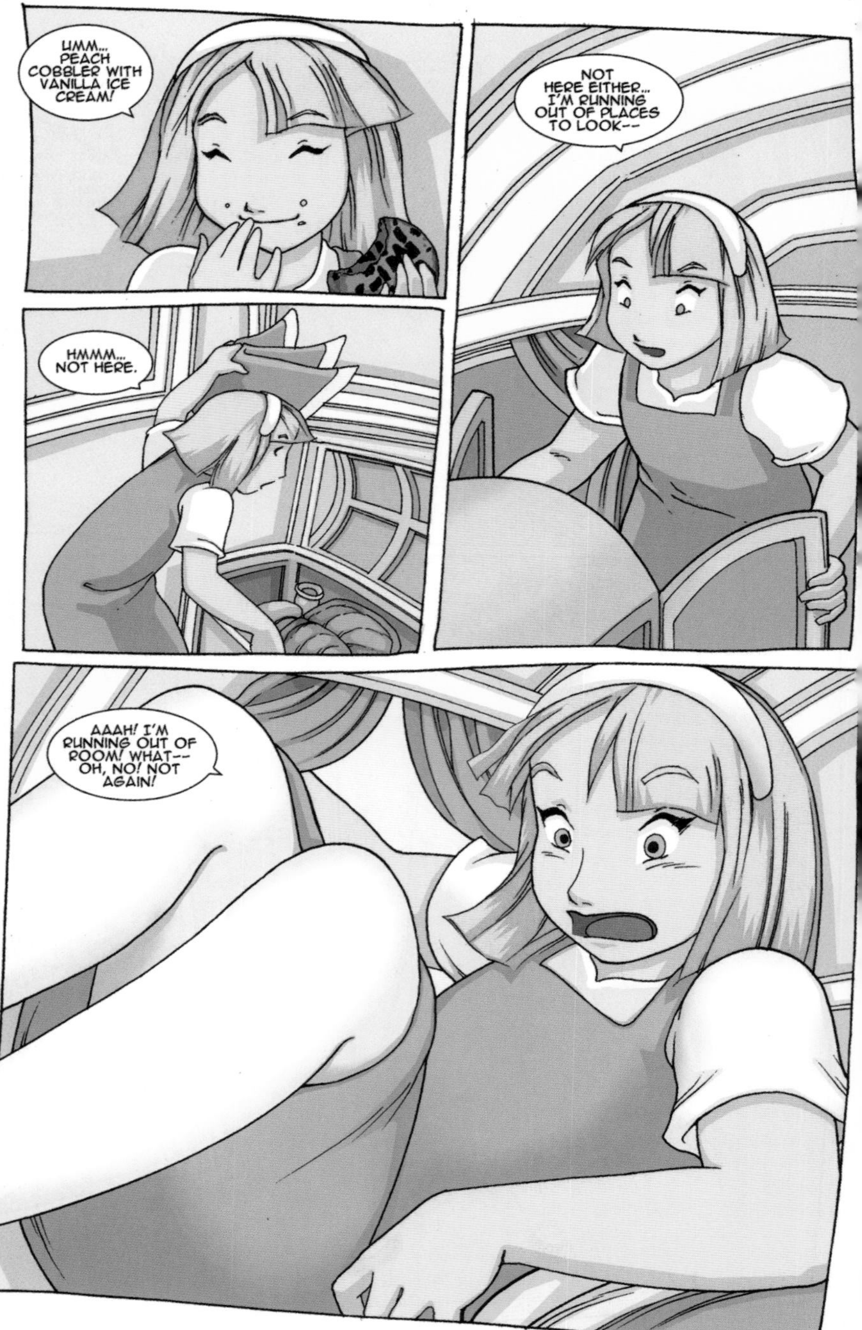
UMM... PEACH COBBLER WITH VANILLA ICE CREAM!
HMMM... NOT HERE.
NOT HERE EITHER... I'M RUNNING OUT OF PLACES TO LOOK--
AAAH! I'M RUNNING OUT OF ROOM! WHAT-- OH, NO! NOT AGAIN!

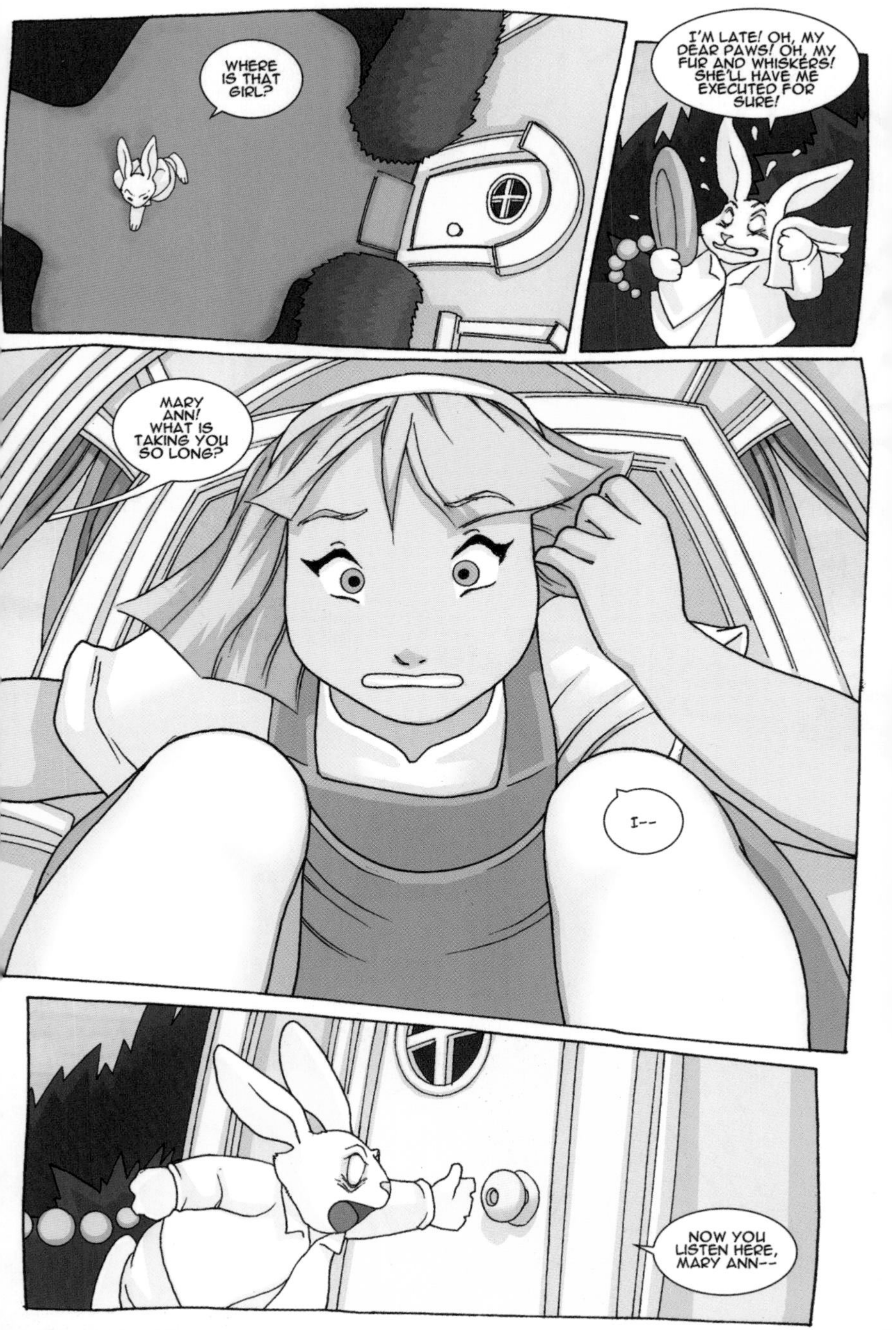
WHERE IS THAT GIRL?
I'M LATE! OH, MY DEAR PAWS! OH, MY FUR AND WHISKERS! SHE'LL HAVE ME EXECUTED FOR SURE!
MARY ANN! WHAT IS TAKING YOU SO LONG?
I--
NOW YOU LISTEN HERE, MARY ANN--

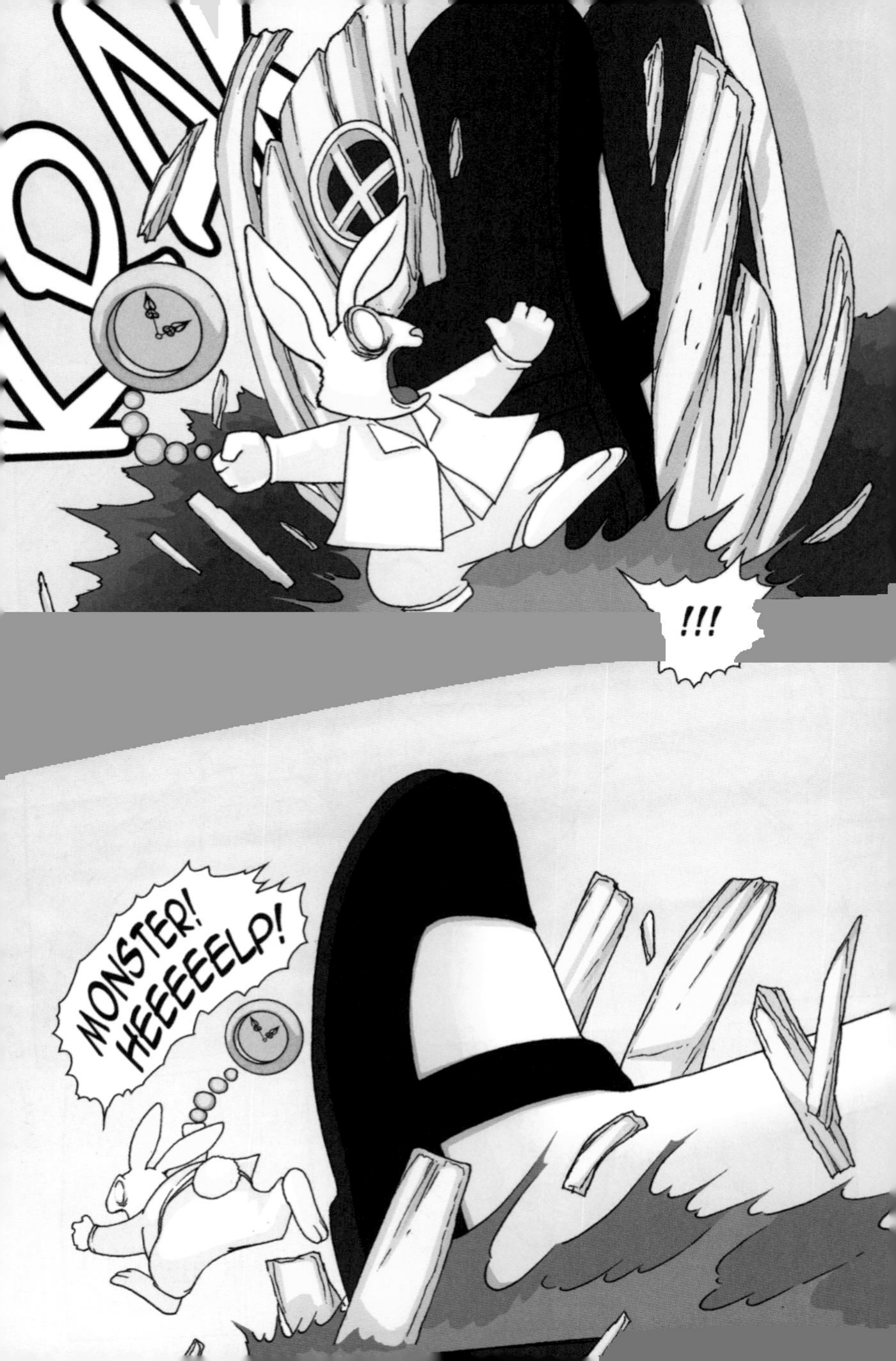
!!!
MONSTER! HEEEEELP!

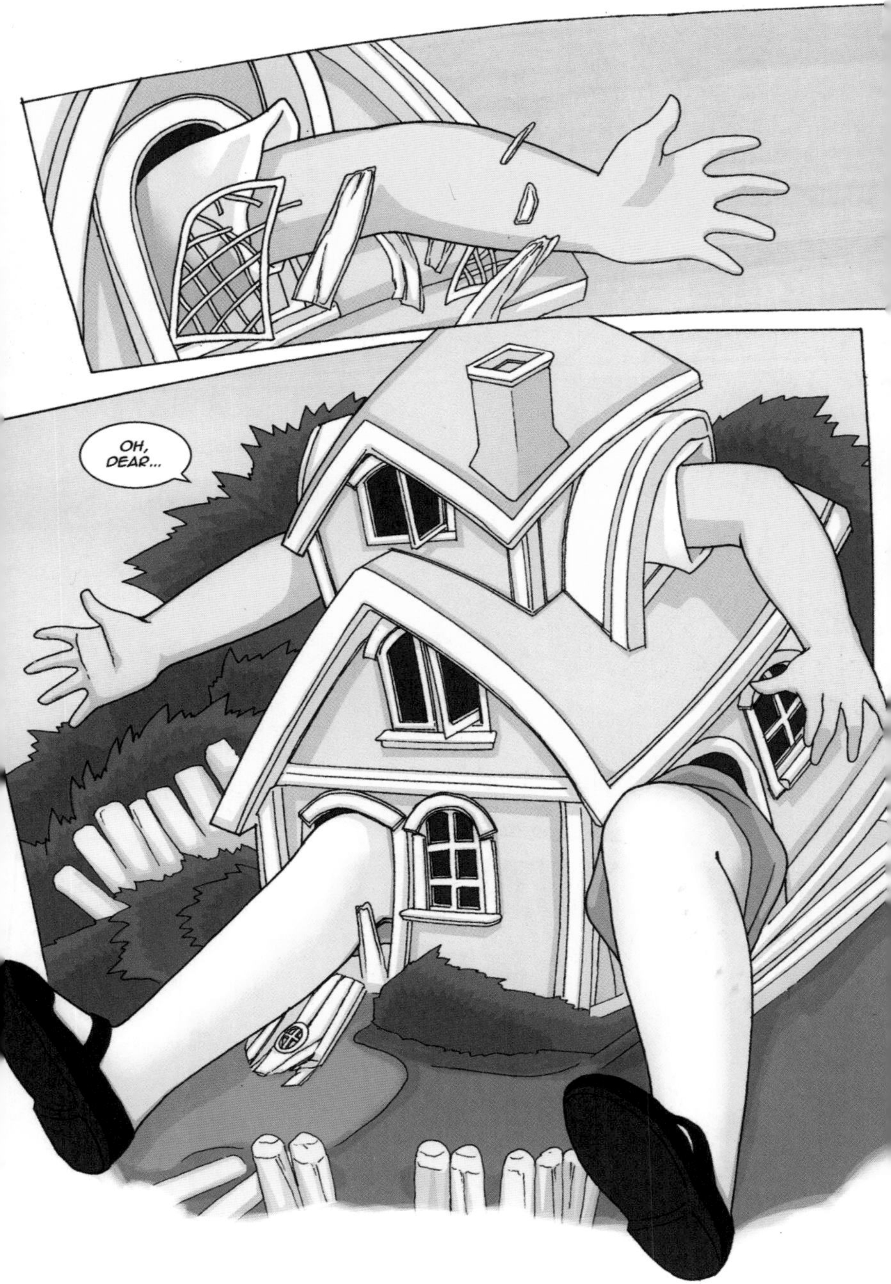
OH, DEAR...

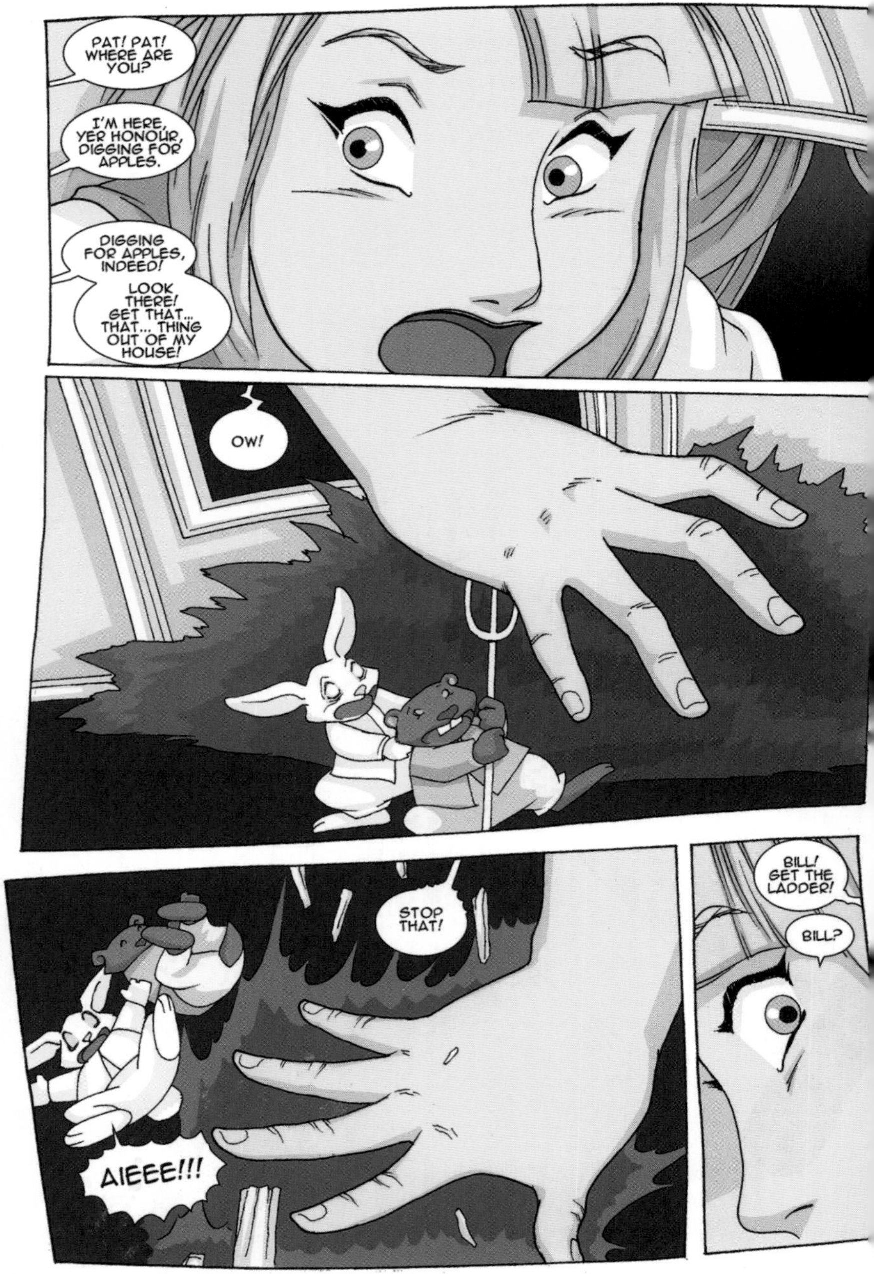
PAT! PAT! WHERE ARE YOU?
I'M HERE, YER HONOUR, DIGGING FOR APPLES.
DIGGING FOR APPLES, INDEED!
LOOK THERE! GET THAT... THAT... THING OUT OF MY HOUSE!
OW!
STOP THAT!
AIEEE!!!
BILL! GET THE LADDER!
BILL?

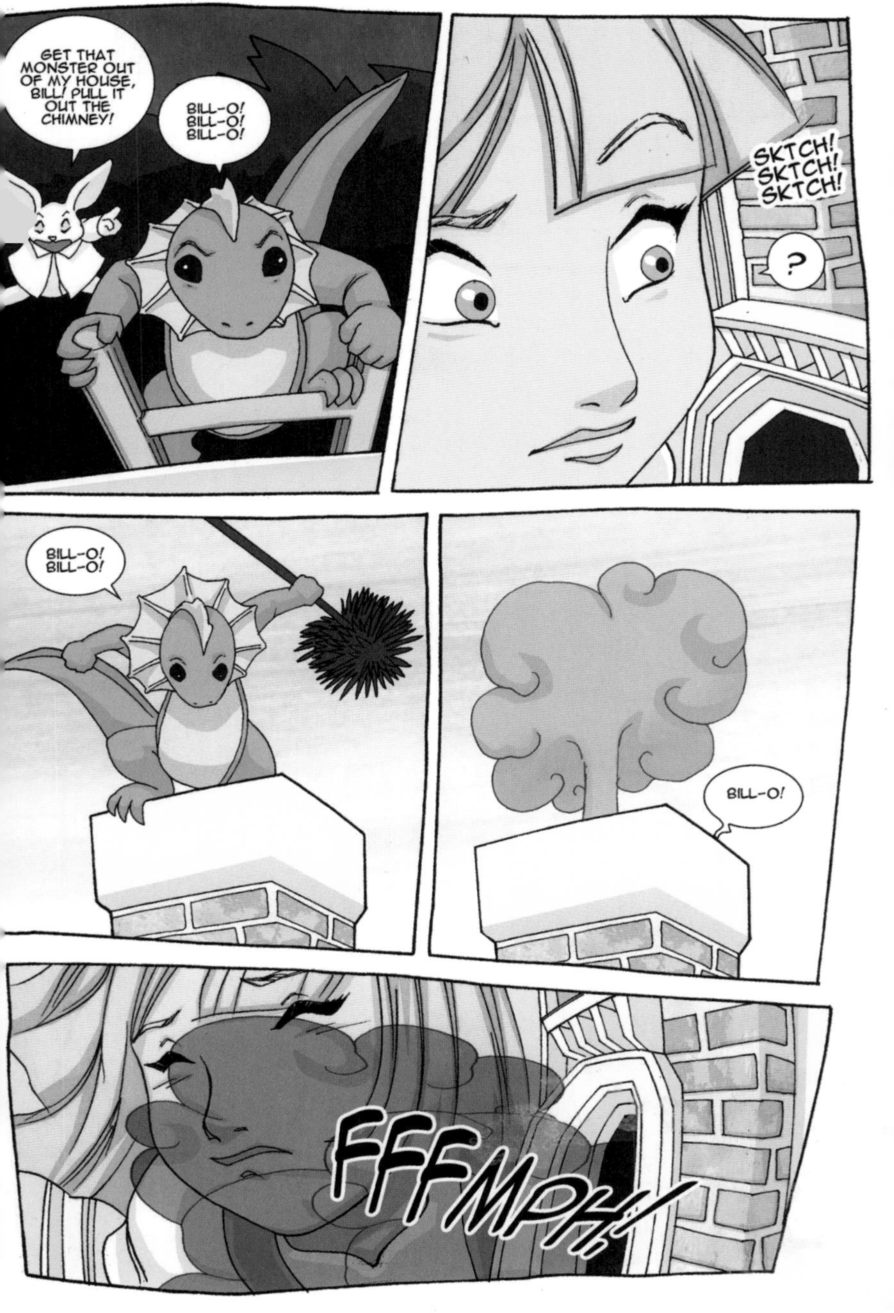
GET THAT MONSTER OUT OF MY HOUSE, BILL! PULL IT OUT THE CHIMNEY!
BILL-O! BILL-O! BILL-O!
SKTCH! SKTCH! SKTCH!
?
BILL-O! BILL-O!
BILL-O!
FFFMPH!!

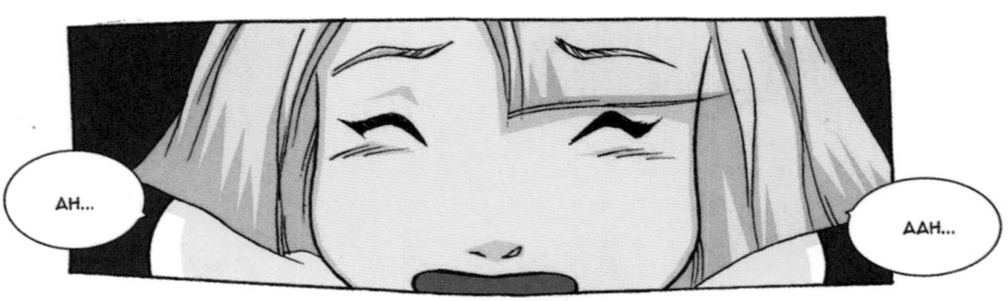
AH...
AAH...

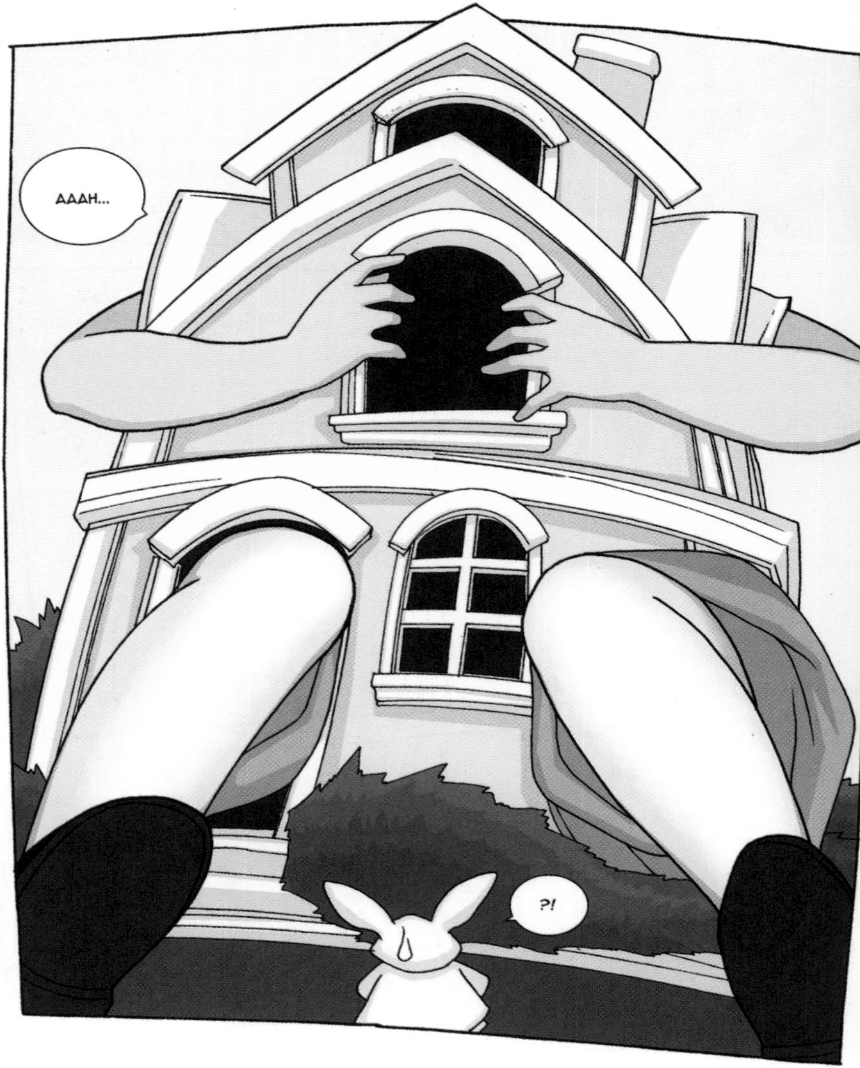
AAAH...
?!

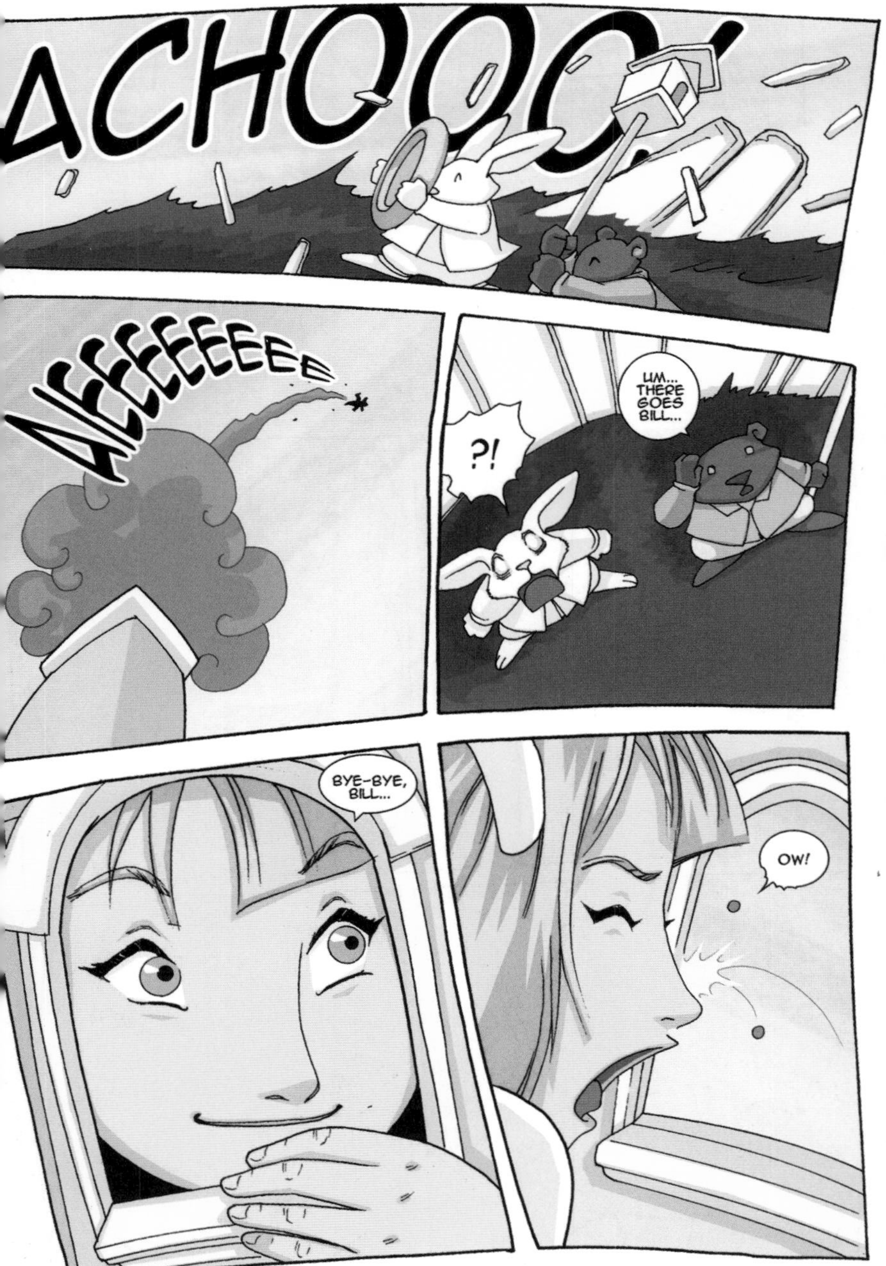
ACHOOO!
AEEEEEEEEE
UM... THERE GOES BILL...
?!
BYE-BYE, BILL...
OW!

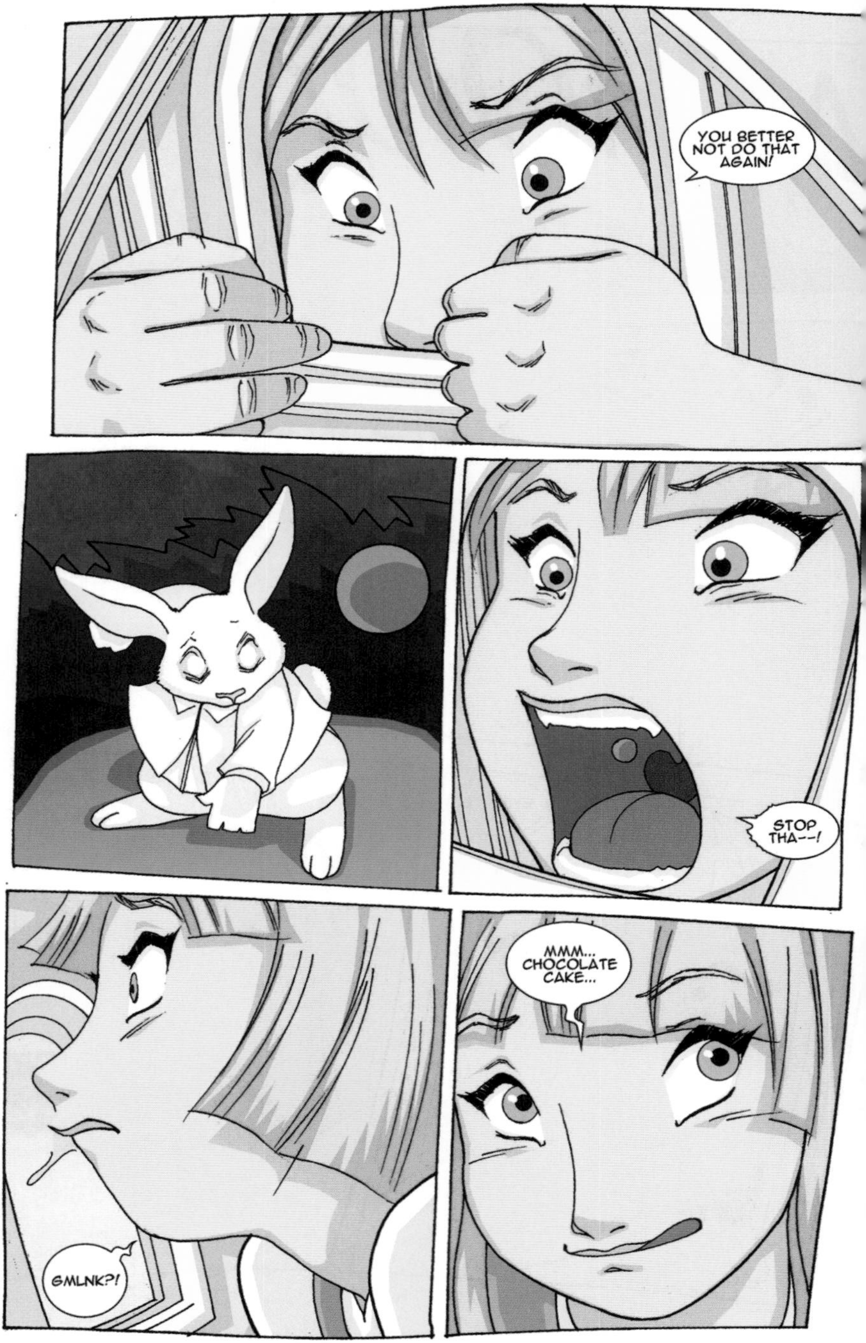
YOU BETTER NOT DO THAT AGAIN!
STOP THA--!
GMLNK?!
MMM... CHOCOLATE CAKE...

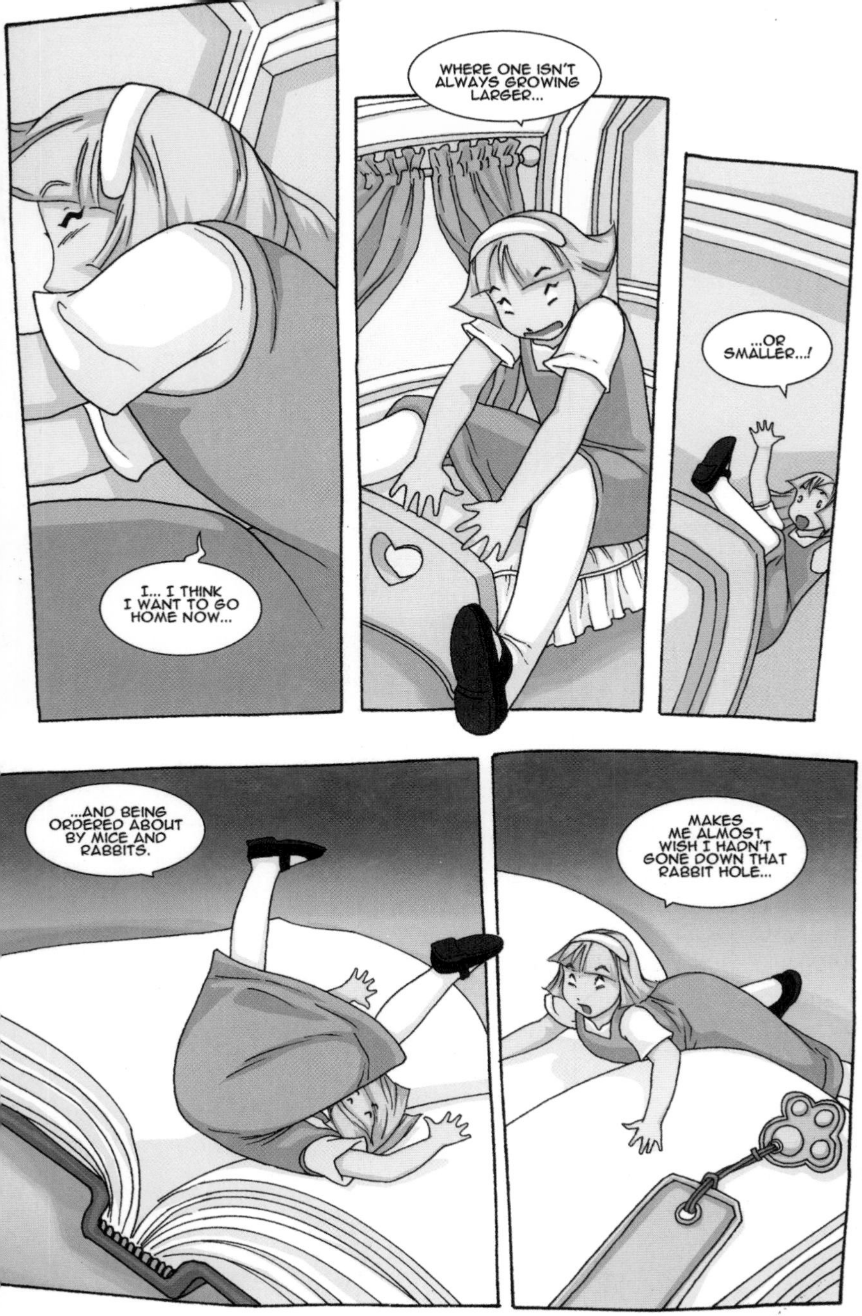
I... I THINK I WANT TO GO HOME NOW...
WHERE ONE ISN'T ALWAYS GROWING LARGER...
...OR SMALLER...!
...AND BEING ORDERED ABOUT BY MICE AND RABBITS.
MAKES ME ALMOST WISH I HADN'T GONE DOWN THAT RABBIT HOLE...

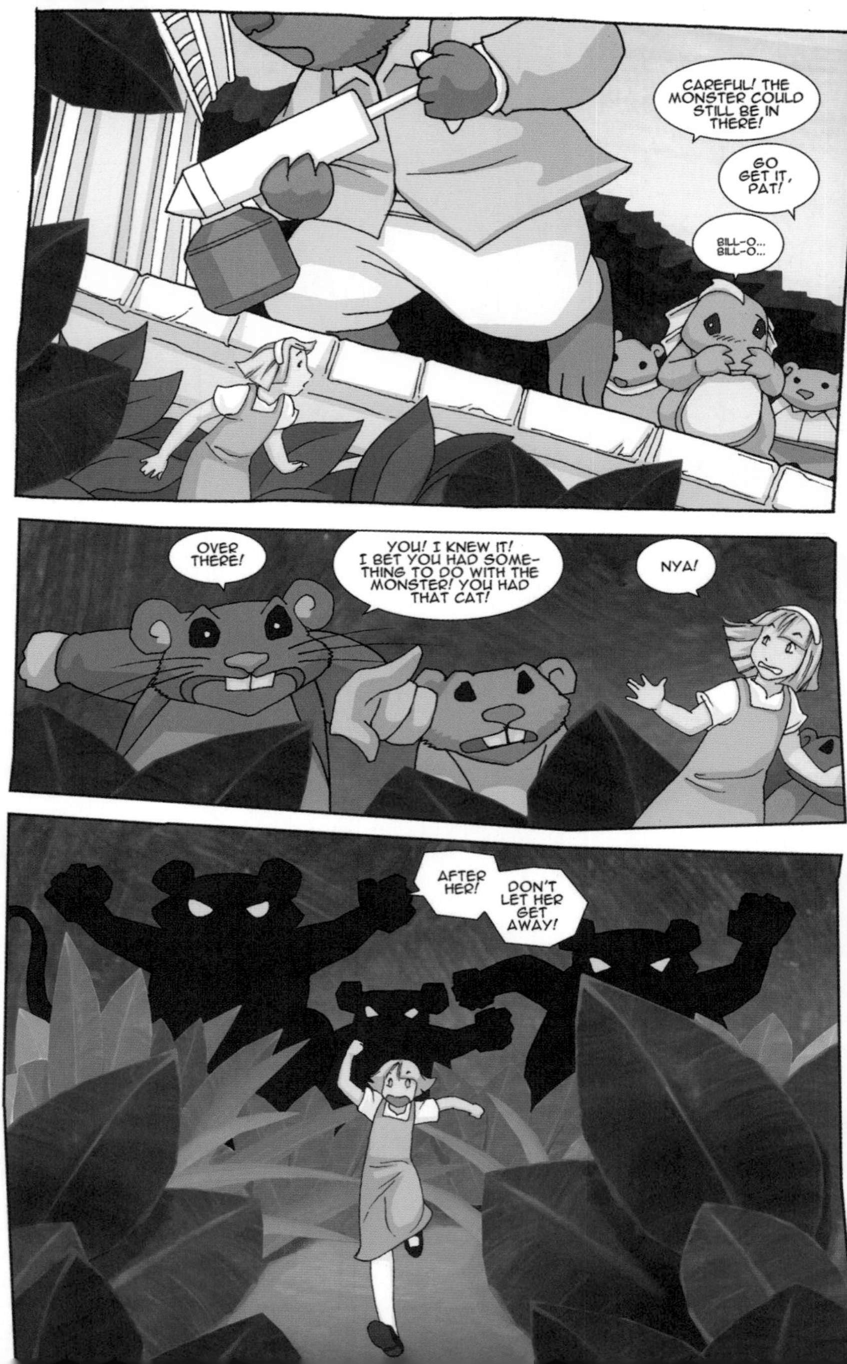
CAREFUL! THE MONSTER COULD STILL BE IN THERE!
GO GET IT, PAT!
BILL-O... BILL-O...
OVER THERE!
YOU! I KNEW IT! I BET YOU HAD SOME-THING TO DO WITH THE MONSTER! YOU HAD THAT CAT!
NYA!
AFTER HER!
DON'T LET HER GET AWAY!

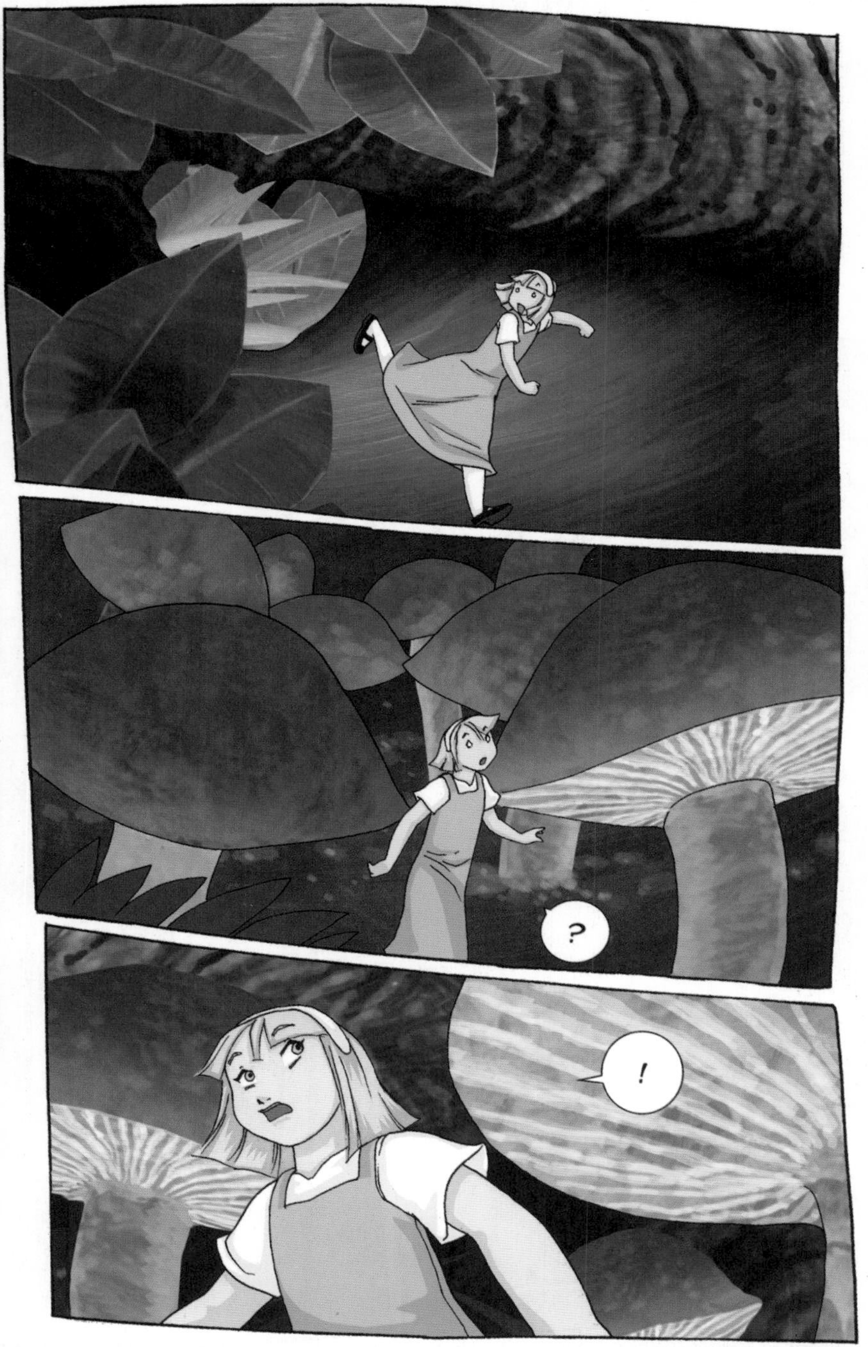
?
!

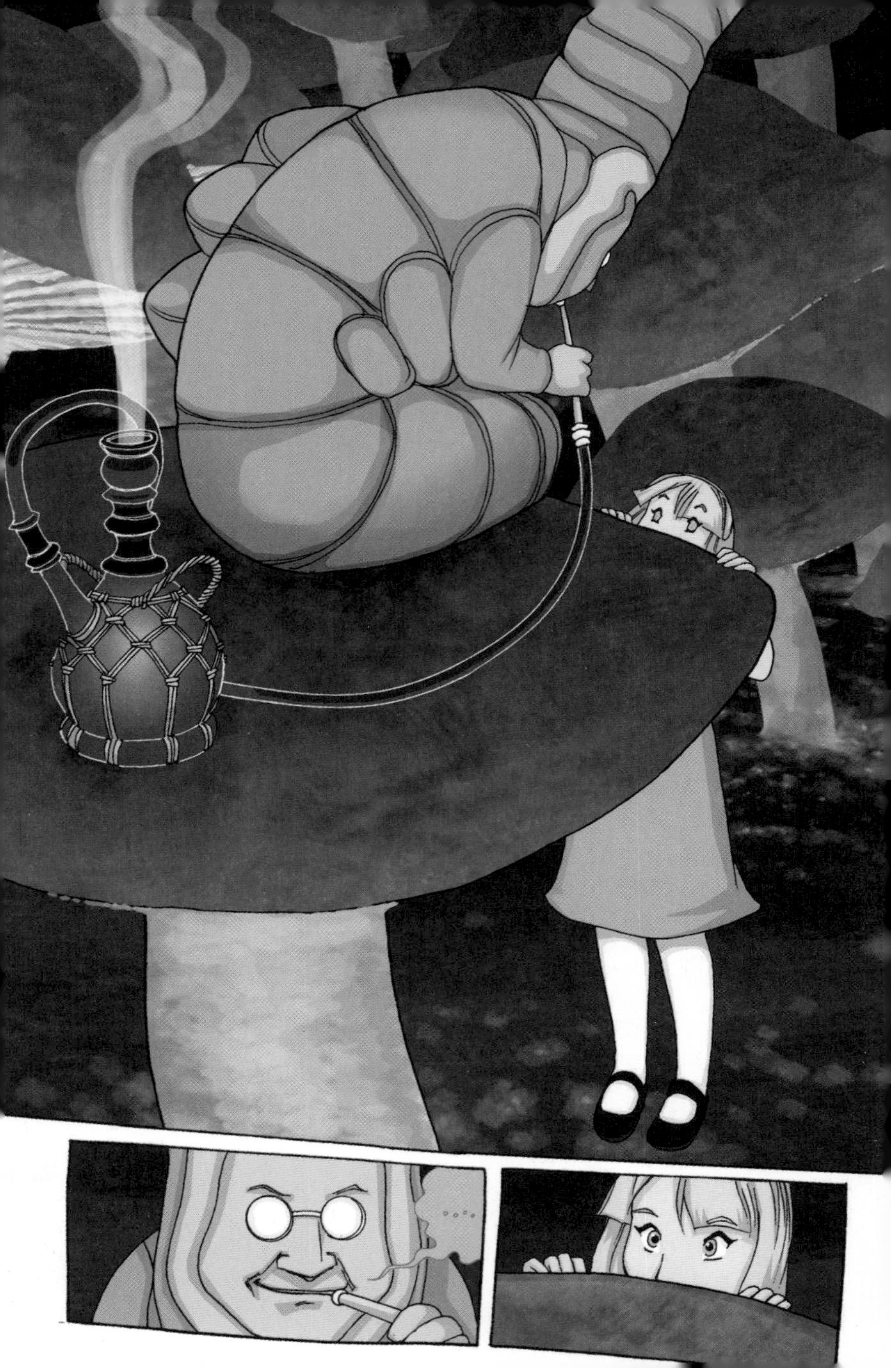

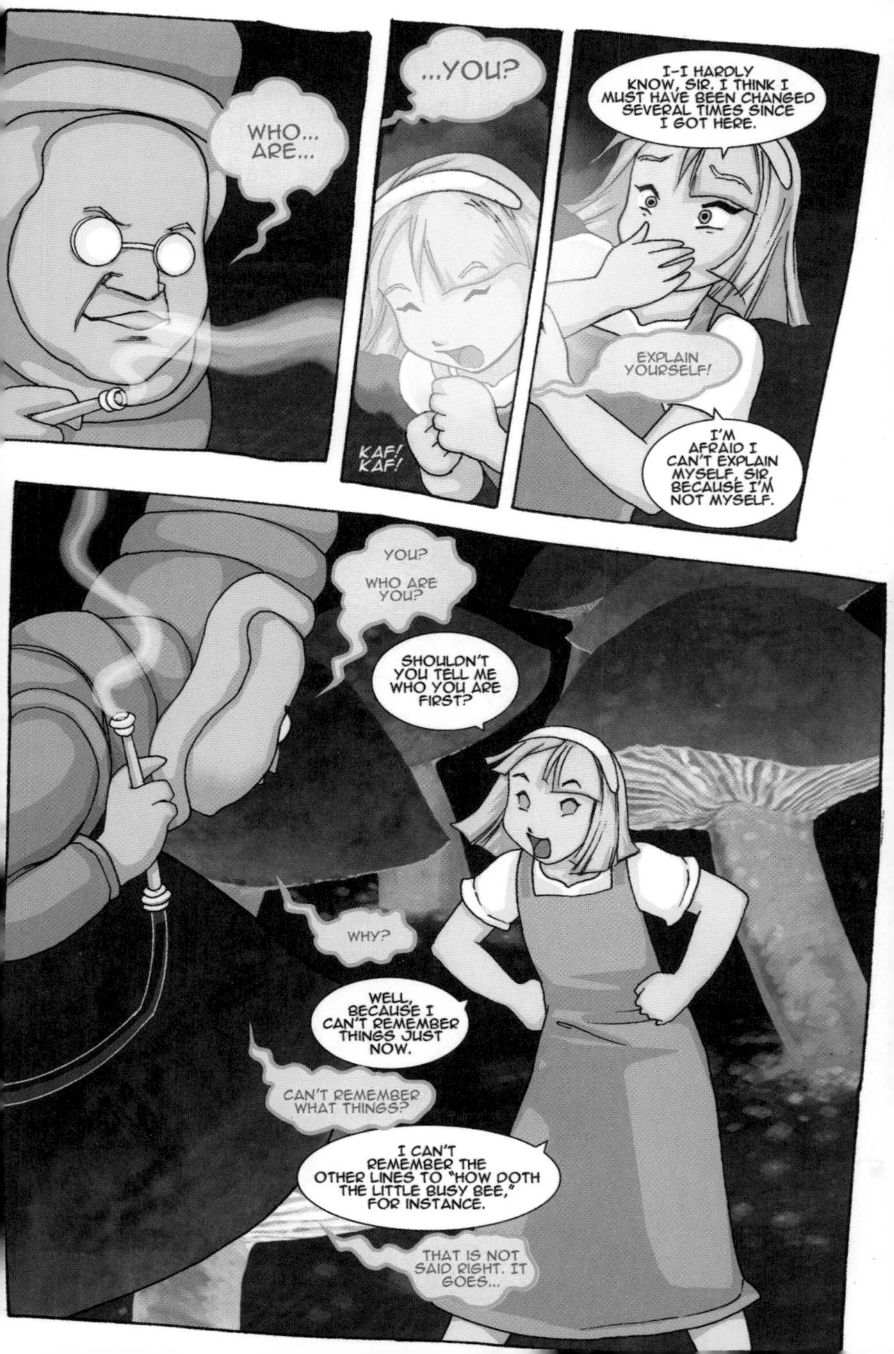
WHO... ARE...
...YOU?
KAF! KAF!
I-I HARDLY KNOW, SIR. I THINK I MUST HAVE BEEN CHANGED SEVERAL TIMES SINCE I GOT HERE.
EXPLAIN YOURSELF!
I'M AFRAID I CAN'T EXPLAIN MYSELF, SIR, BECAUSE I'M NOT MYSELF.
YOU?
WHO ARE YOU?
SHOULDN'T YOU TELL ME WHO YOU ARE FIRST?
WHY?
WELL, BECAUSE I CAN'T REMEMBER THINGS JUST NOW.
CAN'T REMEMBER WHAT THINGS?
I CAN'T REMEMBER THE OTHER LINES TO "HOW DOTH THE LITTLE BUSY BEE," FOR INSTANCE.
THAT IS NOT SAID RIGHT. IT GOES...

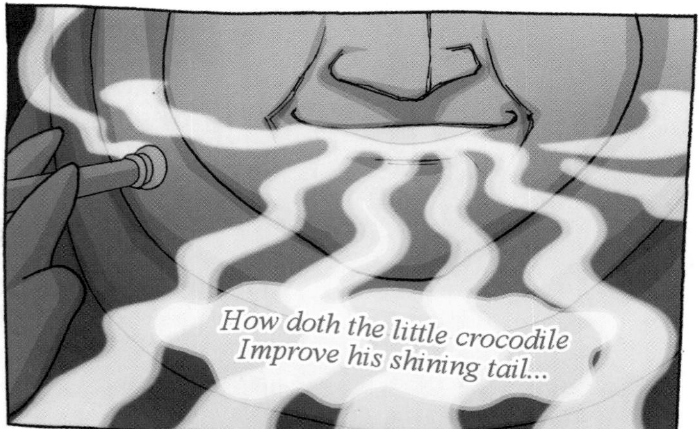
How doth the little crocodile
Improve his shining tail...

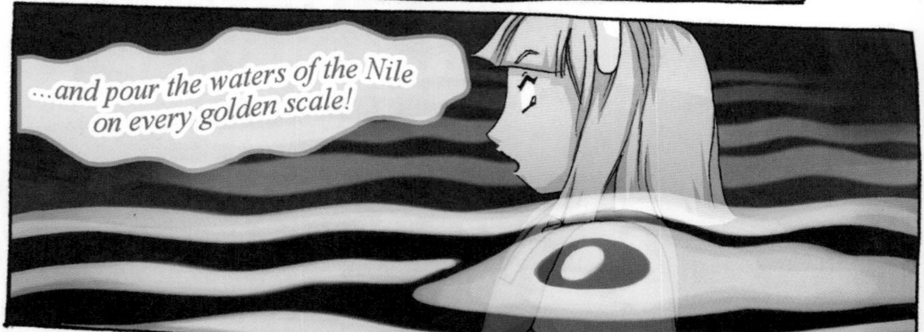
...and pour the waters of the Nile
on every golden scale!

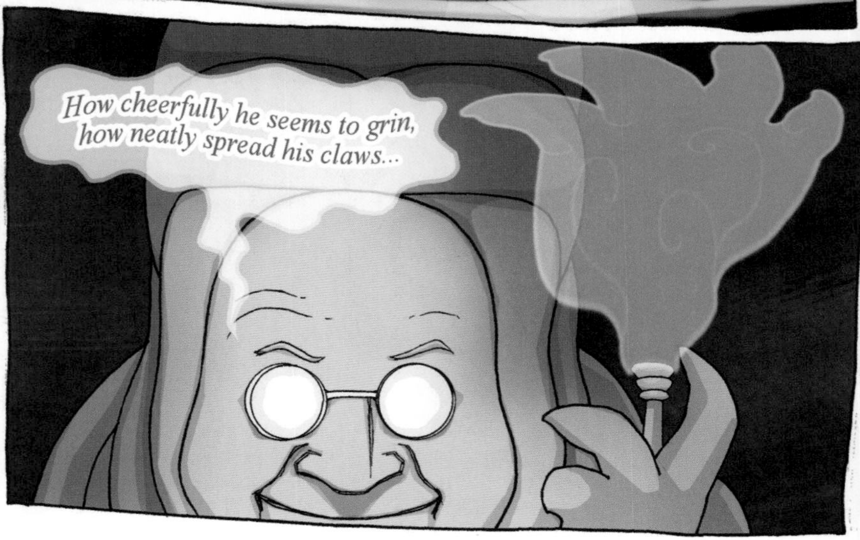
How cheerfully he seems to grin,
how neatly spread his claws...

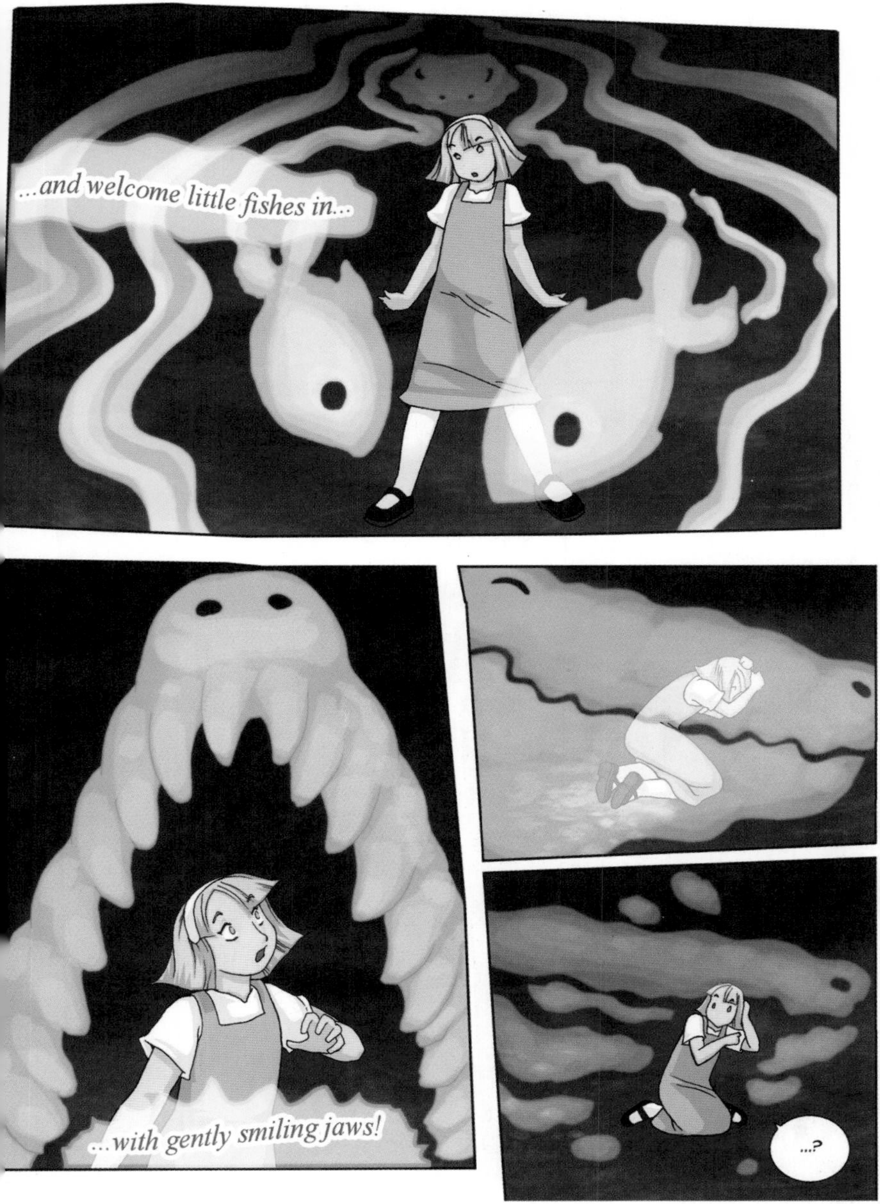
...and welcome little fishes in...
...with gently smiling jaws!
...?

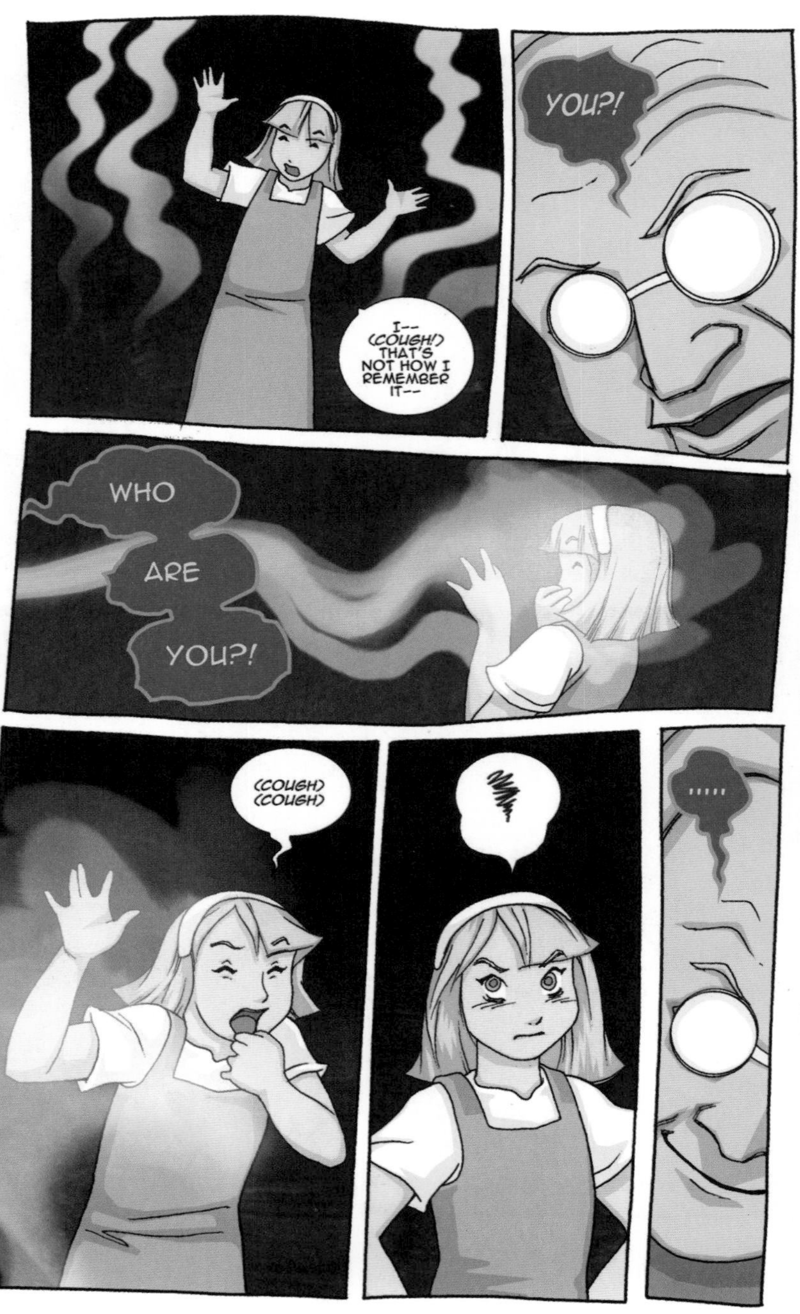
I-- (COUGH!) THAT'S NOT HOW I REMEMBER IT--
YOU?!
WHO ARE YOU?!
(COUGH) (COUGH)
.....

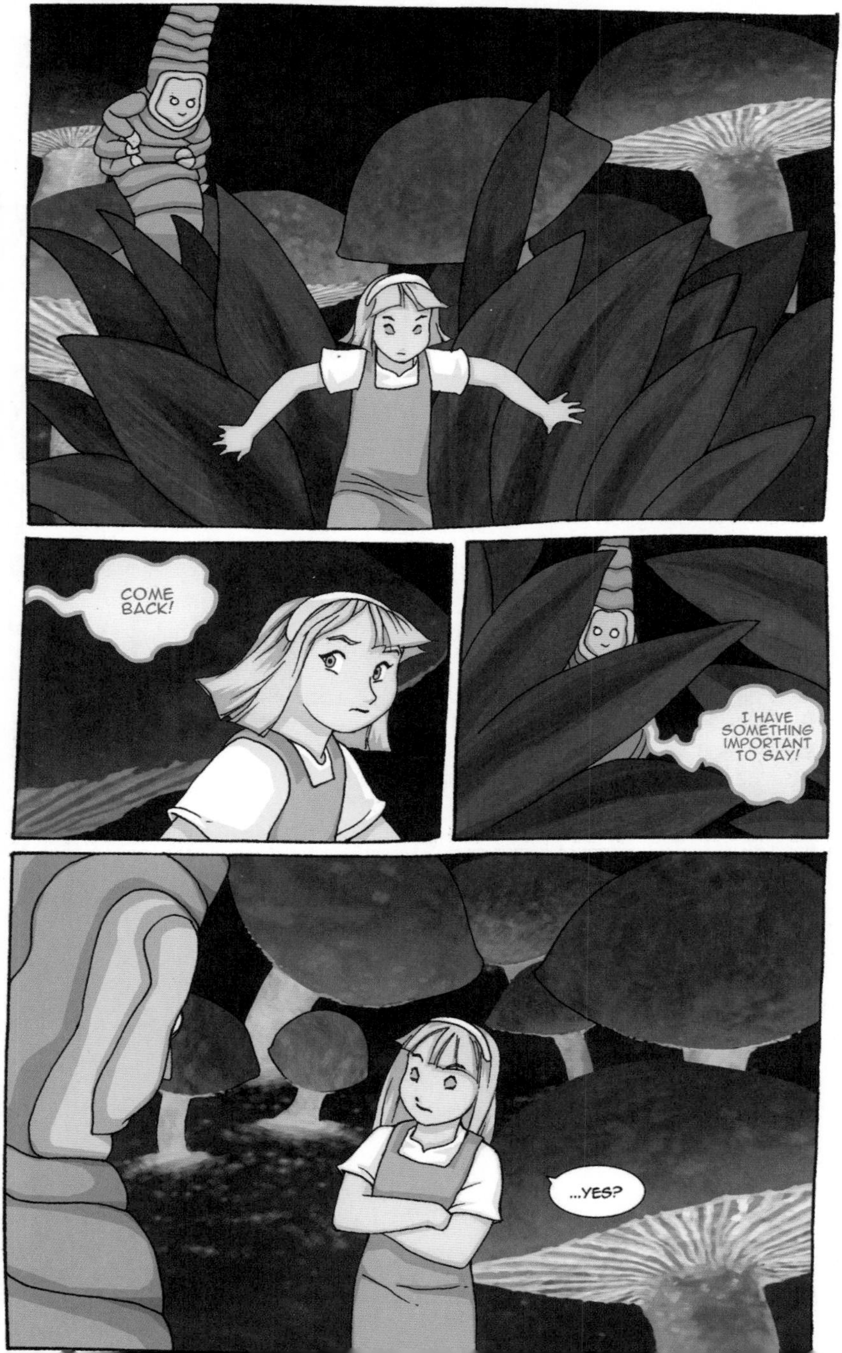
COME BACK!
I HAVE SOMETHING IMPORTANT TO SAY!
...YES?

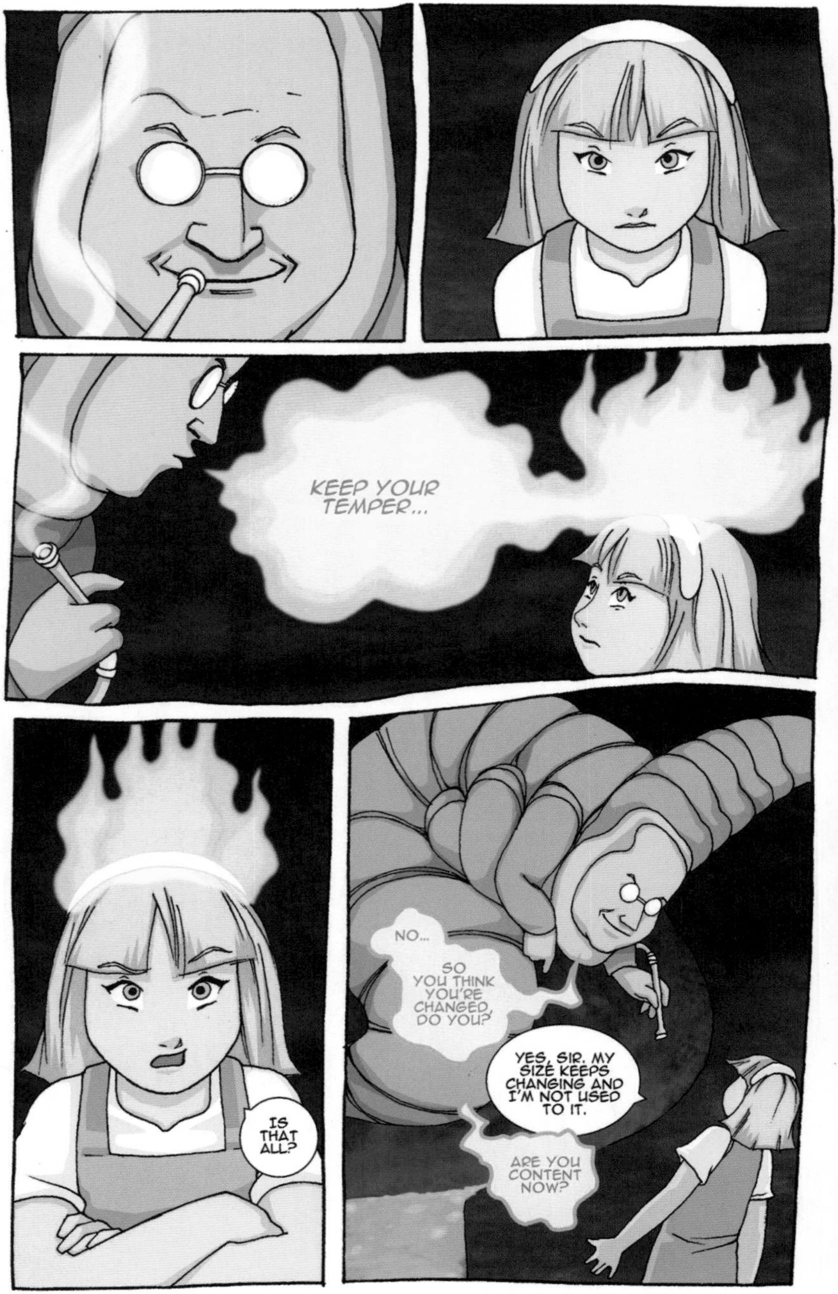
KEEP YOUR TEMPER...
IS THAT ALL?
NO...
SO YOU THINK YOU'RE CHANGED, DO YOU?
YES, SIR. MY SIZE KEEPS CHANGING AND I'M NOT USED TO IT.
ARE YOU CONTENT NOW?

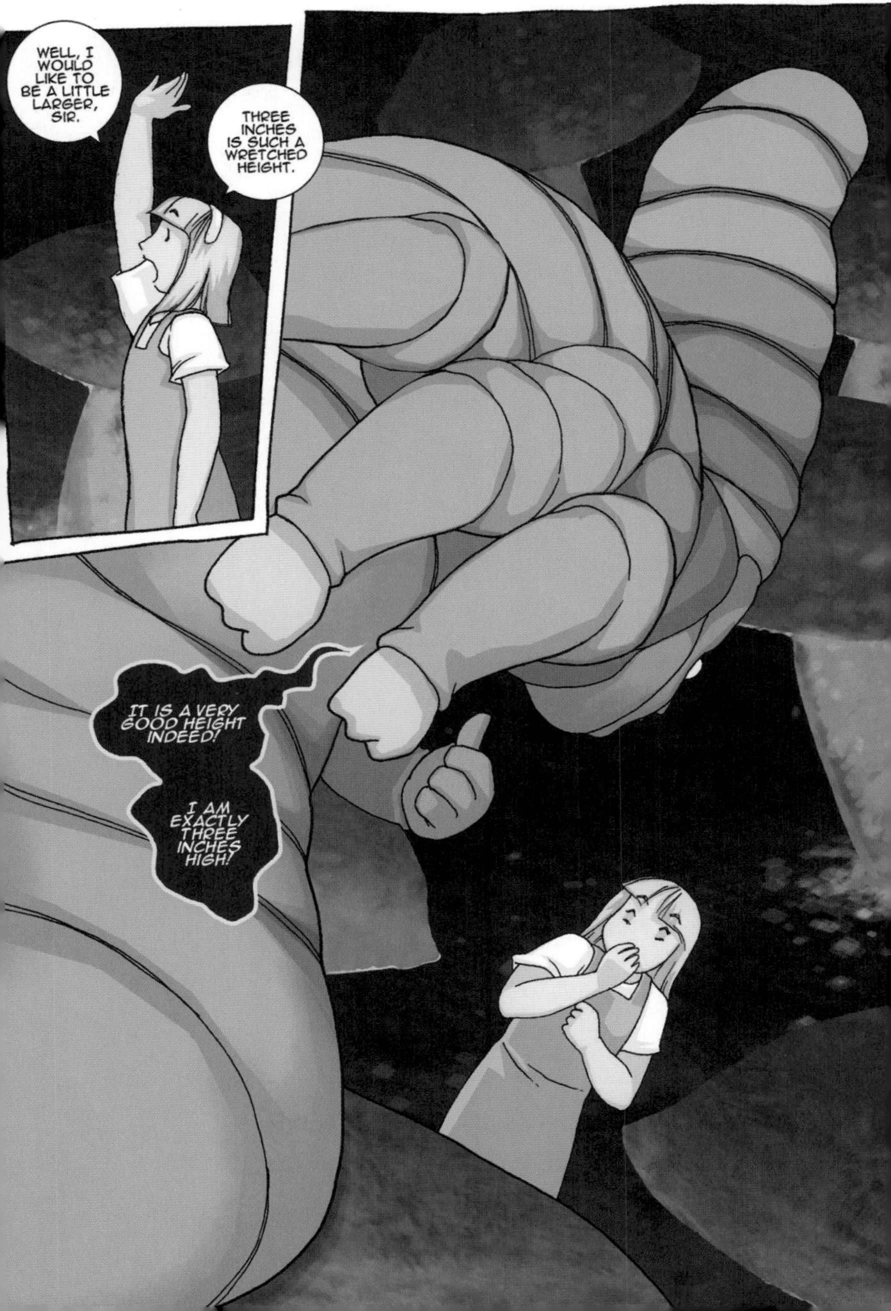

WELL, I WOULD LIKE TO BE A LITTLE LARGER, SIR.
THREE INCHES IS SUCH A WRETCHED HEIGHT.
IT IS A VERY GOOD HEIGHT INDEED!
I AM EXACTLY THREE INCHES HIGH!

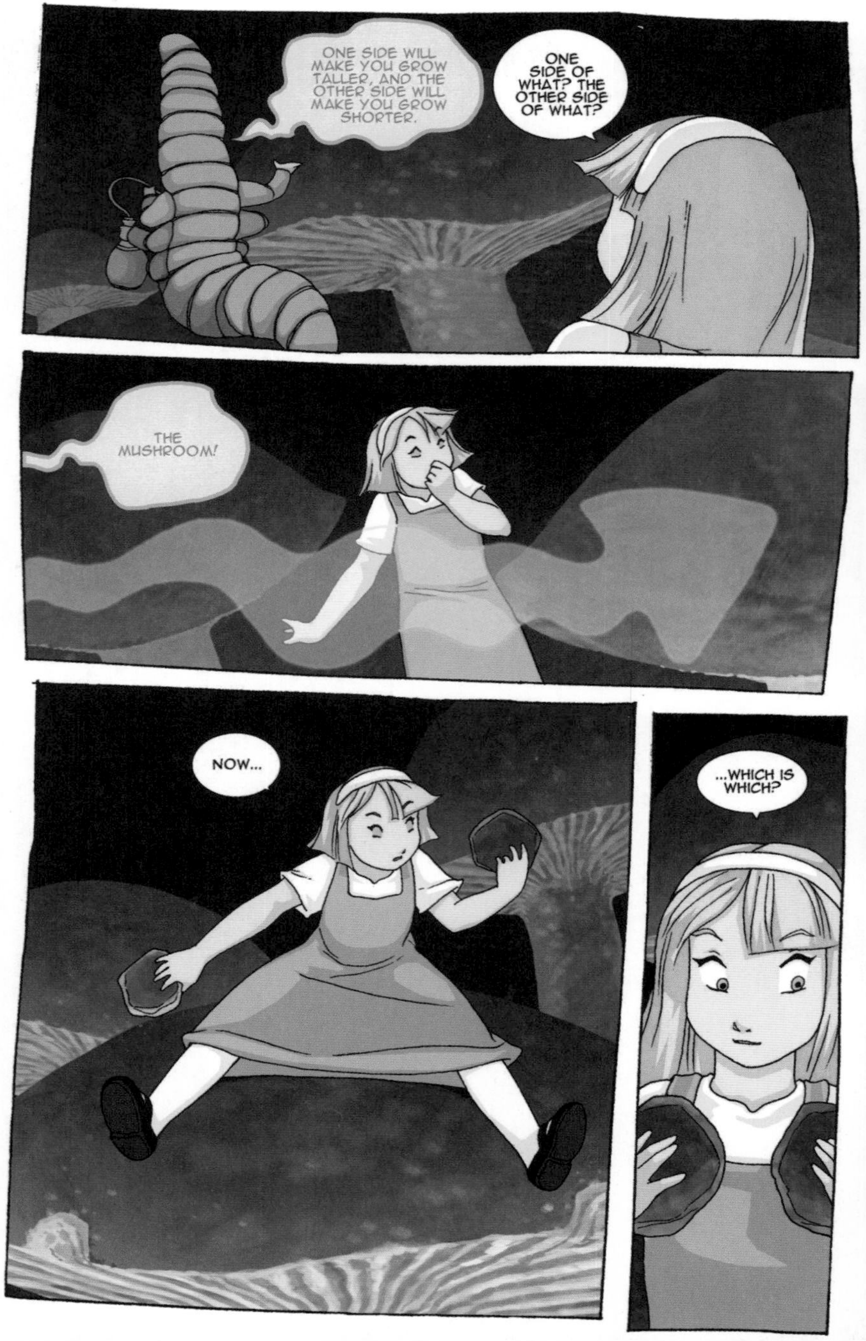
ONE SIDE WILL MAKE YOU GROW TALLER, AND THE OTHER SIDE WILL MAKE YOU GROW SHORTER.
ONE SIDE OF WHAT? THE OTHER SIDE OF WHAT?
THE MUSHROOM!
NOW...
...WHICH IS WHICH?

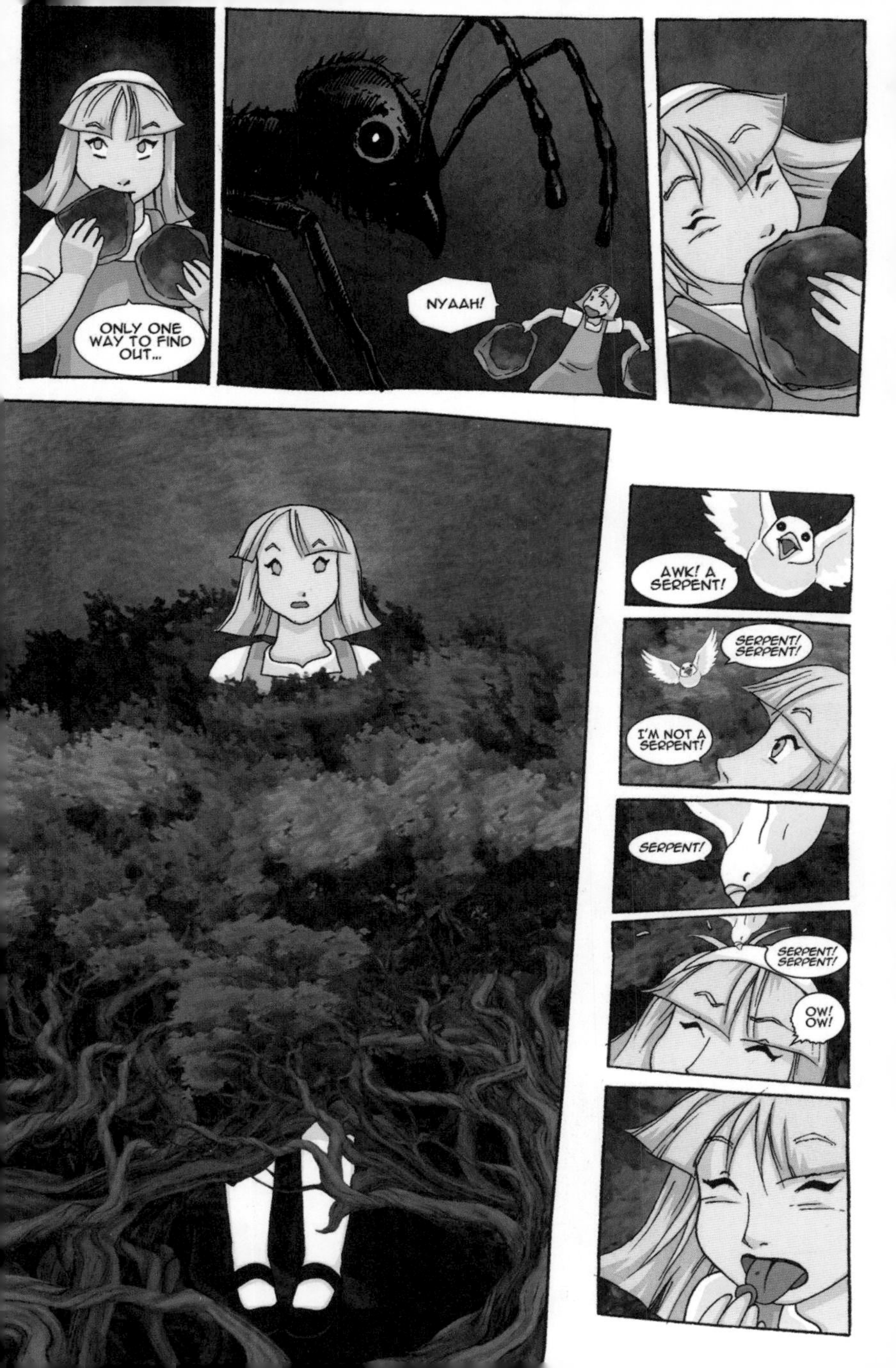
ONLY ONE WAY TO FIND OUT...
NYAAH!
AWK! A SERPENT!
SERPENT! SERPENT!
I'M NOT A SERPENT!
SERPENT!
SERPENT! SERPENT!
OW! OW!

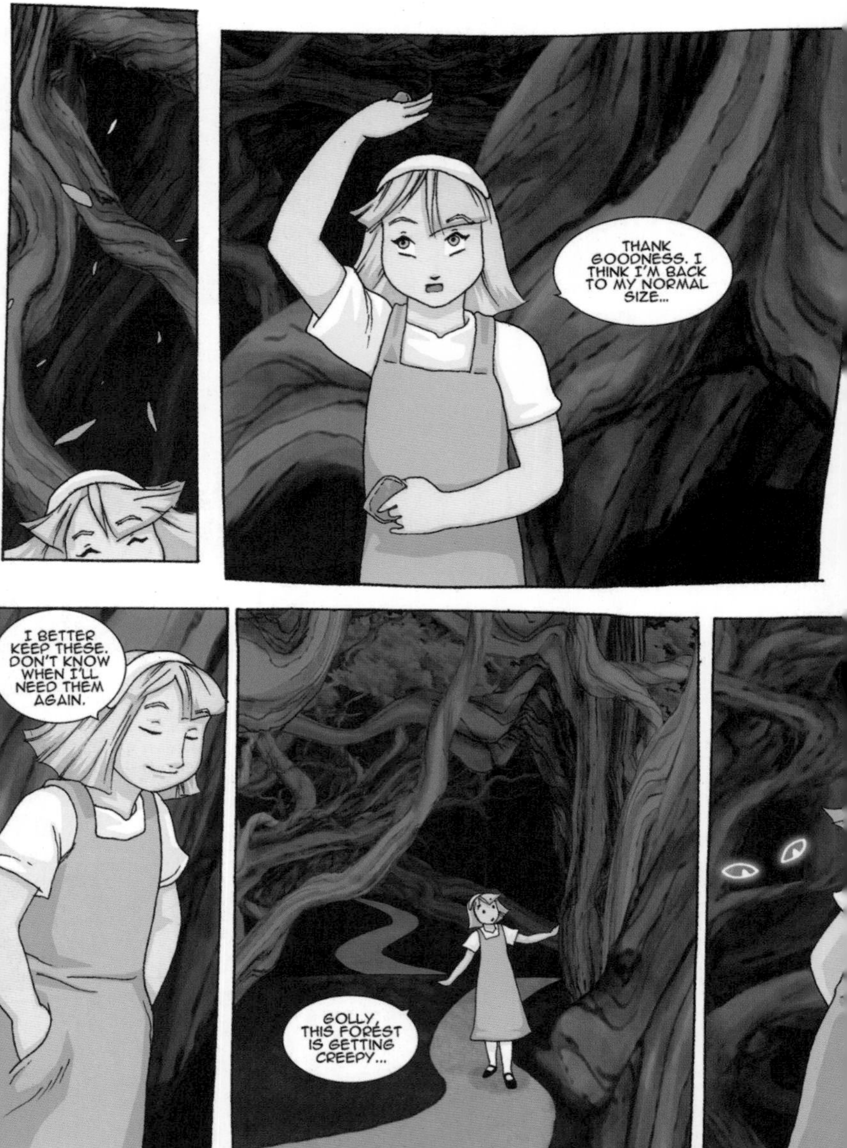
THANK GOODNESS. I THINK I'M BACK TO MY NORMAL SIZE...
I BETTER KEEP THESE. DON'T KNOW WHEN I'LL NEED THEM AGAIN.
GOLLY, THIS FOREST IS GETTING CREEPY...

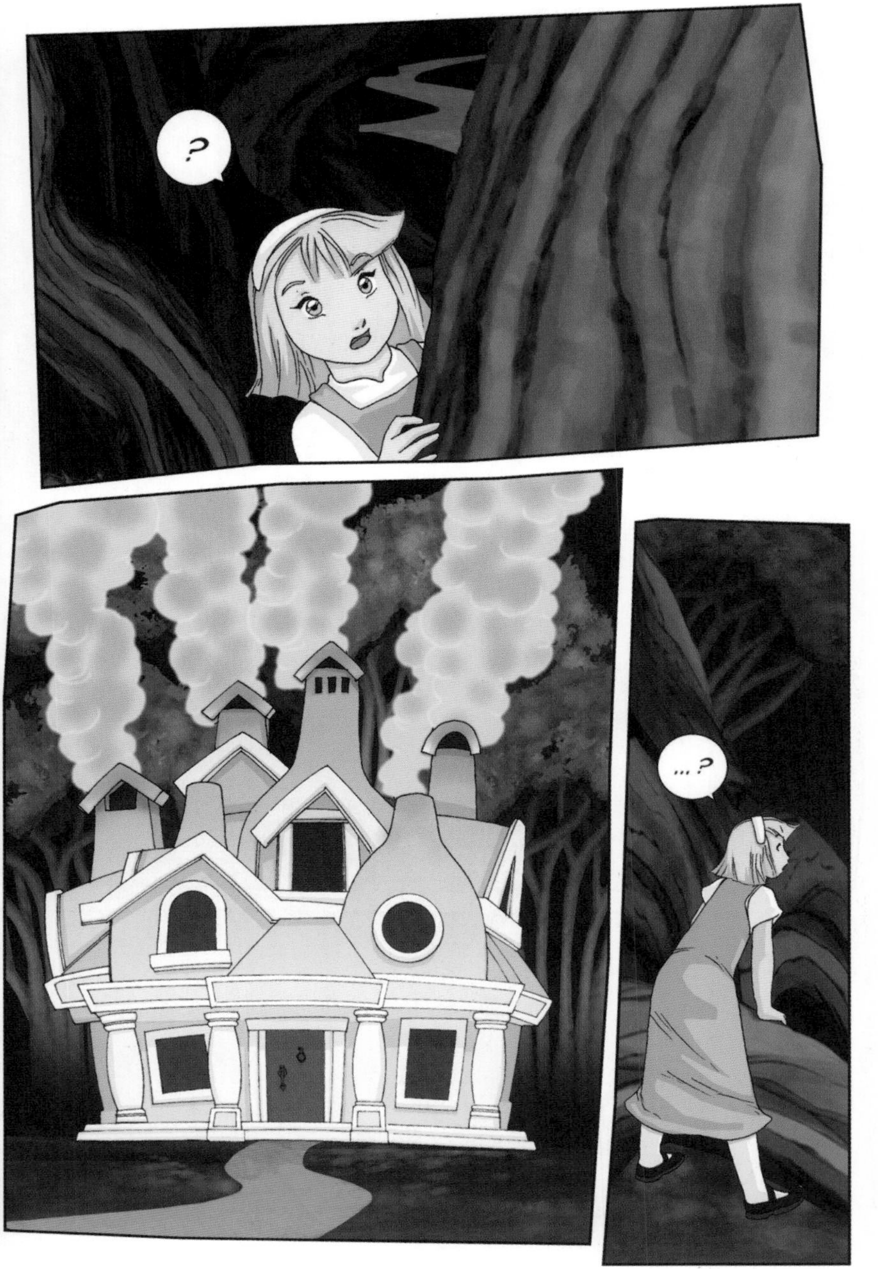
?
...?

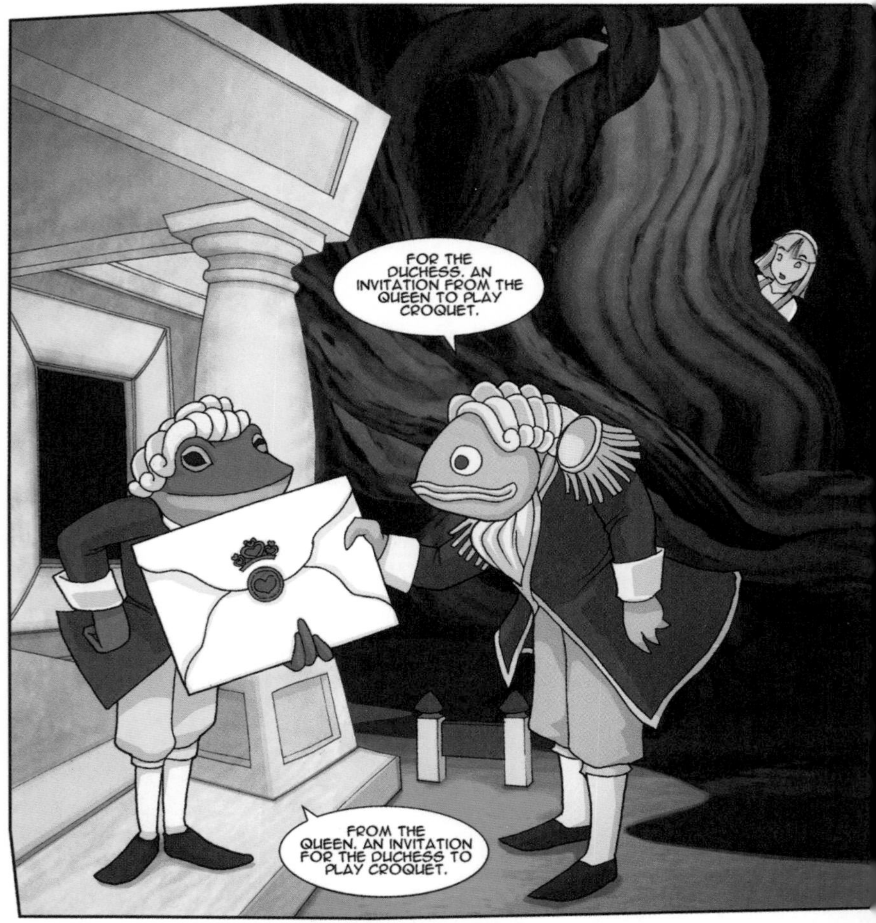
FOR THE DUCHESS. AN INVITATION FROM THE QUEEN TO PLAY CROQUET.
FROM THE QUEEN. AN INVITATION FOR THE DUCHESS TO PLAY CROQUET.

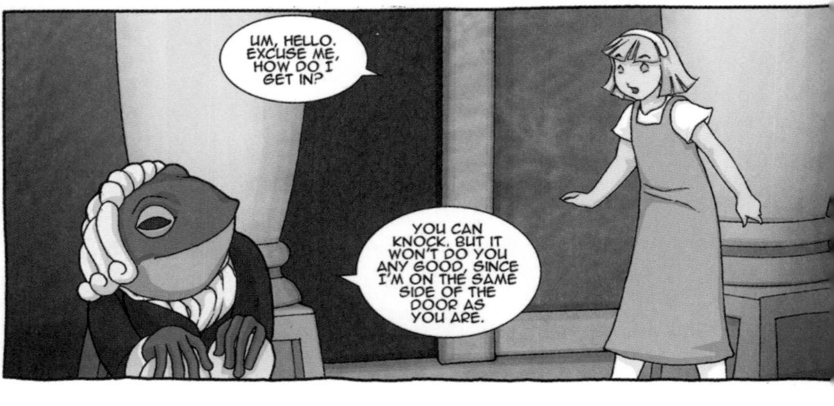
UM, HELLO. EXCUSE ME, HOW DO I GET IN?
YOU CAN KNOCK. BUT IT WON'T DO YOU ANY GOOD, SINCE I'M ON THE SAME SIDE OF THE DOOR AS YOU ARE.

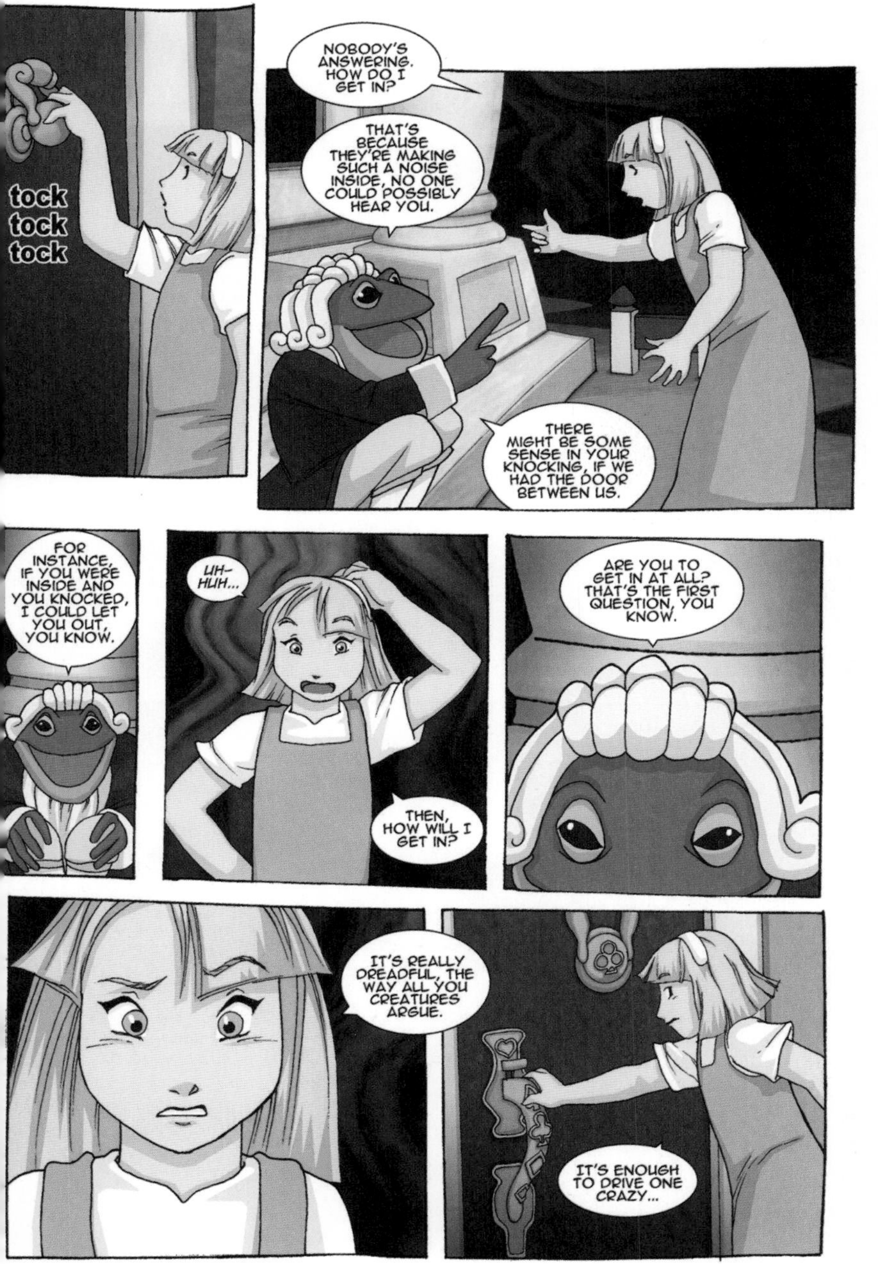
tock
tock
tock
NOBODY'S ANSWERING. HOW DO I GET IN?
THAT'S BECAUSE THEY'RE MAKING SUCH A NOISE INSIDE, NO ONE COULD POSSIBLY HEAR YOU.
THERE MIGHT BE SOME SENSE IN YOUR KNOCKING, IF WE HAD THE DOOR BETWEEN US.
FOR INSTANCE, IF YOU WERE INSIDE AND YOU KNOCKED, I COULD LET YOU OUT, YOU KNOW.
UH-HUH...
THEN, HOW WILL I GET IN?
ARE YOU TO GET IN AT ALL? THAT'S THE FIRST QUESTION, YOU KNOW.
IT'S REALLY DREADFUL, THE WAY ALL YOU CREATURES ARGUE.
IT'S ENOUGH TO DRIVE ONE CRAZY...

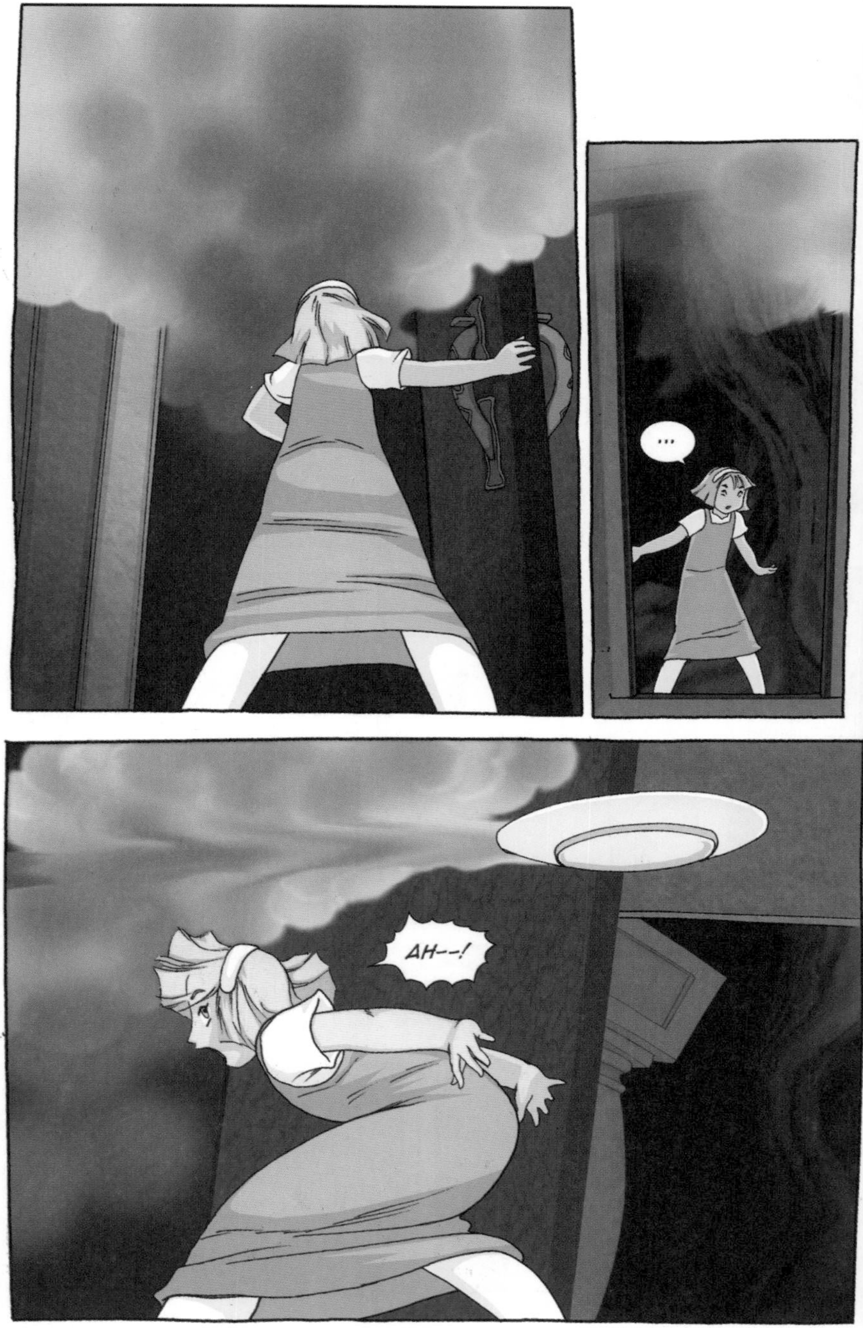
...
AH--!

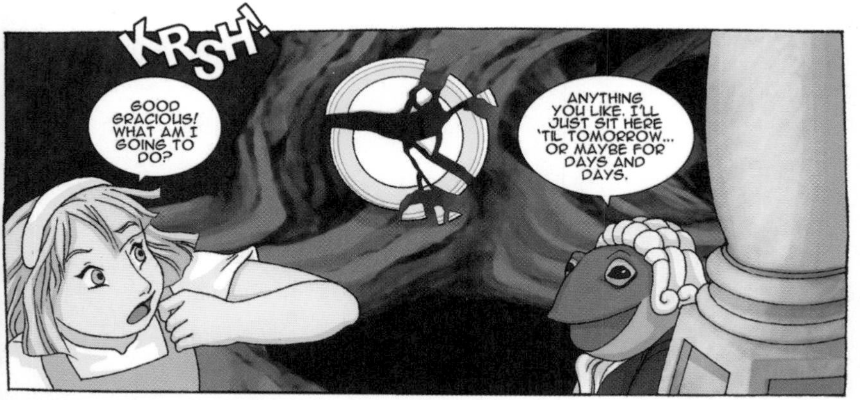
KRSH!
GOOD GRACIOUS! WHAT AM I GOING TO DO?
ANYTHING YOU LIKE. I'LL JUST SIT HERE 'TIL TOMORROW... OR MAYBE FOR DAYS AND DAYS.

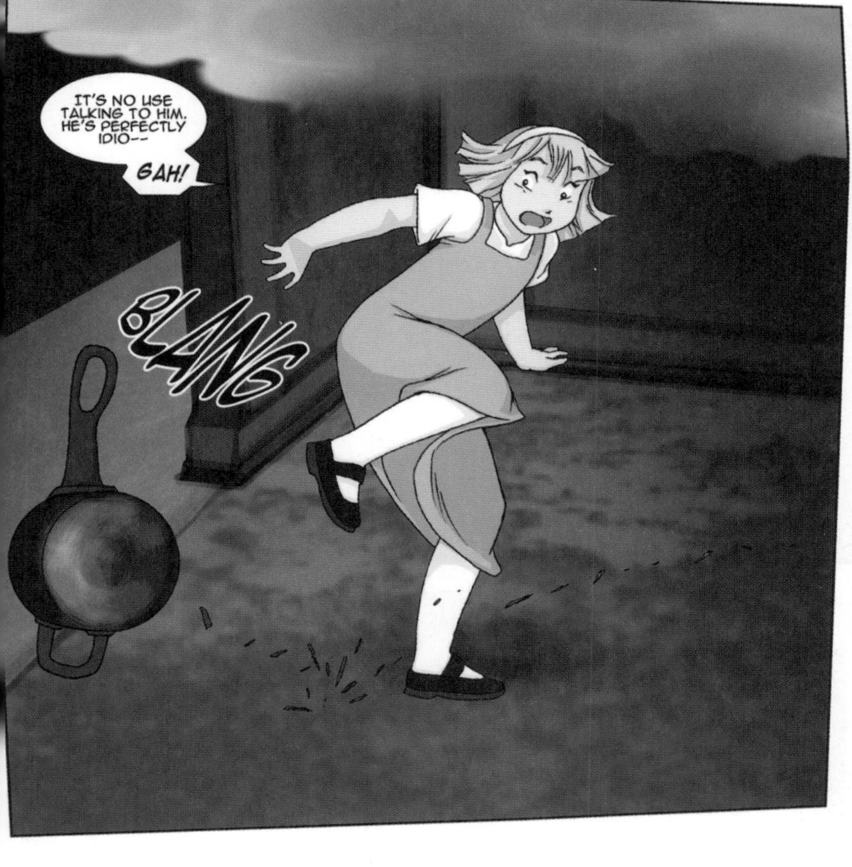
IT'S NO USE TALKING TO HIM. HE'S PERFECTLY IDIO--
GAH!
BLANG

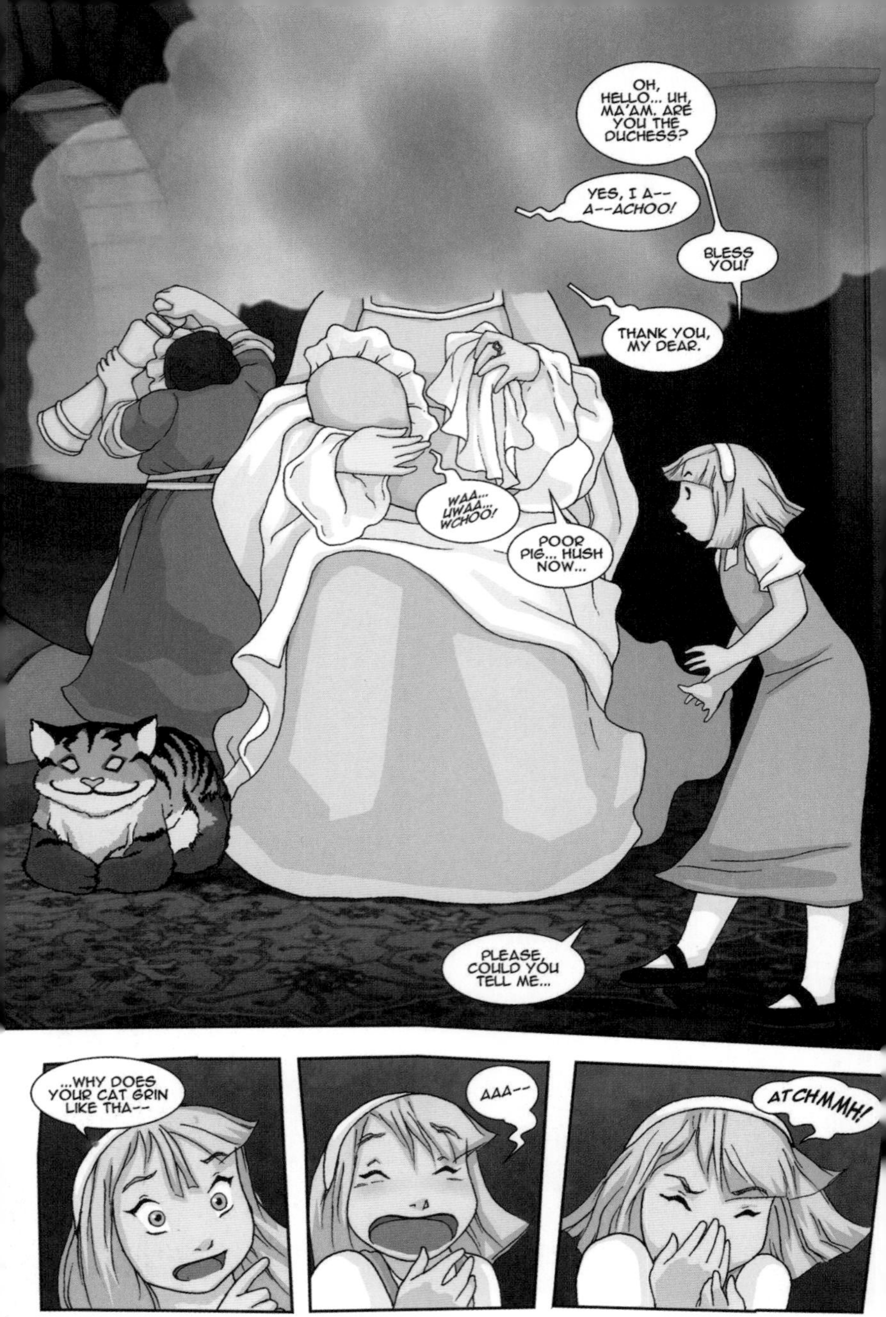
OH, HELLO... UH, MA'AM. ARE YOU THE DUCHESS?
YES, I A-- A--ACHOO!
BLESS YOU!
THANK YOU, MY DEAR.
WAA... UWAA... WCHOO!
POOR PIG... HUSH NOW...
PLEASE, COULD YOU TELL ME...
...WHY DOES YOUR CAT GRIN LIKE THA--
AAA--
ATCHMMH!

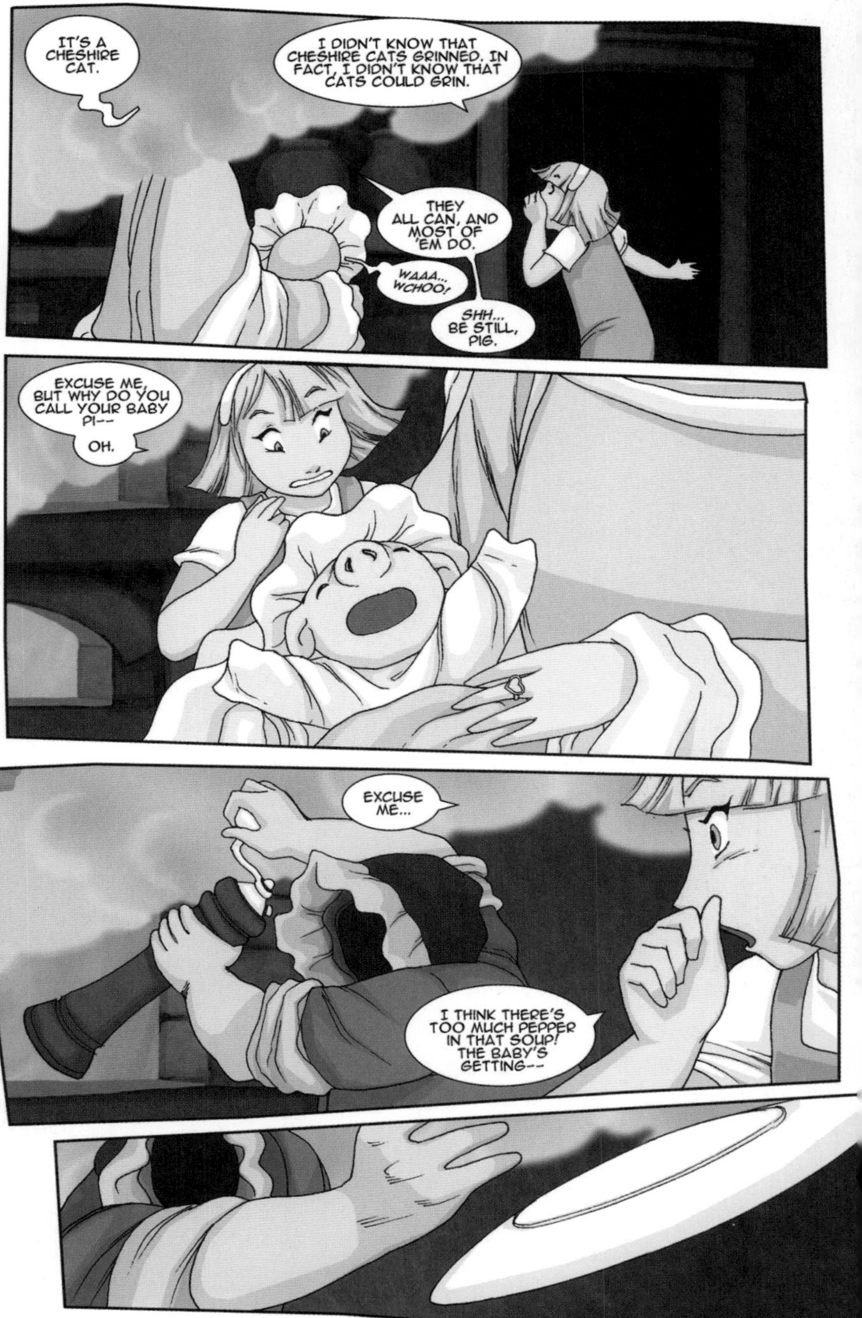
IT'S A CHESHIRE CAT.
I DIDN'T KNOW THAT CHESHIRE CATS GRINNED. IN FACT, I DIDN'T KNOW THAT CATS COULD GRIN.
THEY ALL CAN, AND MOST OF 'EM DO.
WAAA... WCHOO!
SHH... BE STILL, PIG.
EXCUSE ME, BUT WHY DO YOU CALL YOUR BABY PI--
OH.
EXCUSE ME...
I THINK THERE'S TOO MUCH PEPPER IN THAT SOUP! THE BABY'S GETTING--

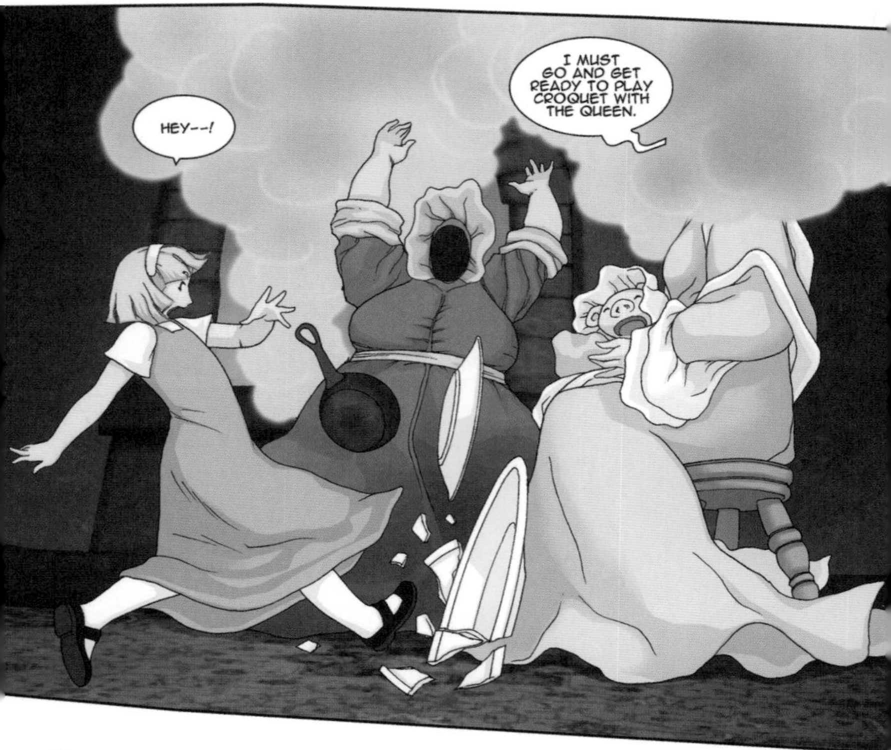
HEY--!
I MUST GO AND GET READY TO PLAY CROQUET WITH THE QUEEN.

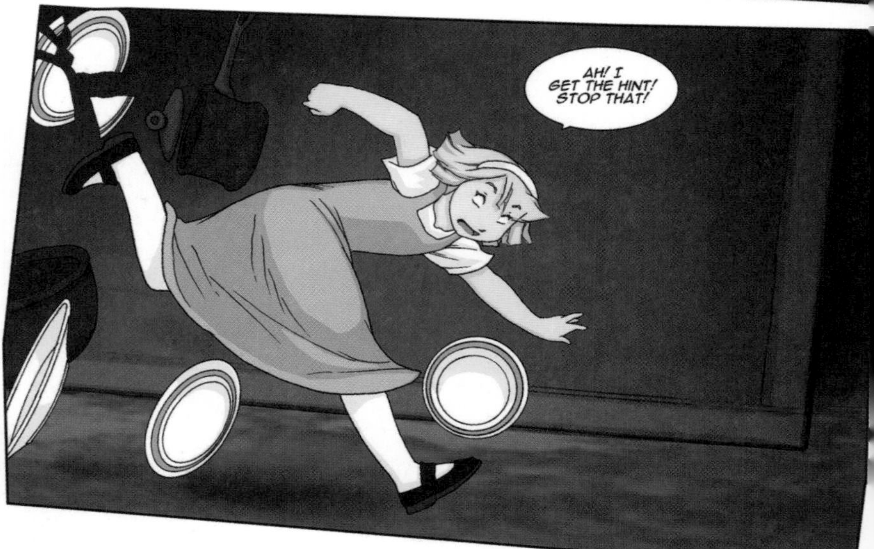
AH! I GET THE HINT! STOP THAT!

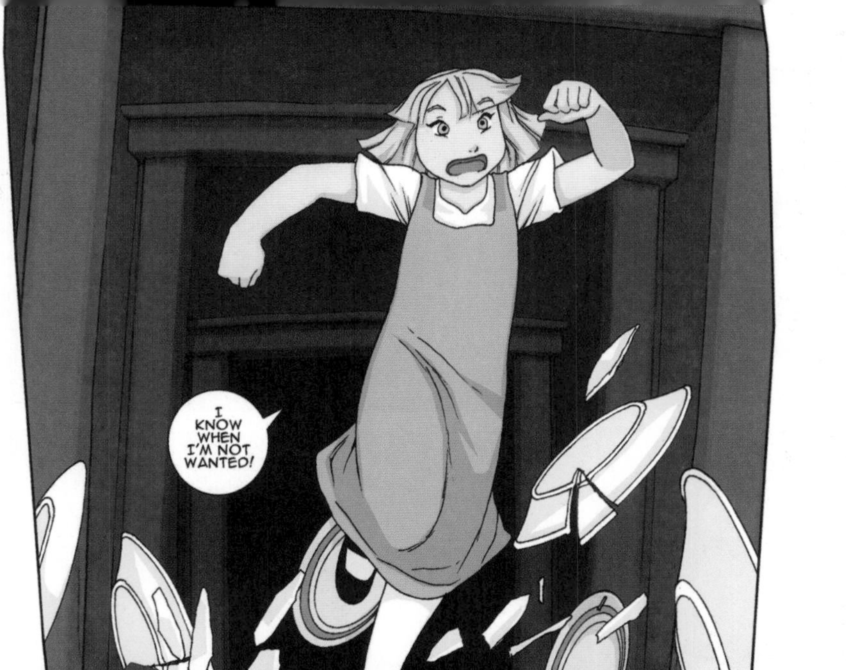
I KNOW WHEN I'M NOT WANTED!

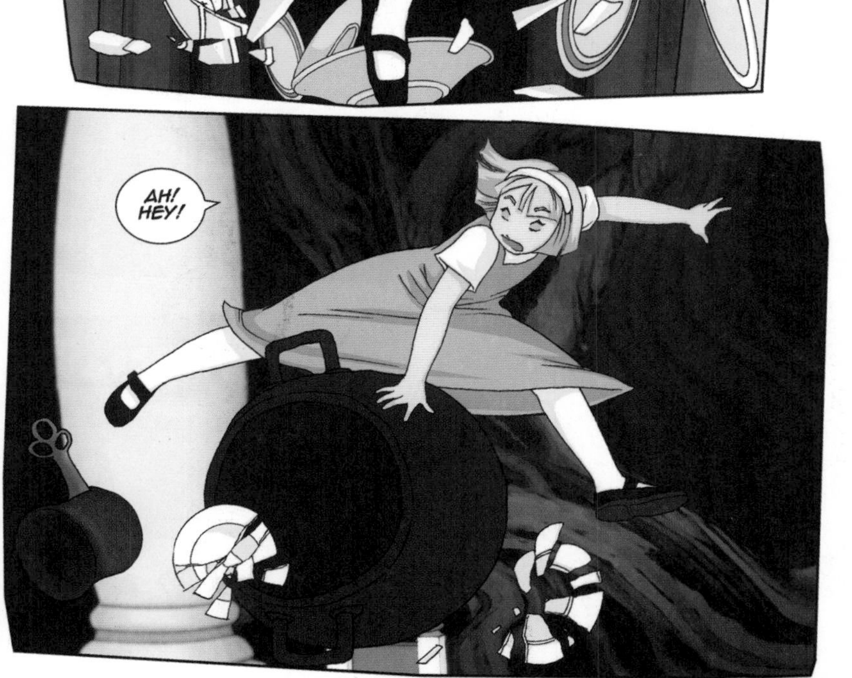
AH! HEY!

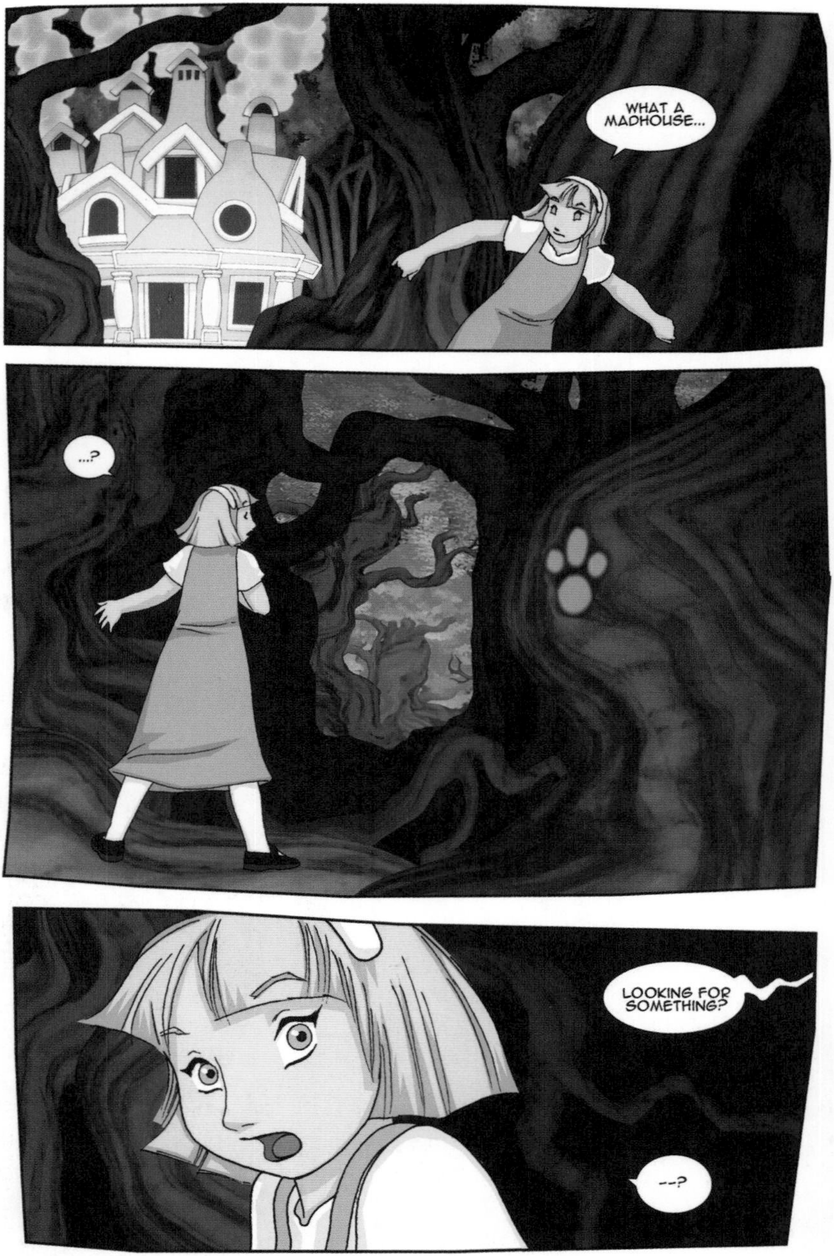
WHAT A MADHOUSE...
...?
LOOKING FOR SOMETHING?
--?

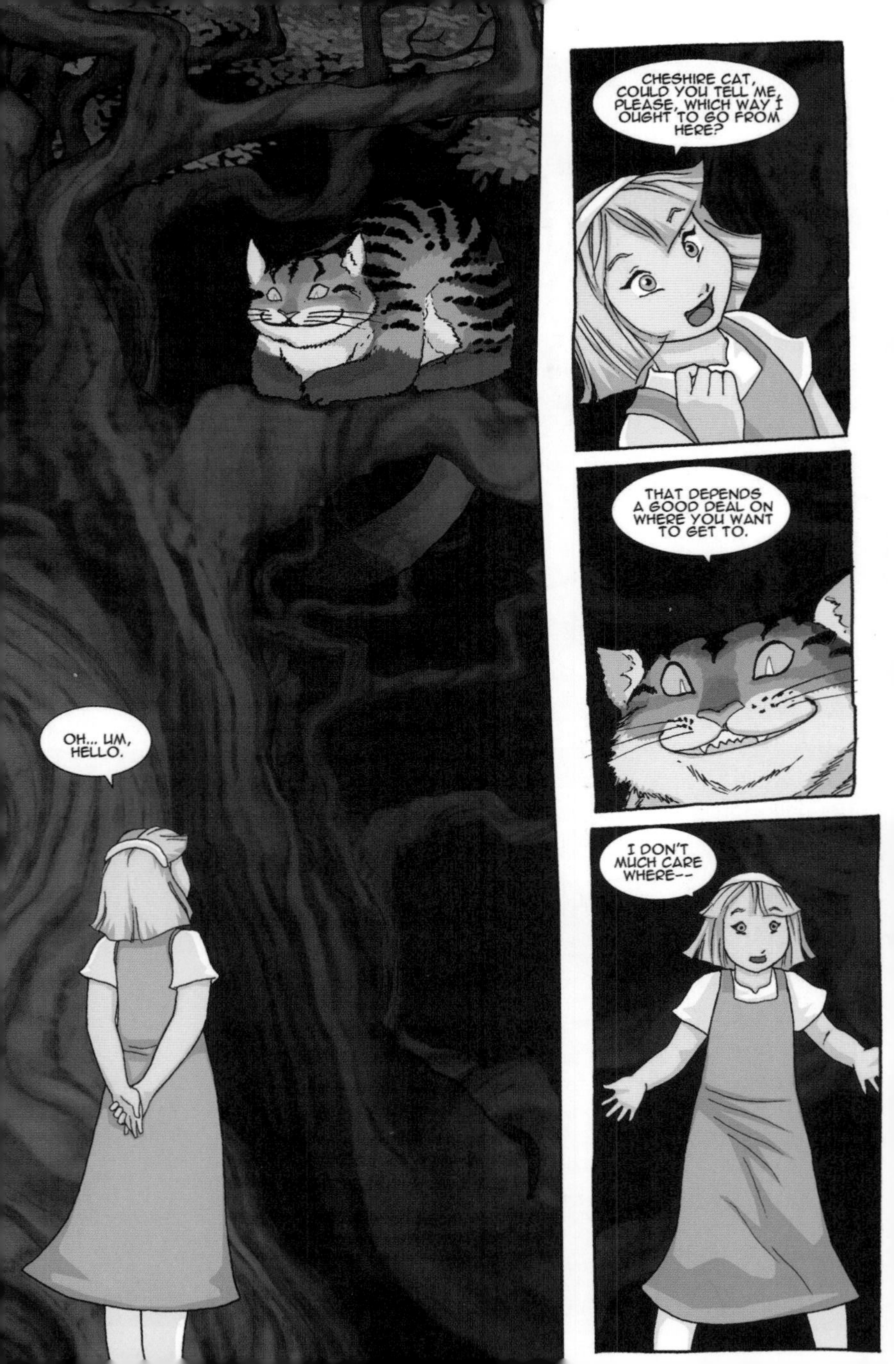
OH... UM, HELLO.
CHESHIRE CAT, COULD YOU TELL ME, PLEASE, WHICH WAY I OUGHT TO GO FROM HERE?
THAT DEPENDS A GOOD DEAL ON WHERE YOU WANT TO GET TO.
I DON'T MUCH CARE WHERE--

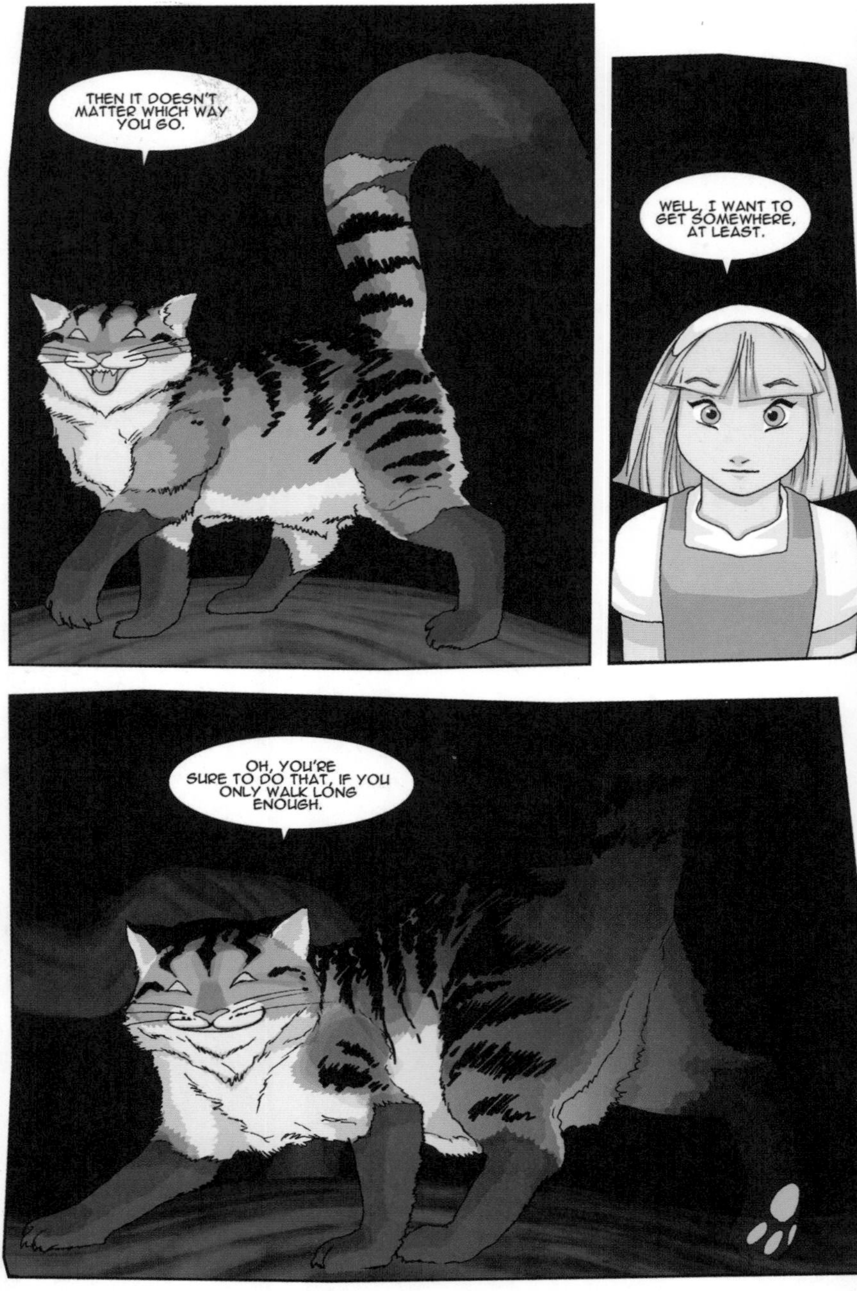
THEN IT DOESN'T MATTER WHICH WAY YOU GO.
WELL, I WANT TO GET SOMEWHERE, AT LEAST.
OH, YOU'RE SURE TO DO THAT, IF YOU ONLY WALK LONG ENOUGH.

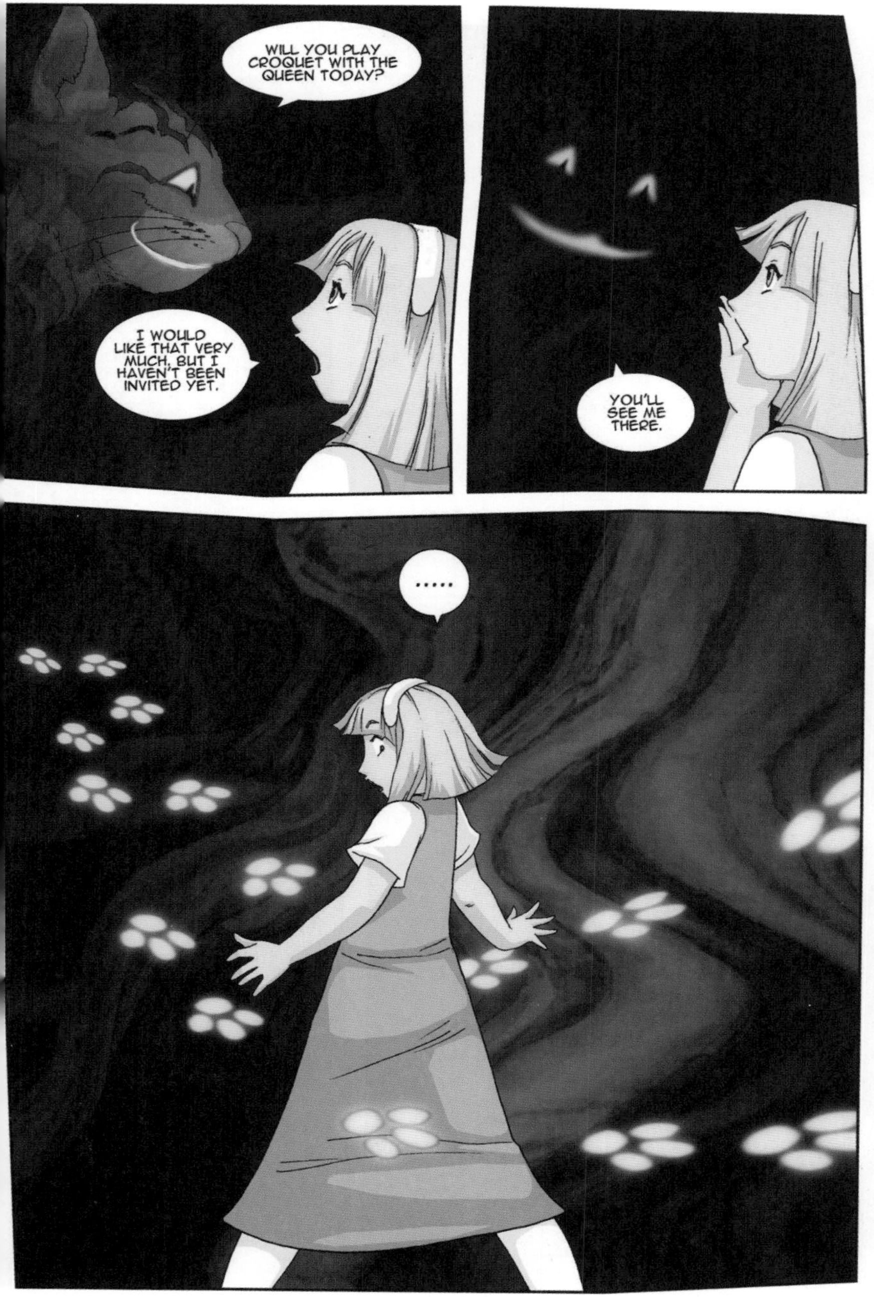
WILL YOU PLAY CROQUET WITH THE QUEEN TODAY?
I WOULD LIKE THAT VERY MUCH, BUT I HAVEN'T BEEN INVITED YET.
YOU'LL SEE ME THERE.
......

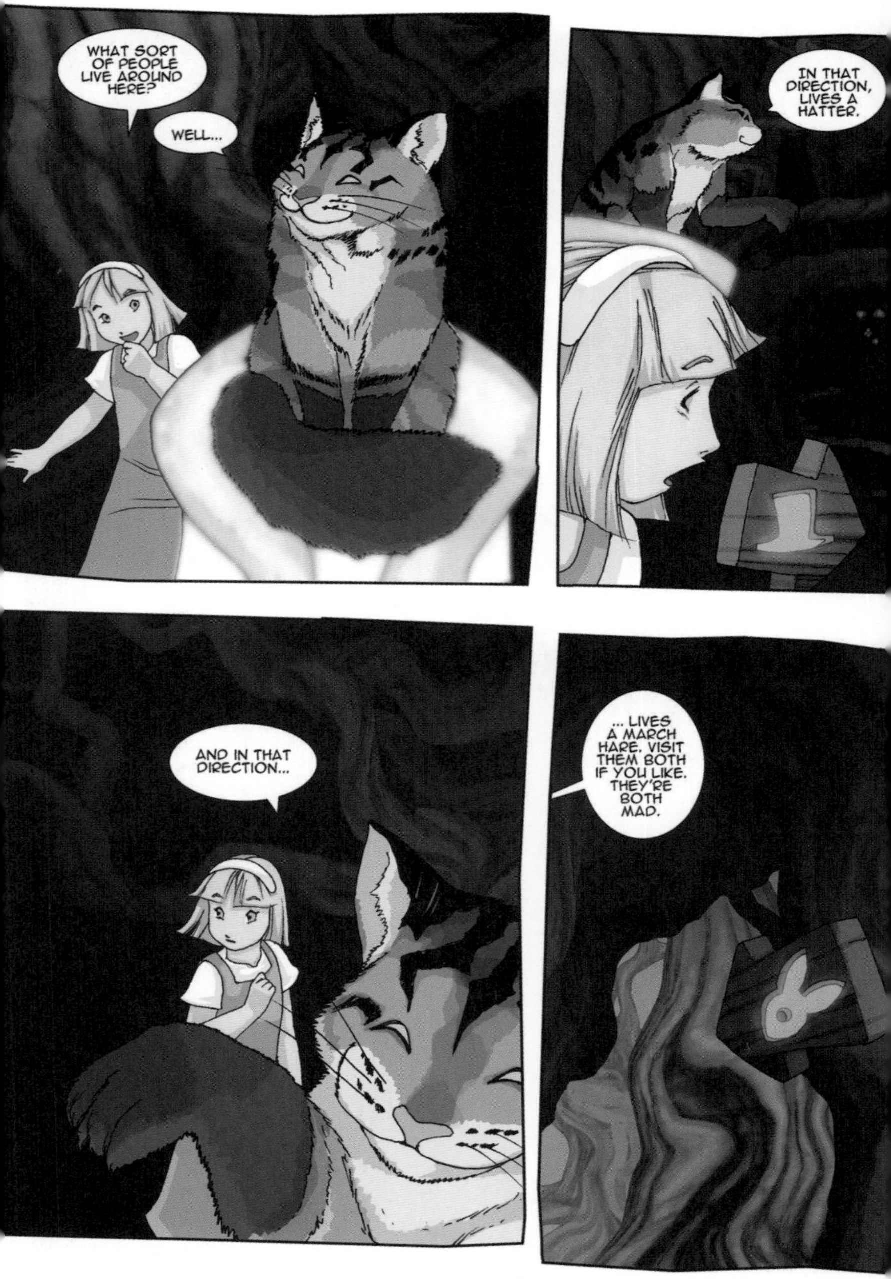
WHAT SORT OF PEOPLE LIVE AROUND HERE?
WELL...
IN THAT DIRECTION, LIVES A HATTER.
AND IN THAT DIRECTION...
... LIVES A MARCH HARE. VISIT THEM BOTH IF YOU LIKE. THEY'RE BOTH MAD.

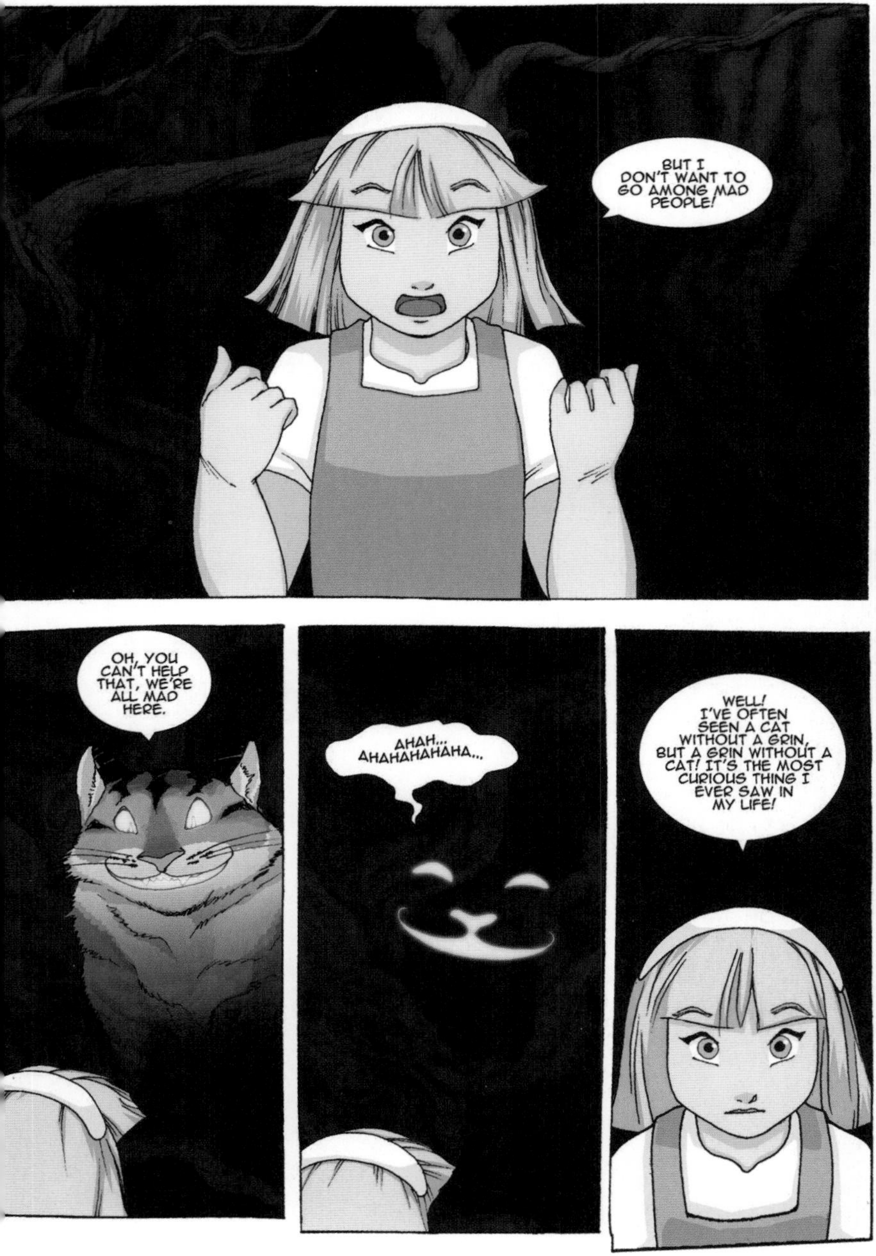
BUT I DON'T WANT TO GO AMONG MAD PEOPLE!
OH, YOU CAN'T HELP THAT, WE'RE ALL MAD HERE.
AHAH... AHAHAHAHAHA...
WELL! I'VE OFTEN SEEN A CAT WITHOUT A GRIN, BUT A GRIN WITHOUT A CAT! IT'S THE MOST CURIOUS THING I EVER SAW IN MY LIFE!

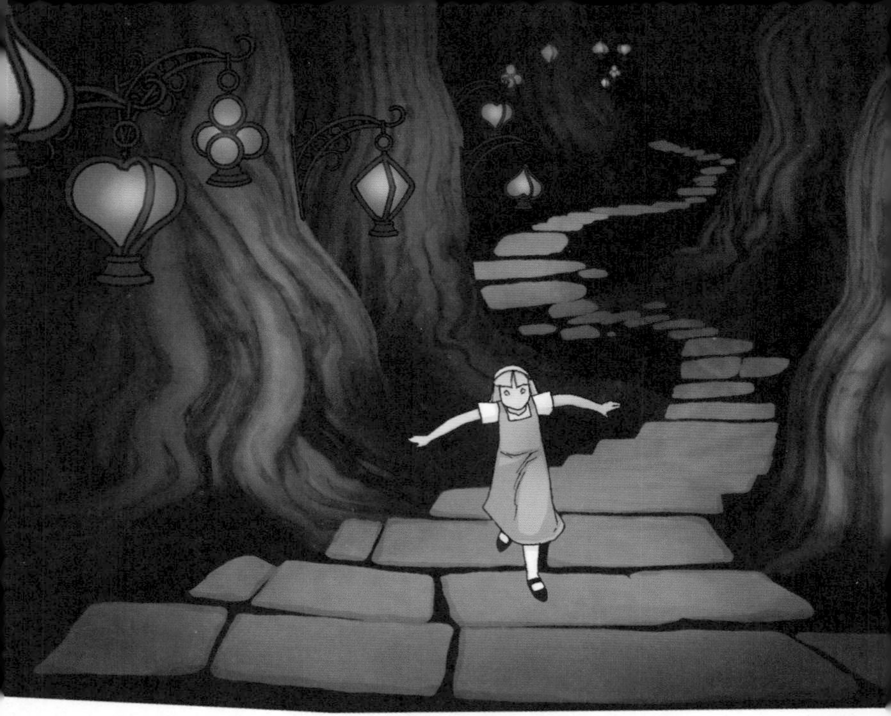

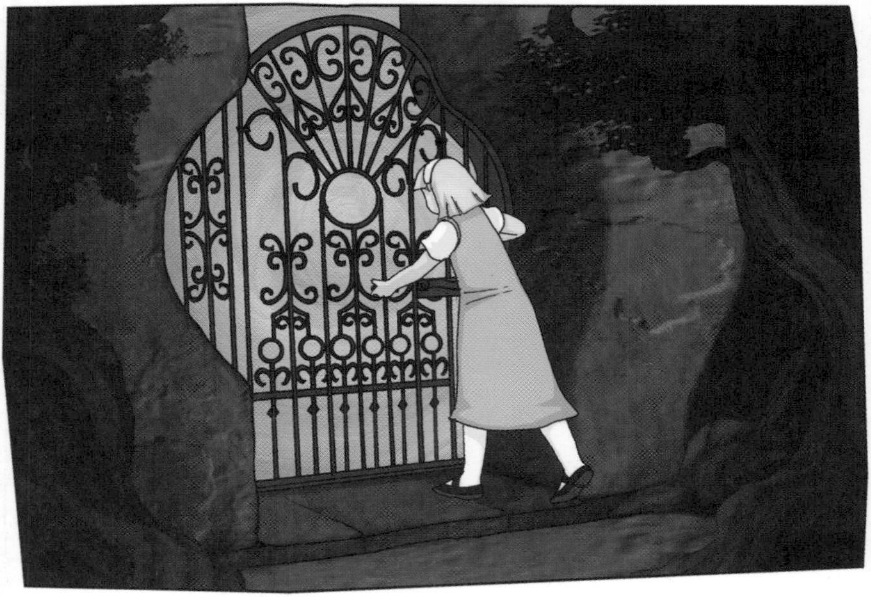

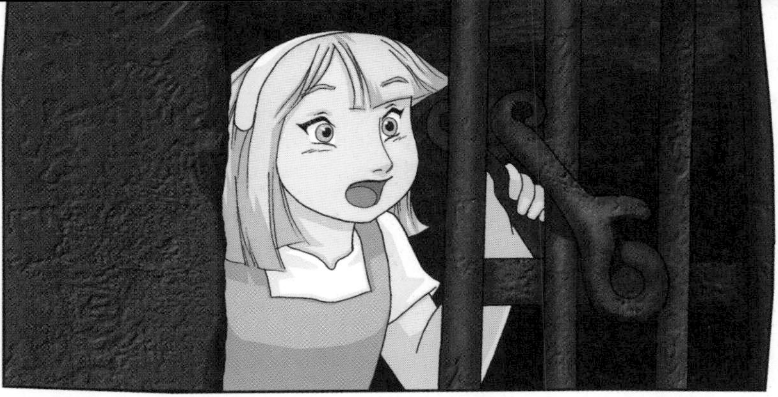

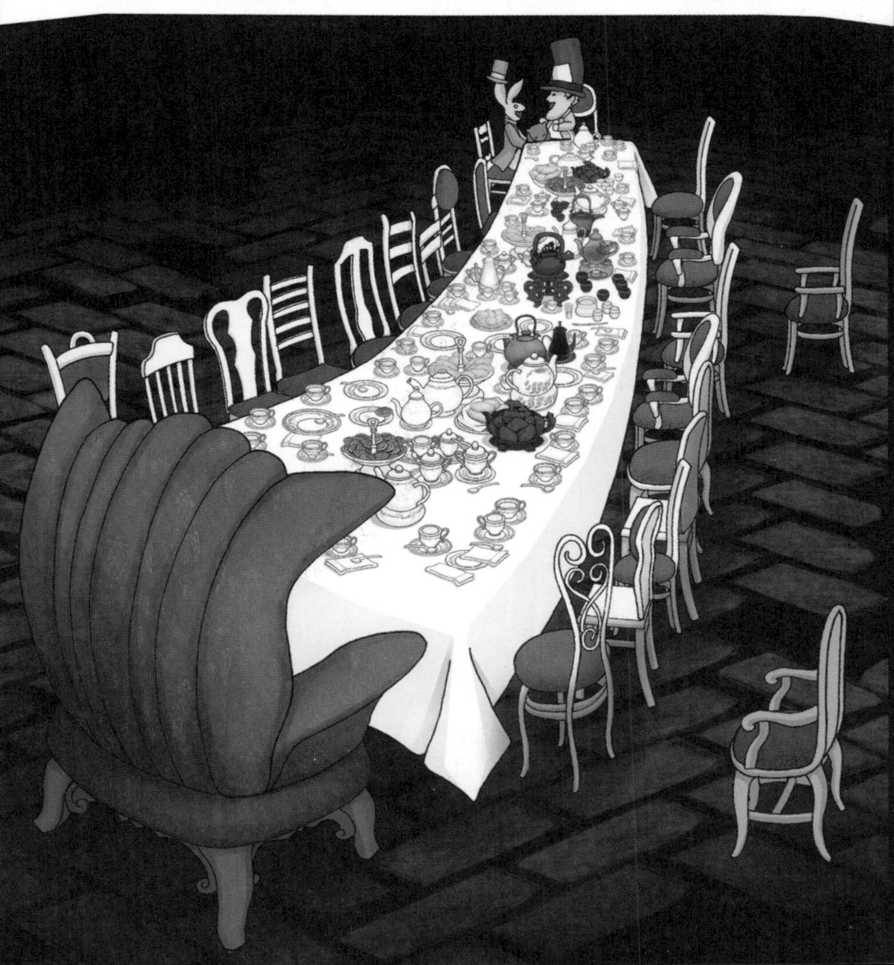

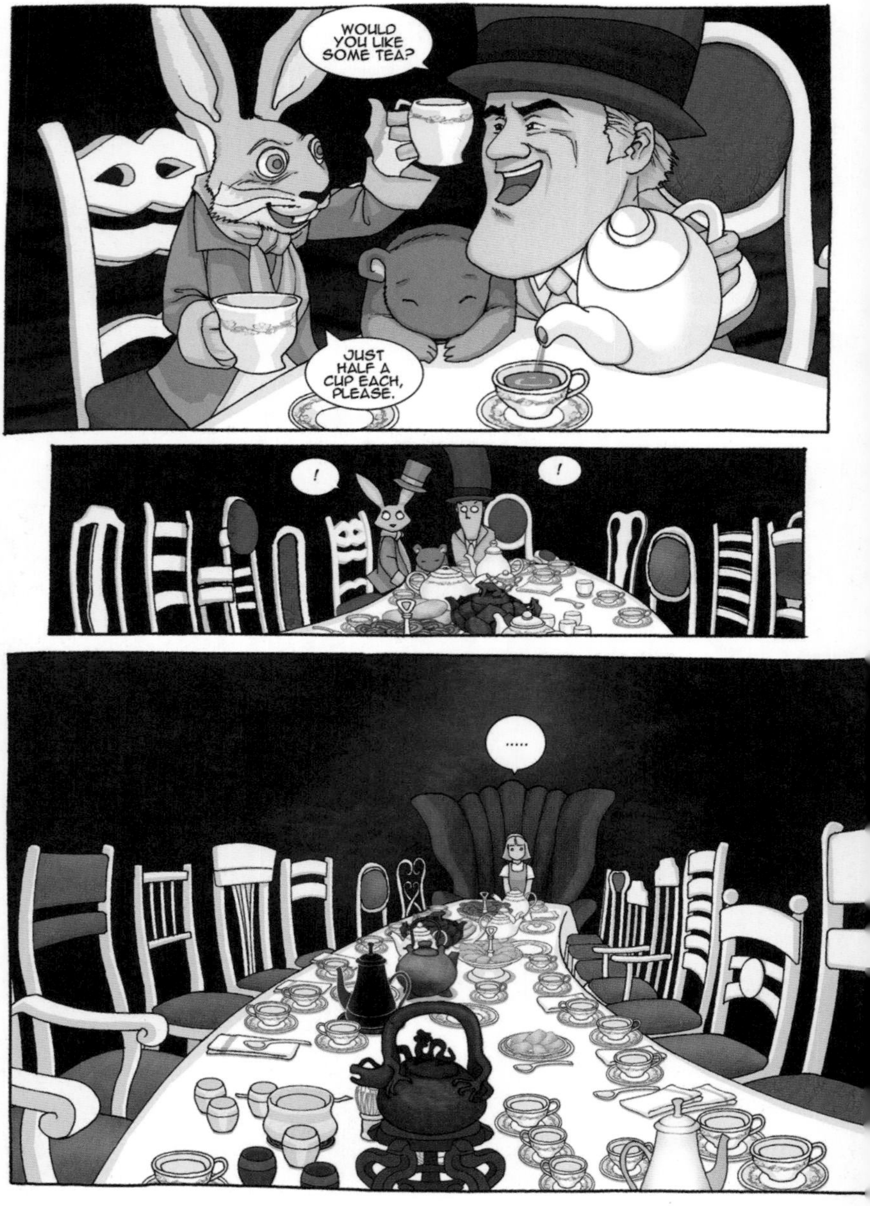
WOULD YOU LIKE SOME TEA?
JUST HALF A CUP EACH, PLEASE.
!
!
.....

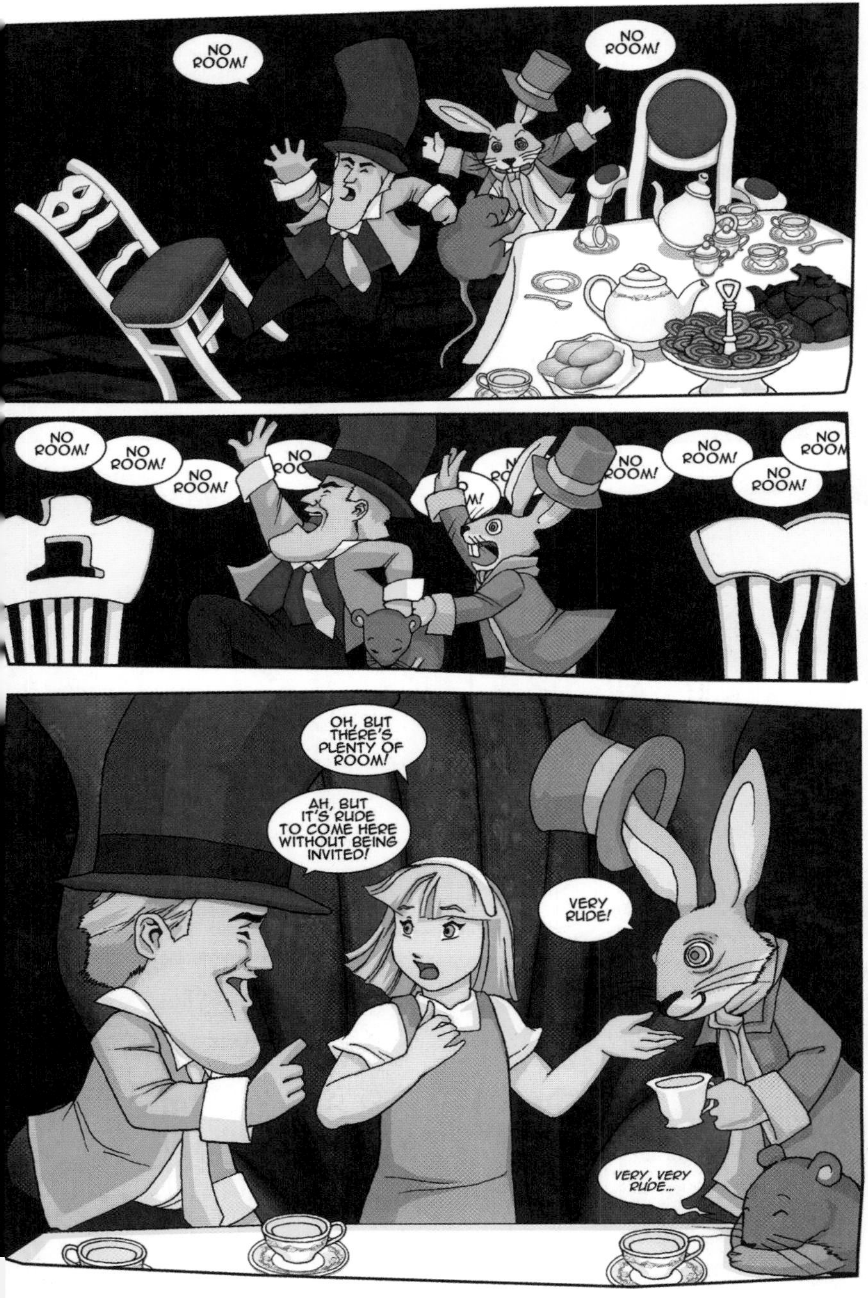
NO ROOM!
NO ROOM!
NO ROOM!
NO ROOM!
NO ROOM!
NO ROOM!
NO ROOM!
OH, BUT THERE'S PLENTY OF ROOM!
AH, BUT IT'S RUDE TO COME HERE WITHOUT BEING INVITED!
VERY RUDE!
VERY, VERY RUDE...

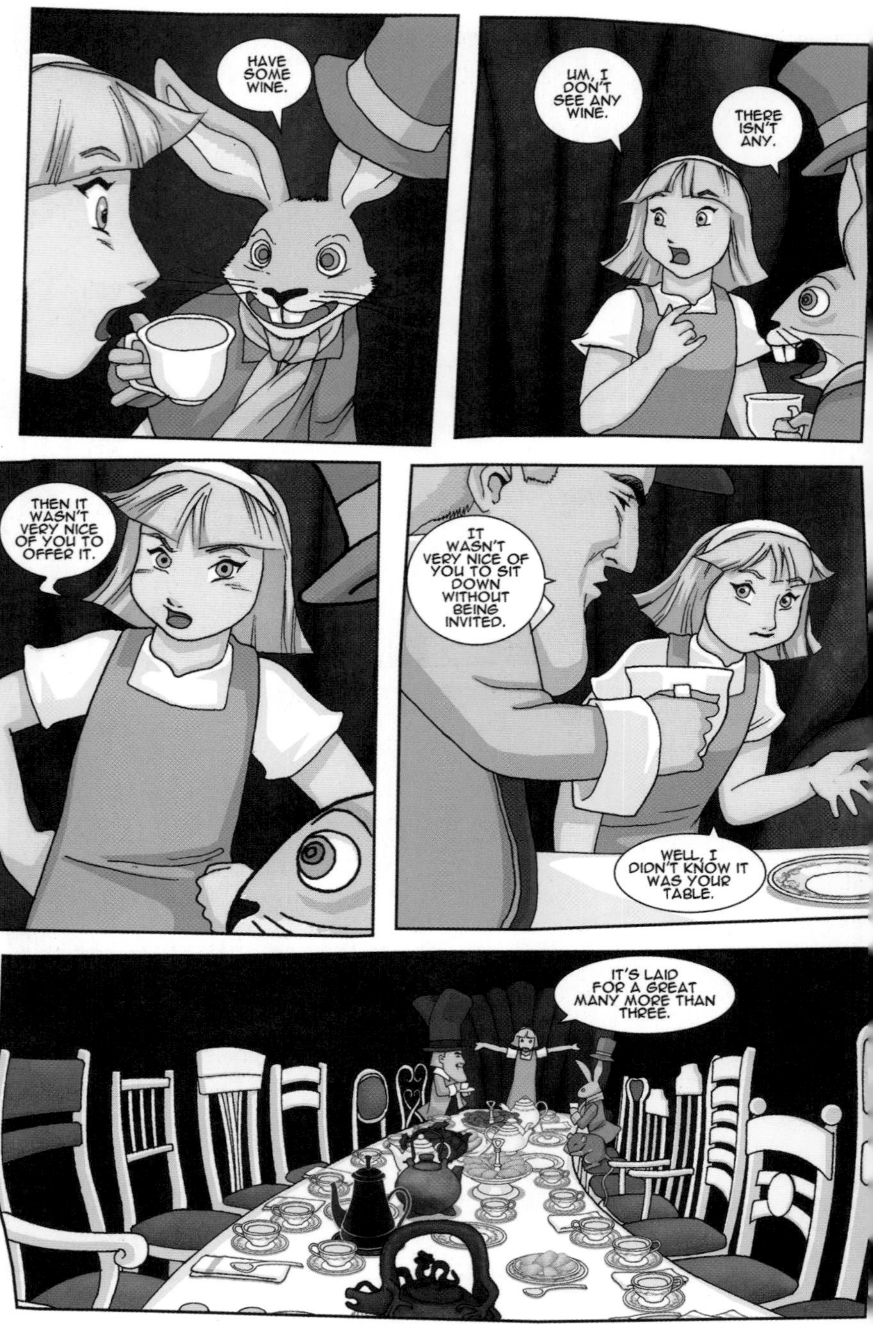
HAVE SOME WINE.
UM, I DON'T SEE ANY WINE.
THERE ISN'T ANY.
THEN IT WASN'T VERY NICE OF YOU TO OFFER IT.
IT WASN'T VERY NICE OF YOU TO SIT DOWN WITHOUT BEING INVITED.
WELL, I DIDN'T KNOW IT WAS YOUR TABLE.
IT'S LAID FOR A GREAT MANY MORE THAN THREE.

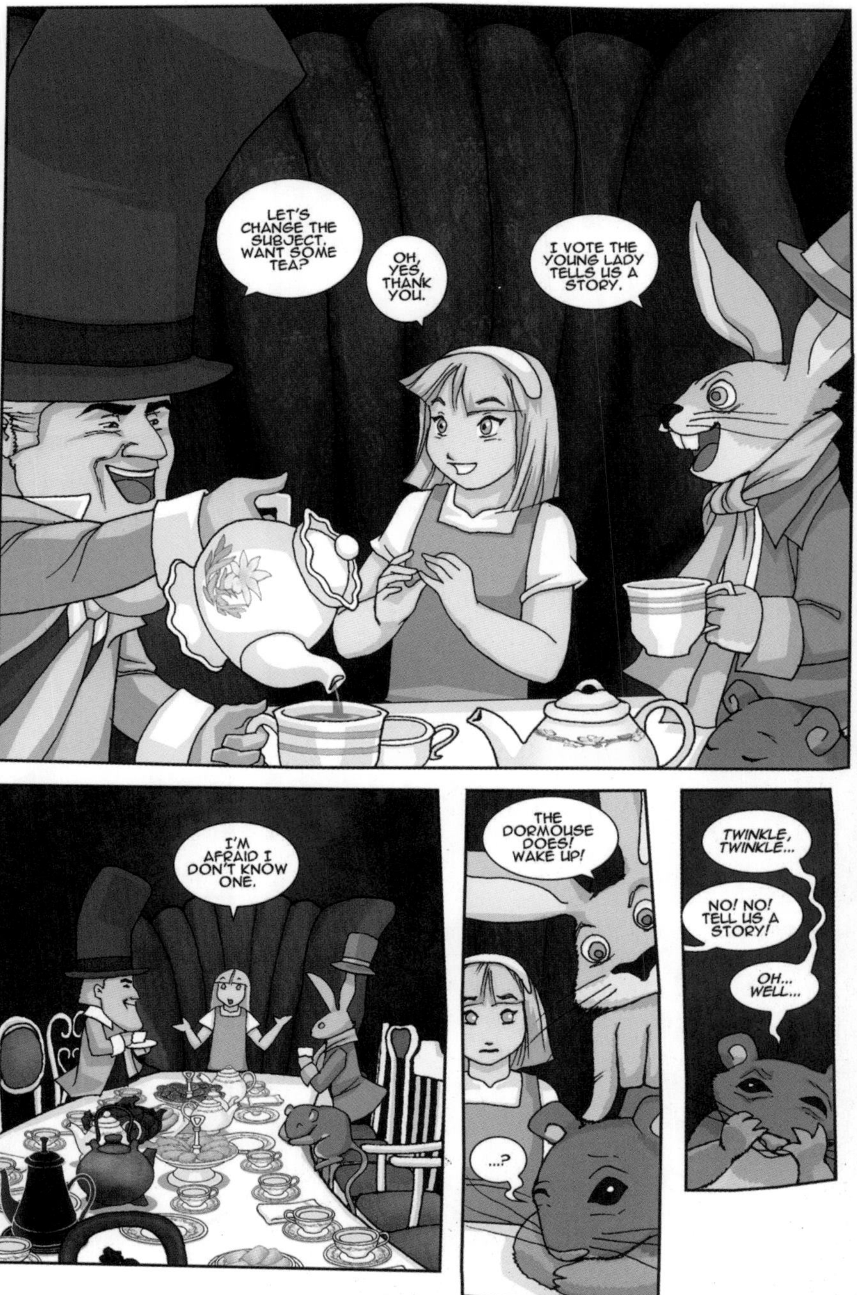
LET'S CHANGE THE SUBJECT. WANT SOME TEA?
OH, YES, THANK YOU.
I VOTE THE YOUNG LADY TELLS US A STORY.
I'M AFRAID I DON'T KNOW ONE.
THE DORMOUSE DOES! WAKE UP!
...?
TWINKLE, TWINKLE...
NO! NO! TELL US A STORY!
OH... WELL...

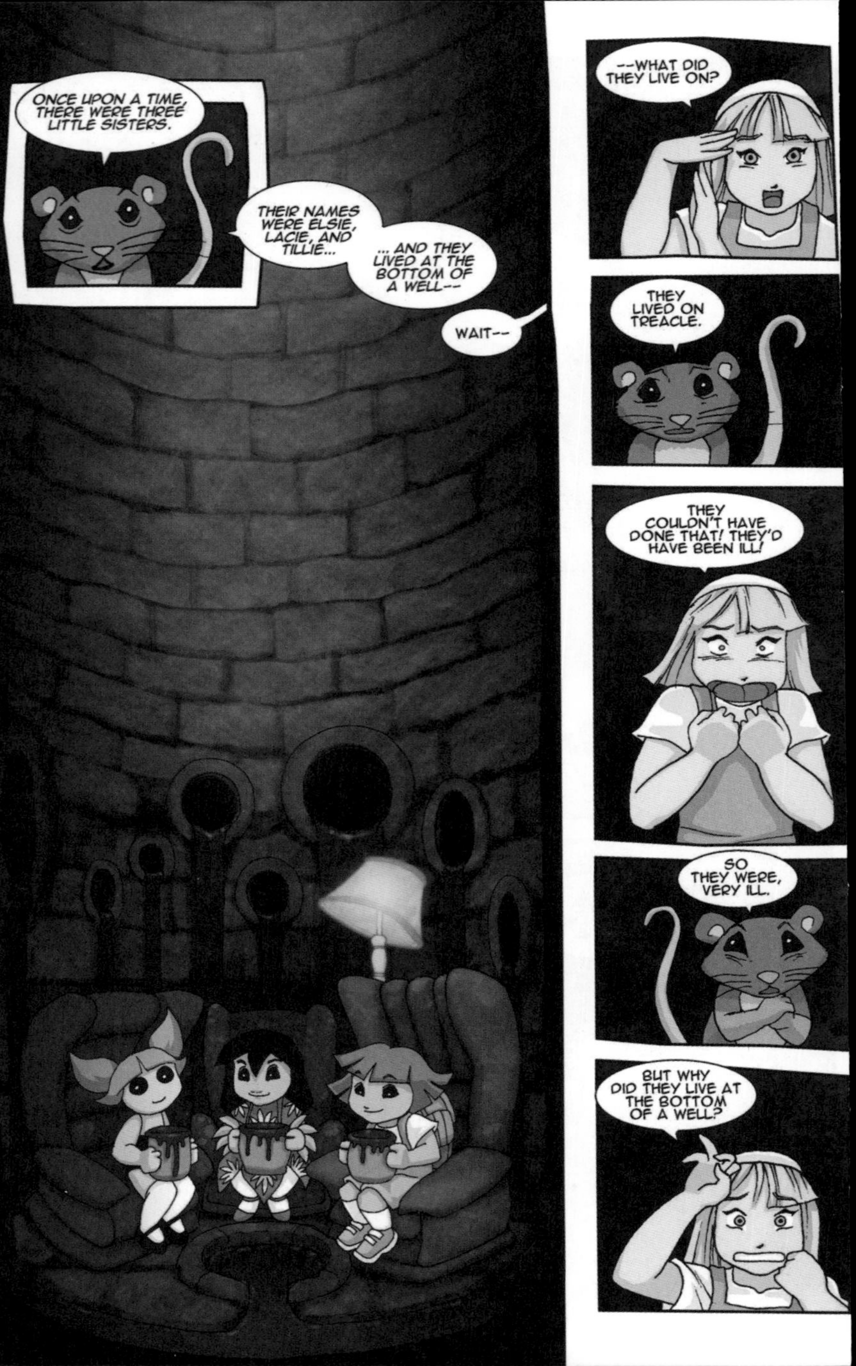
ONCE UPON A TIME, THERE WERE THREE LITTLE SISTERS.
THEIR NAMES WERE ELSIE, LACIE, AND TILLIE...
... AND THEY LIVED AT THE BOTTOM OF A WELL--
WAIT--
--WHAT DID THEY LIVE ON?
THEY LIVED ON TREACLE.
THEY COULDN'T HAVE DONE THAT! THEY'D HAVE BEEN ILL!
SO THEY WERE, VERY ILL.
BUT WHY DID THEY LIVE AT THE BOTTOM OF A WELL?

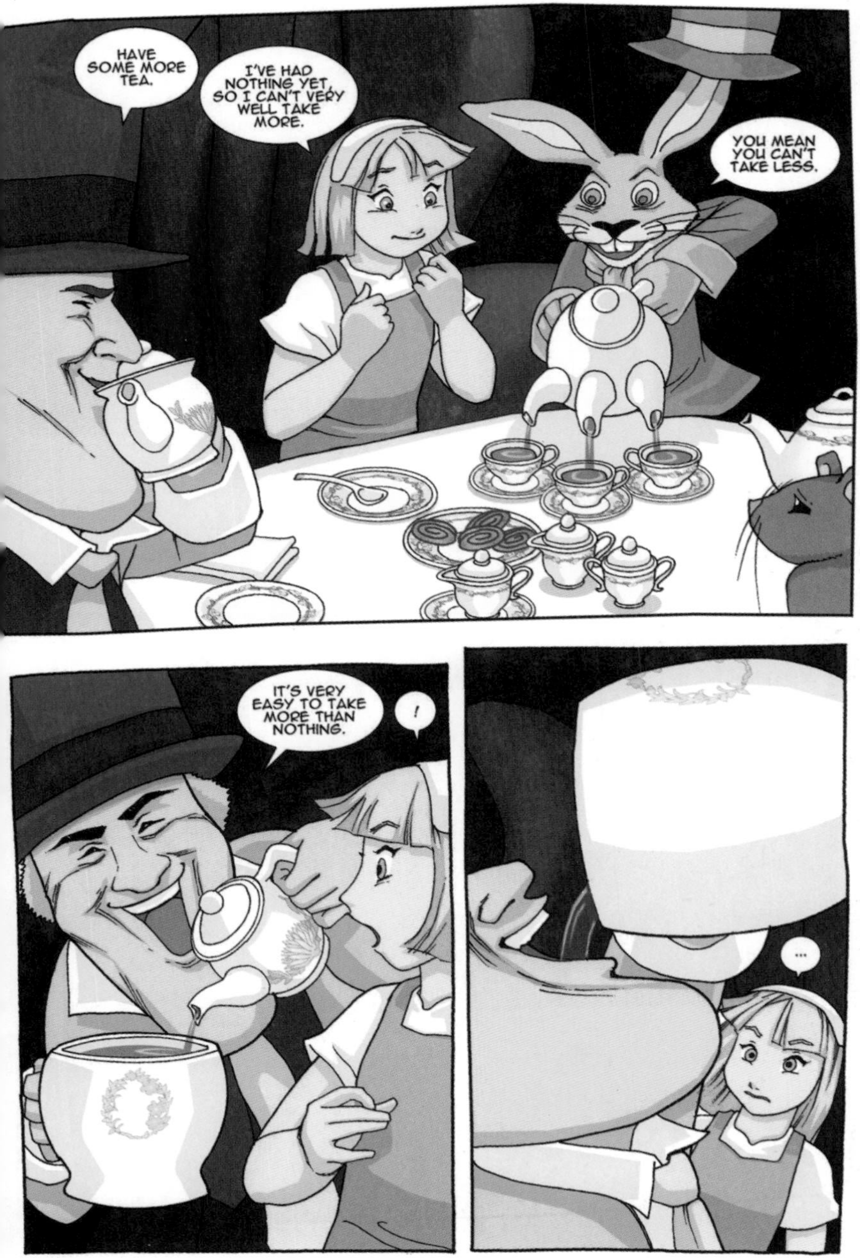
HAVE SOME MORE TEA.
I'VE HAD NOTHING YET, SO I CAN'T VERY WELL TAKE MORE.
YOU MEAN YOU CAN'T TAKE LESS.
IT'S VERY EASY TO TAKE MORE THAN NOTHING.
!
...

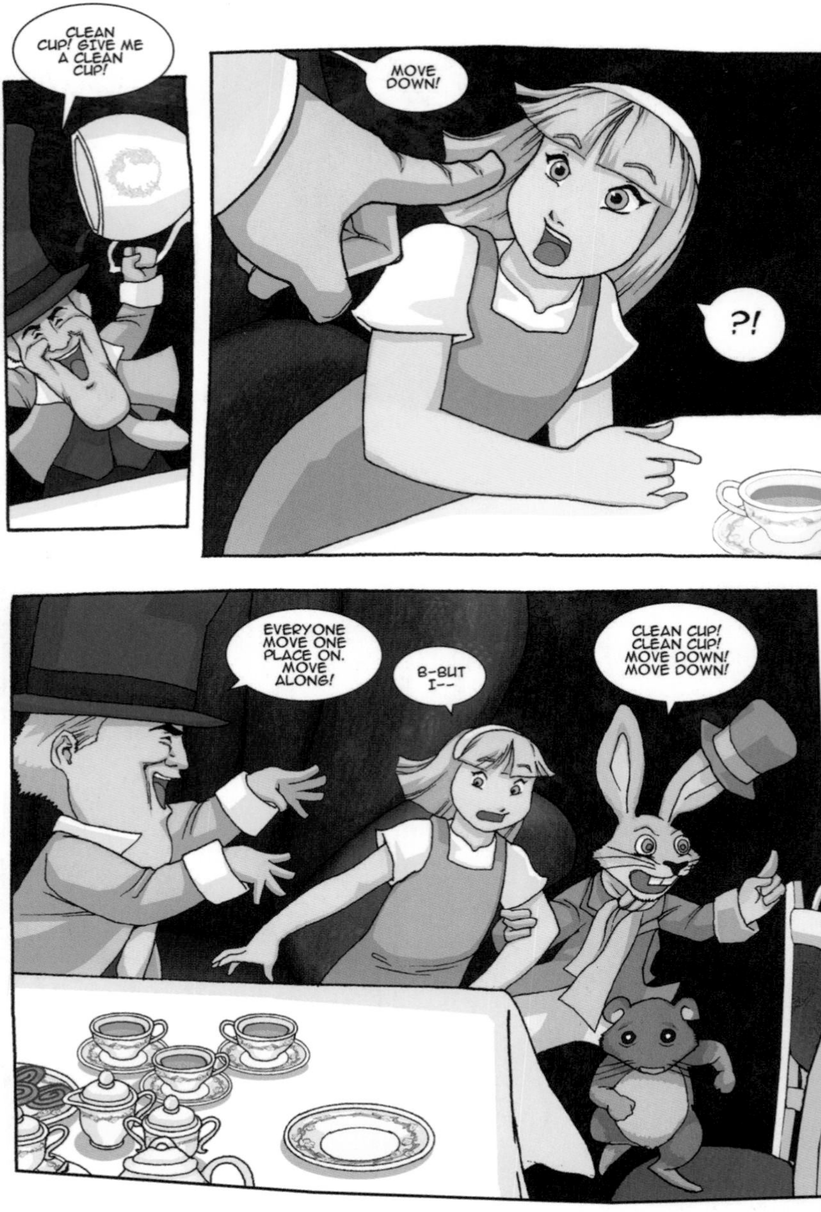

CLEAN CUP! GIVE ME A CLEAN CUP!
MOVE DOWN!
?!
EVERYONE MOVE ONE PLACE ON. MOVE ALONG!
B-BUT I--
CLEAN CUP! CLEAN CUP! MOVE DOWN! MOVE DOWN!

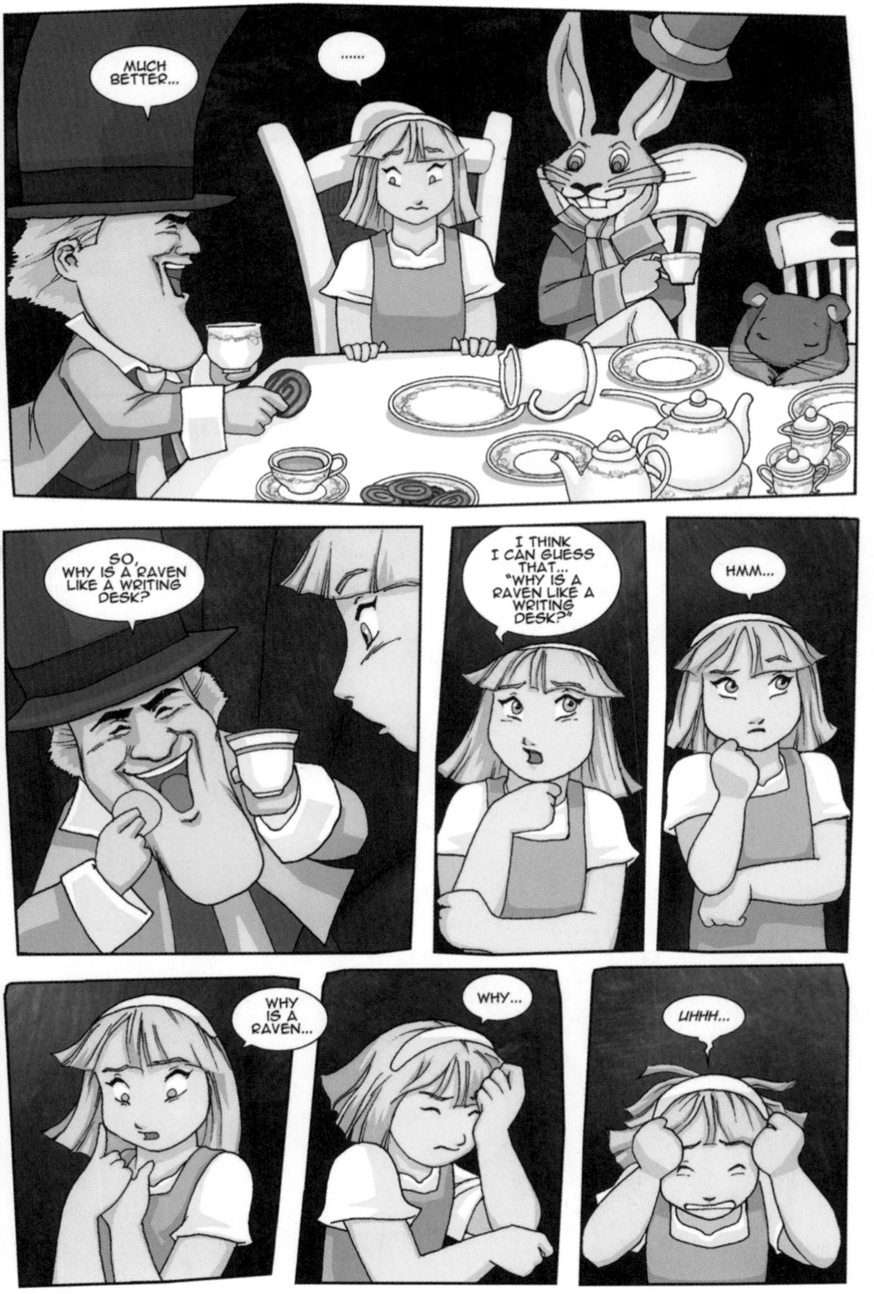
MUCH BETTER...
......
SO, WHY IS A RAVEN LIKE A WRITING DESK?
I THINK I CAN GUESS THAT... "WHY IS A RAVEN LIKE A WRITING DESK?"
HMM...
WHY IS A RAVEN...
WHY...
UHHH...

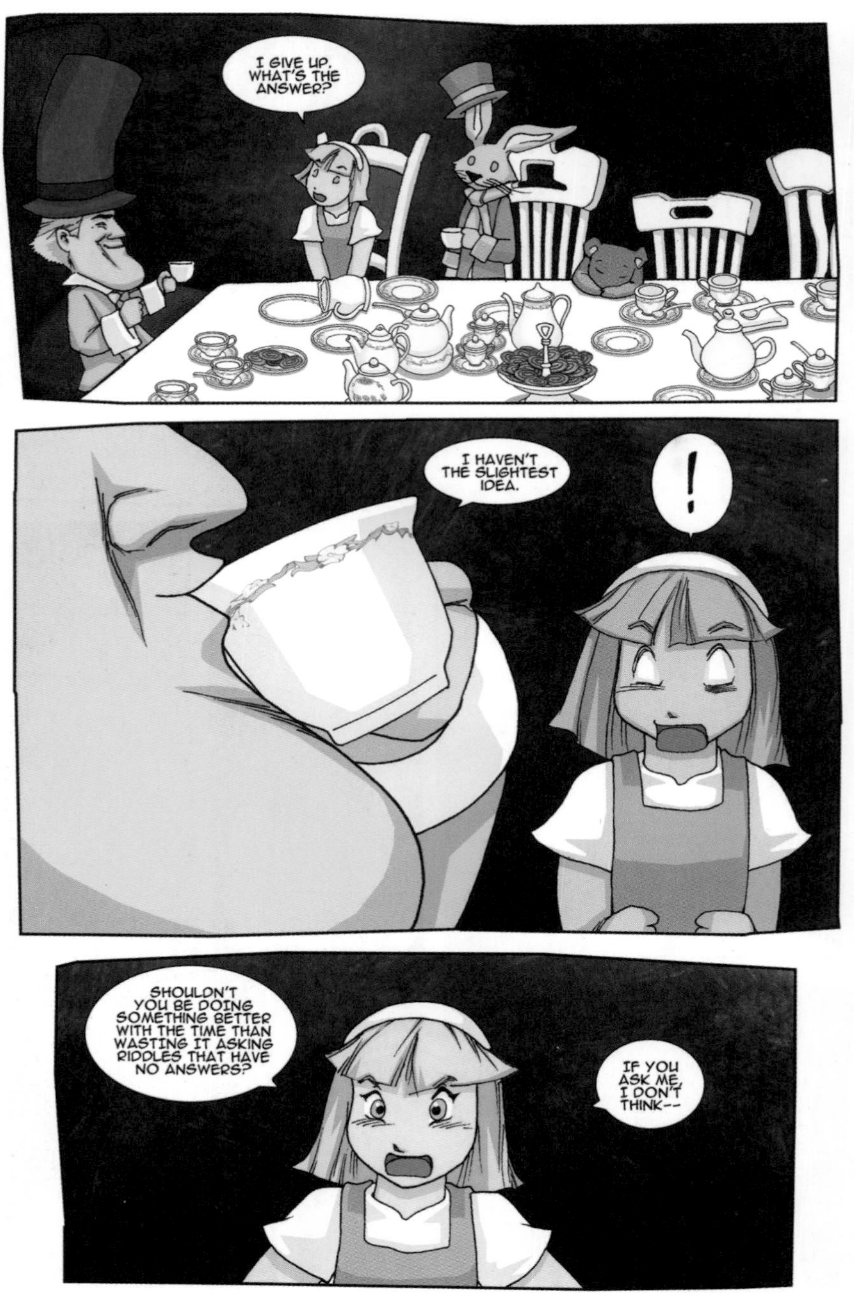
I GIVE UP. WHAT'S THE ANSWER?
I HAVEN'T THE SLIGHTEST IDEA.
!
SHOULDN'T YOU BE DOING SOMETHING BETTER WITH THE TIME THAN WASTING IT ASKING RIDDLES THAT HAVE NO ANSWERS?
IF YOU ASK ME, I DON'T THINK--

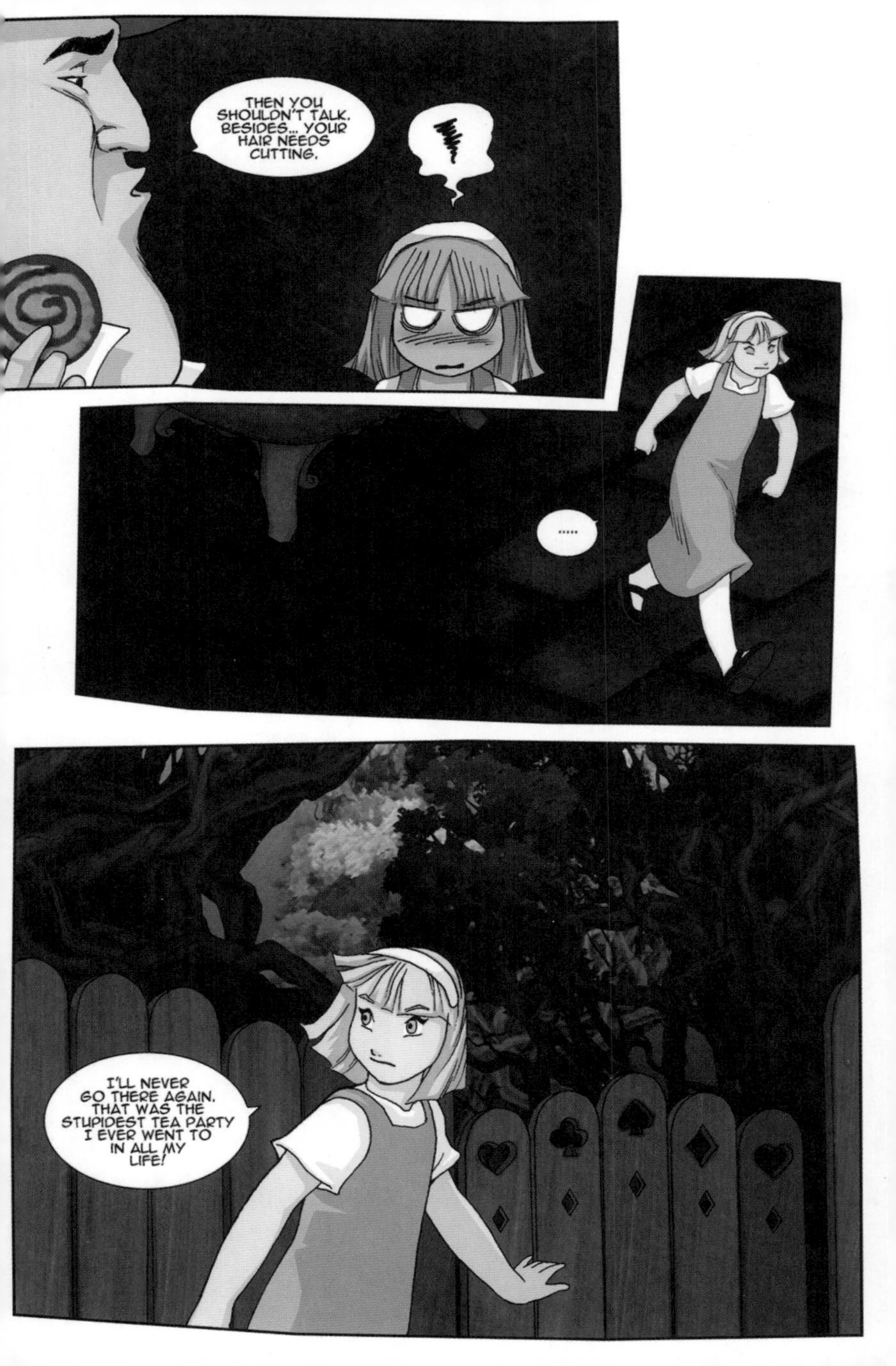
THEN YOU SHOULDN'T TALK. BESIDES... YOUR HAIR NEEDS CUTTING.
......
I'LL NEVER GO THERE AGAIN. THAT WAS THE STUPIDEST TEA PARTY I EVER WENT TO IN ALL MY LIFE!

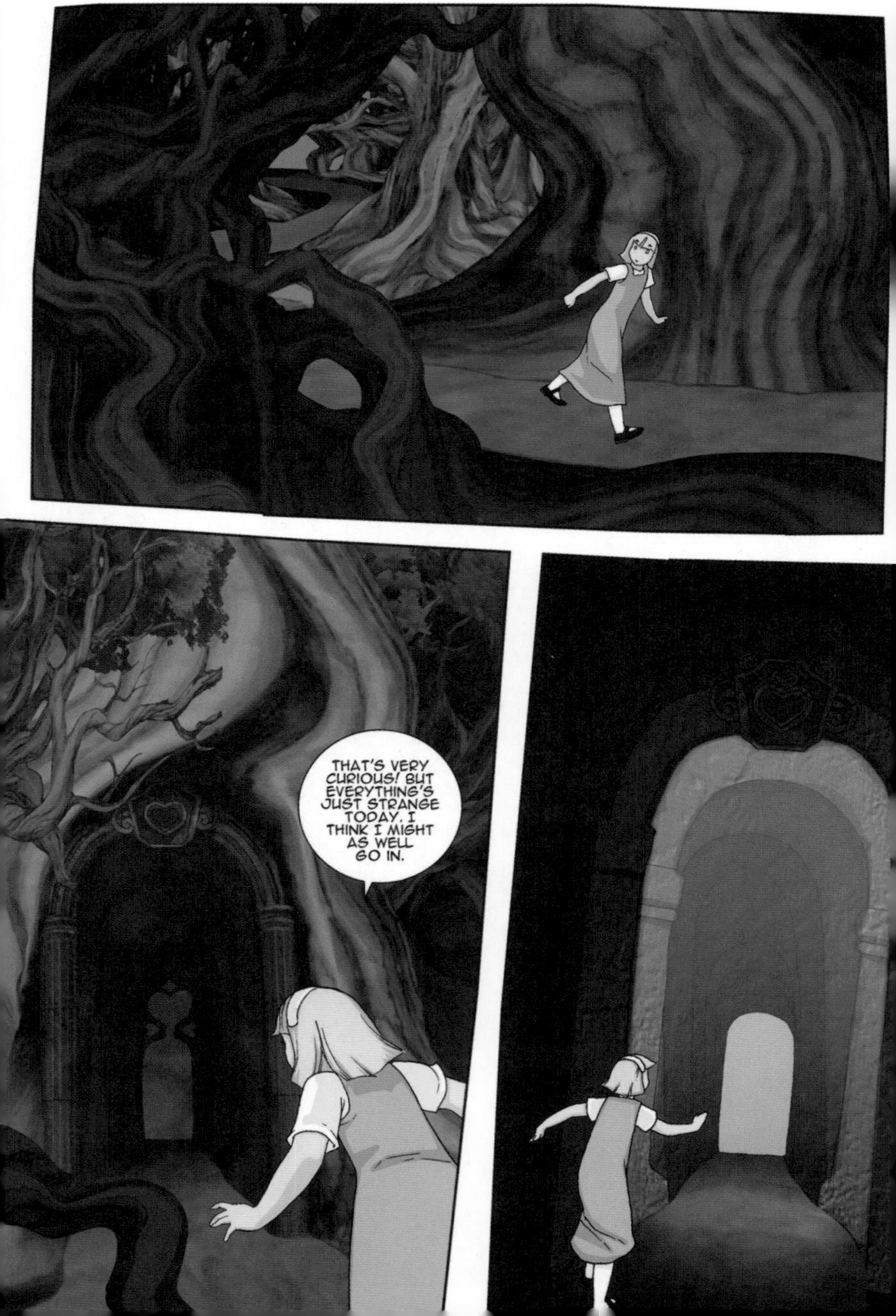
THAT'S VERY CURIOUS! BUT EVERYTHING'S JUST STRANGE TODAY. I THINK I MIGHT AS WELL GO IN.

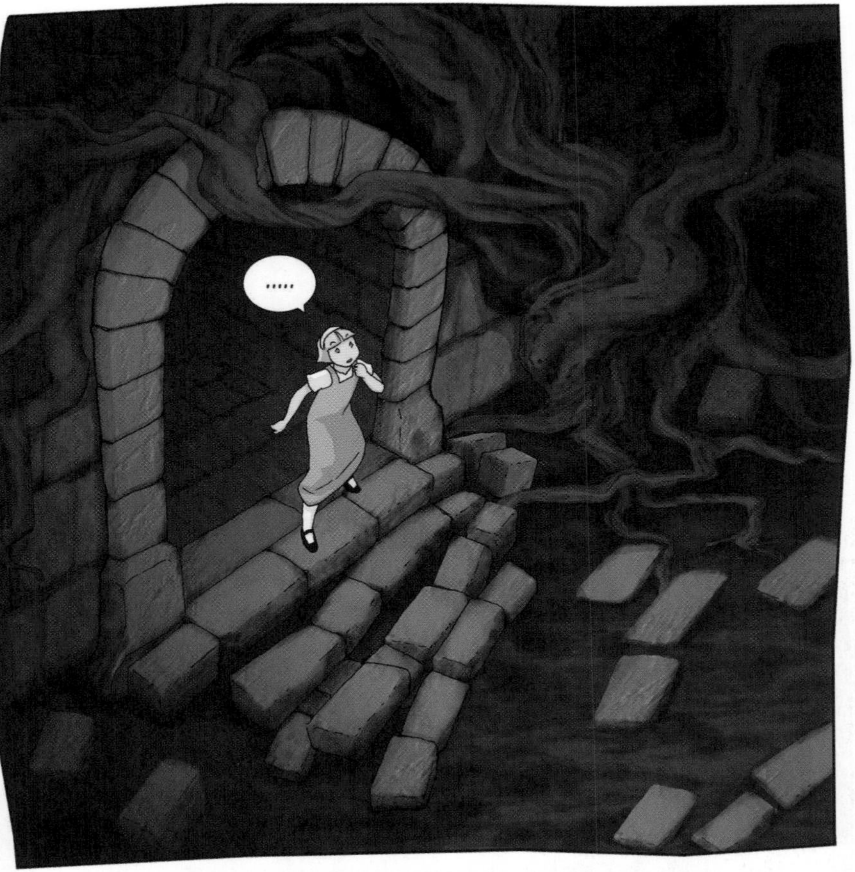
.....

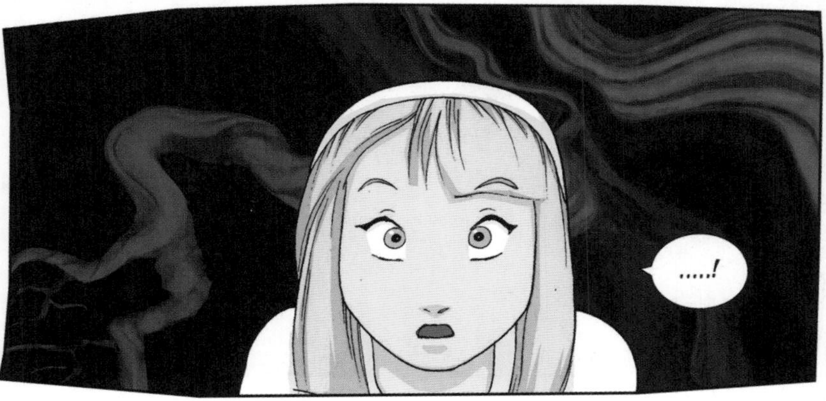
.....!

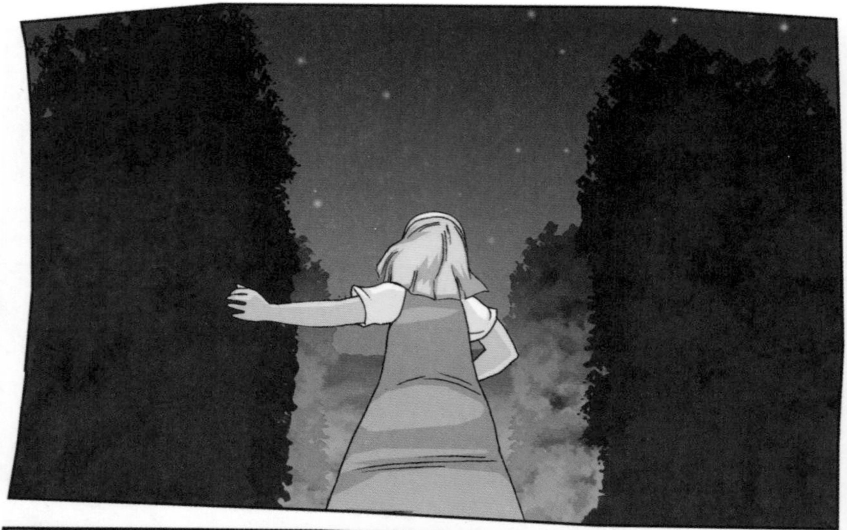

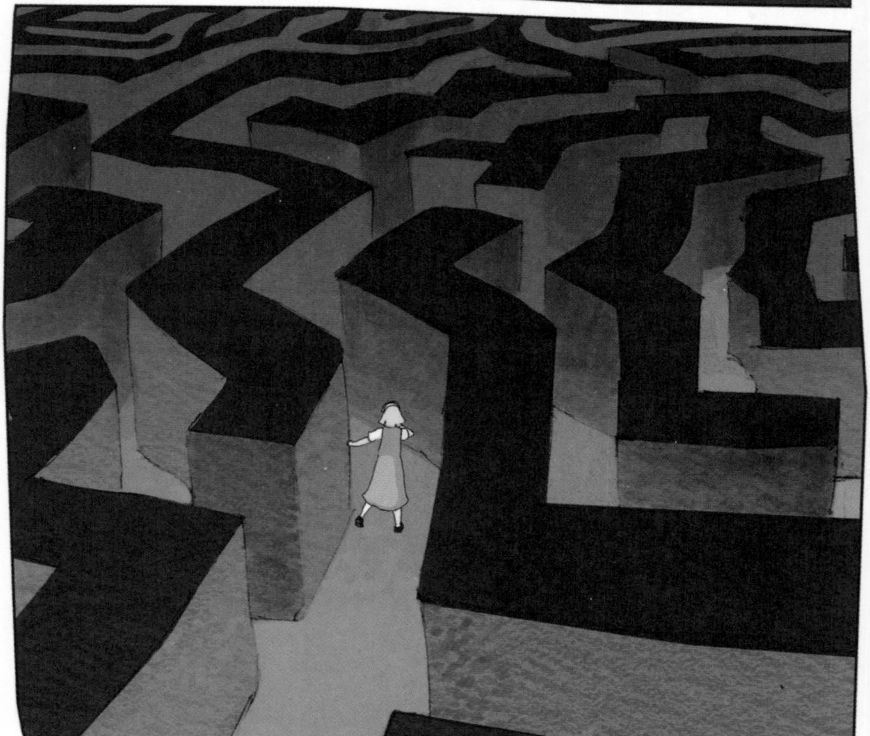

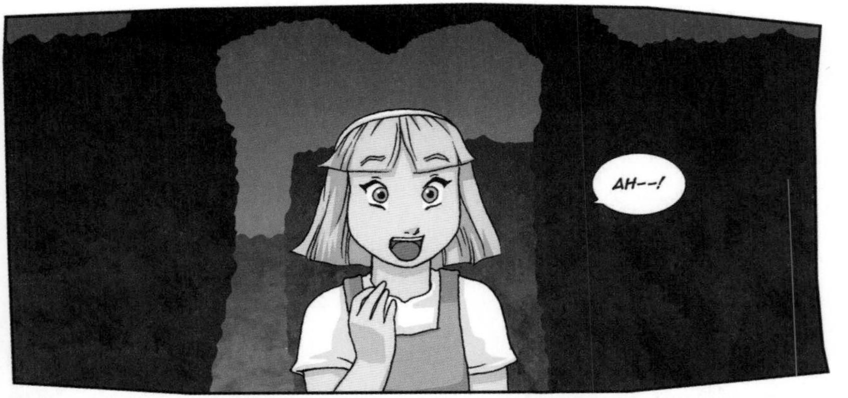
AH--!

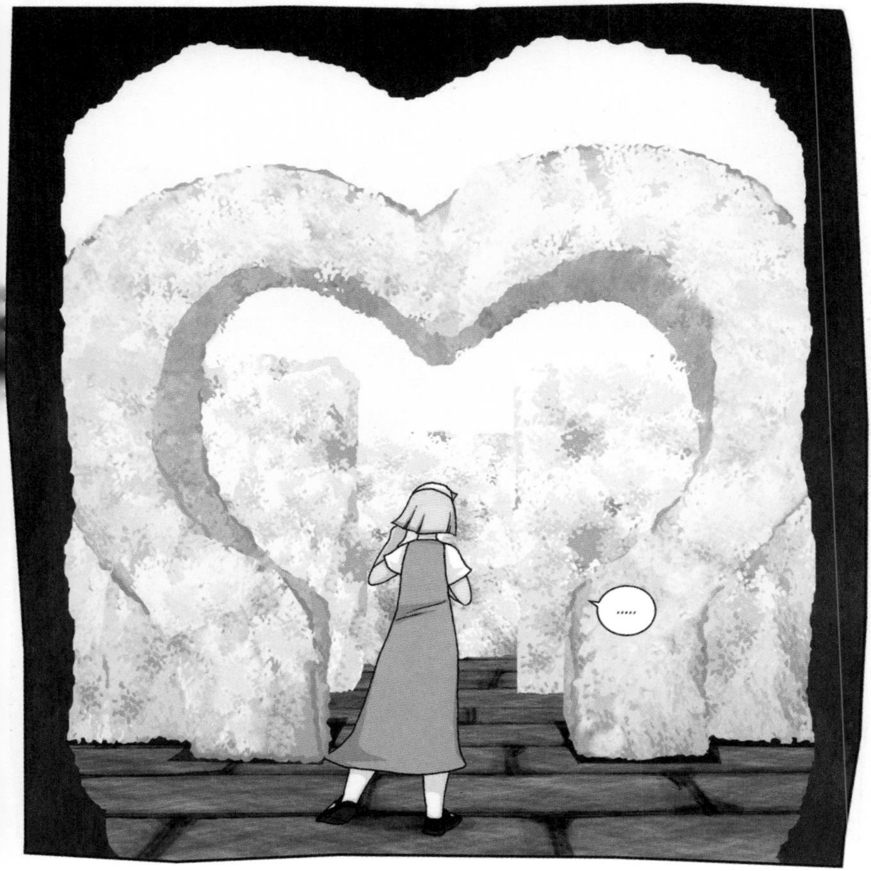
......

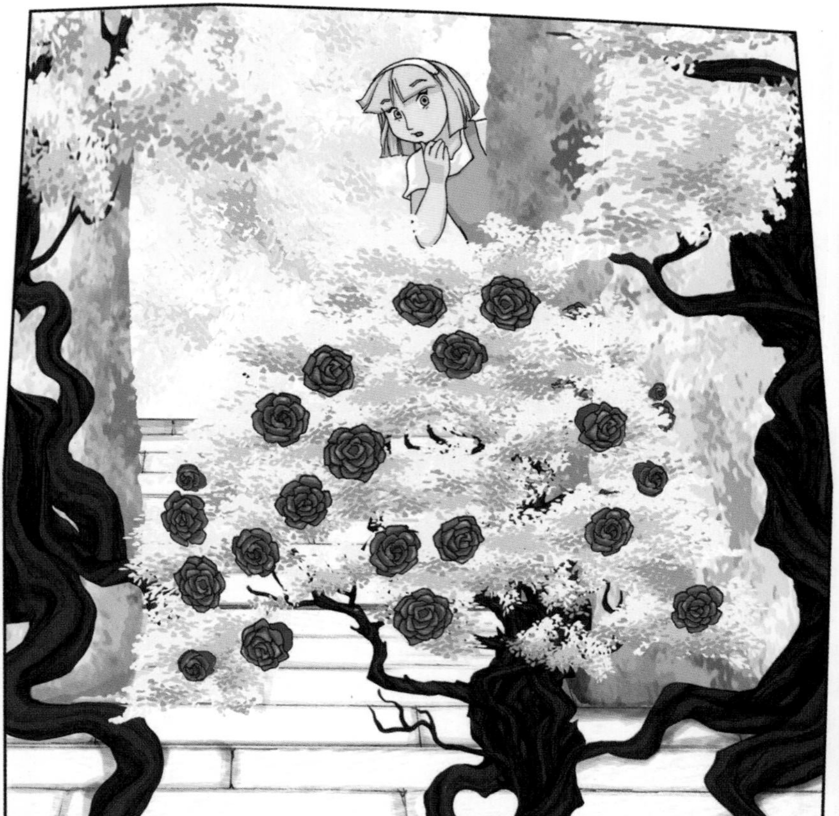

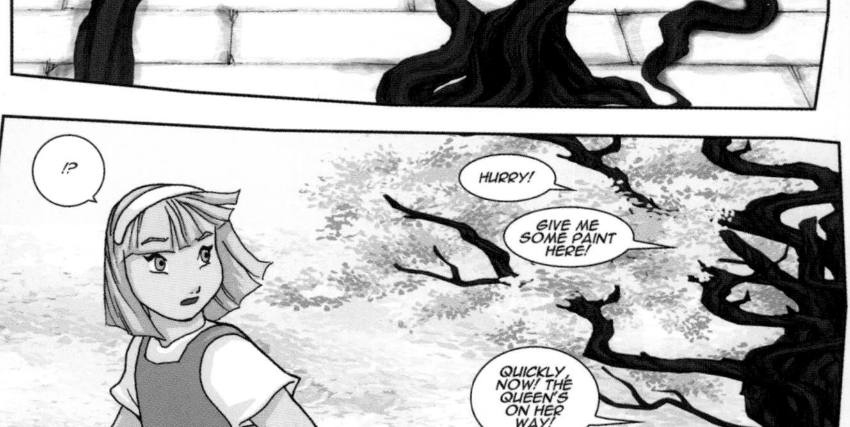
!?
HURRY!
GIVE ME SOME PAINT HERE!
QUICKLY NOW! THE QUEEN'S ON HER WAY!

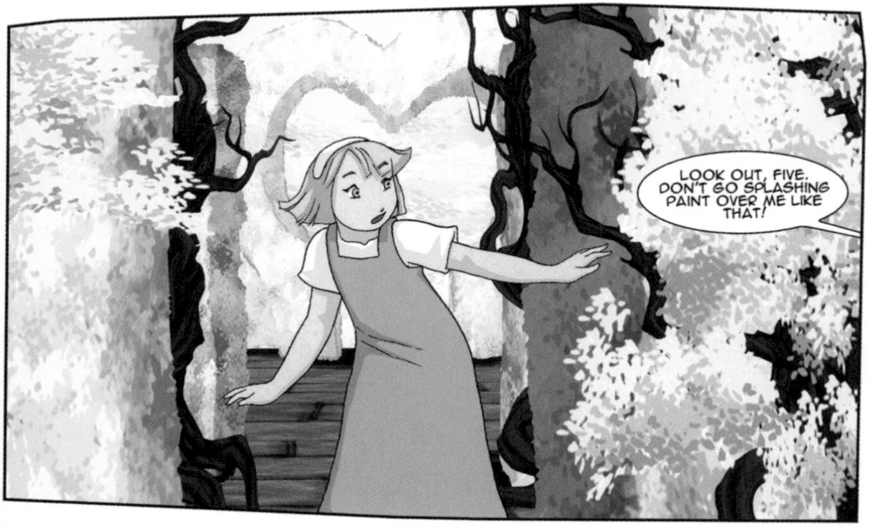
LOOK OUT, FIVE. DON'T GO SPLASHING PAINT OVER ME LIKE THAT!

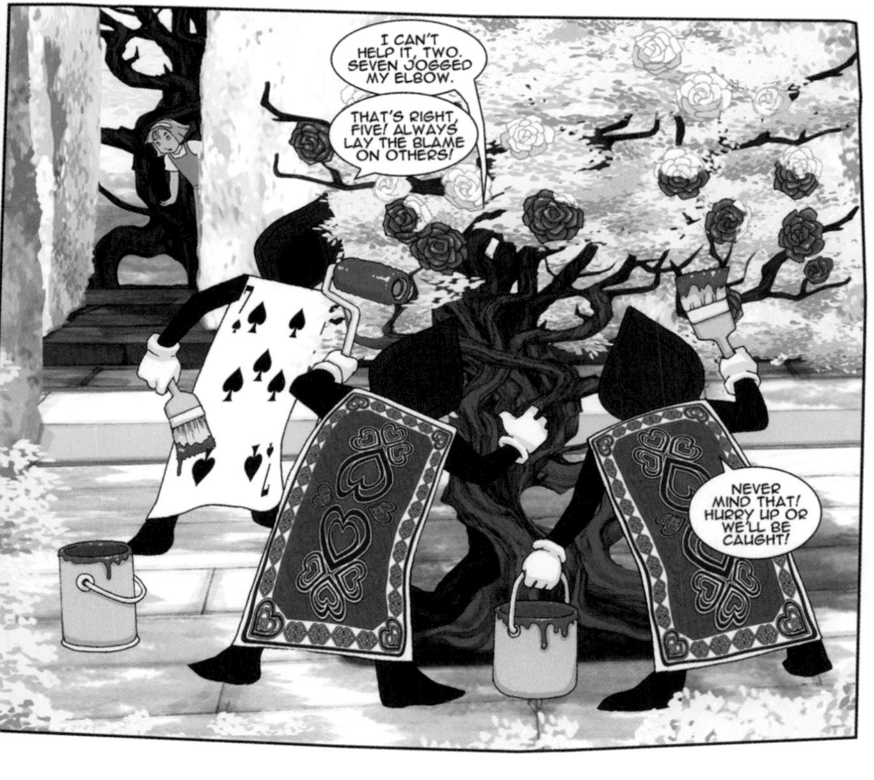
I CAN'T HELP IT, TWO. SEVEN JOGGED MY ELBOW.
THAT'S RIGHT, FIVE! ALWAYS LAY THE BLAME ON OTHERS!
NEVER MIND THAT! HURRY UP OR WE'LL BE CAUGHT!

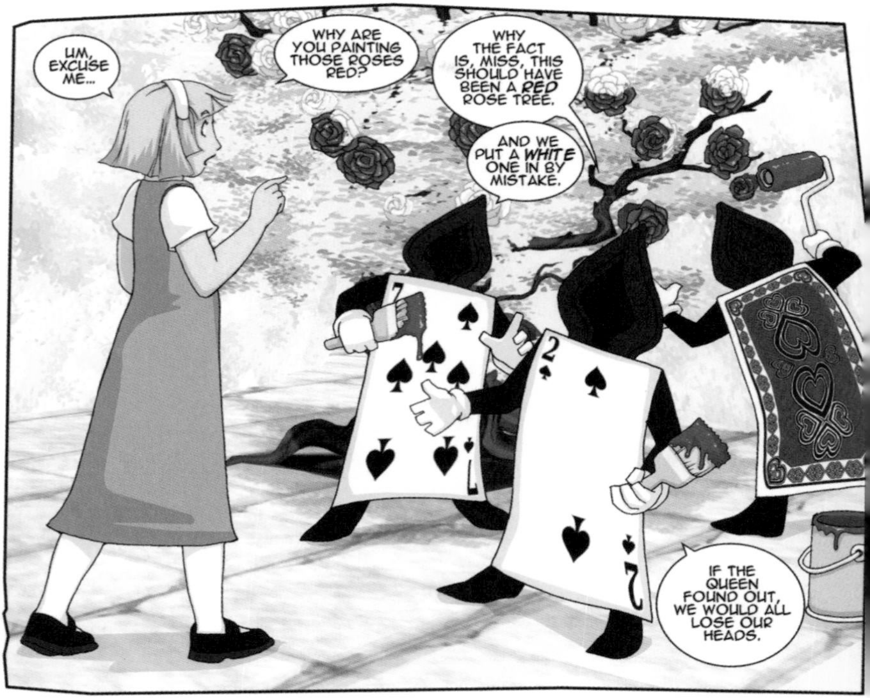
UM, EXCUSE ME...
WHY ARE YOU PAINTING THOSE ROSES RED?
WHY THE FACT IS, MISS, THIS SHOULD HAVE BEEN A RED ROSE TREE.
AND WE PUT A WHITE ONE IN BY MISTAKE.
IF THE QUEEN FOUND OUT, WE WOULD ALL LOSE OUR HEADS.

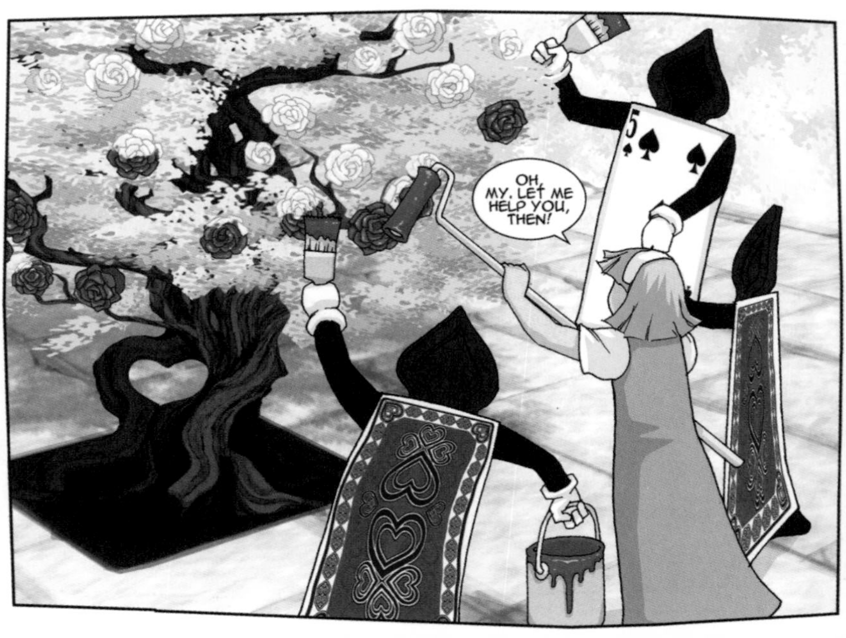
OH, MY. LET ME HELP YOU, THEN!

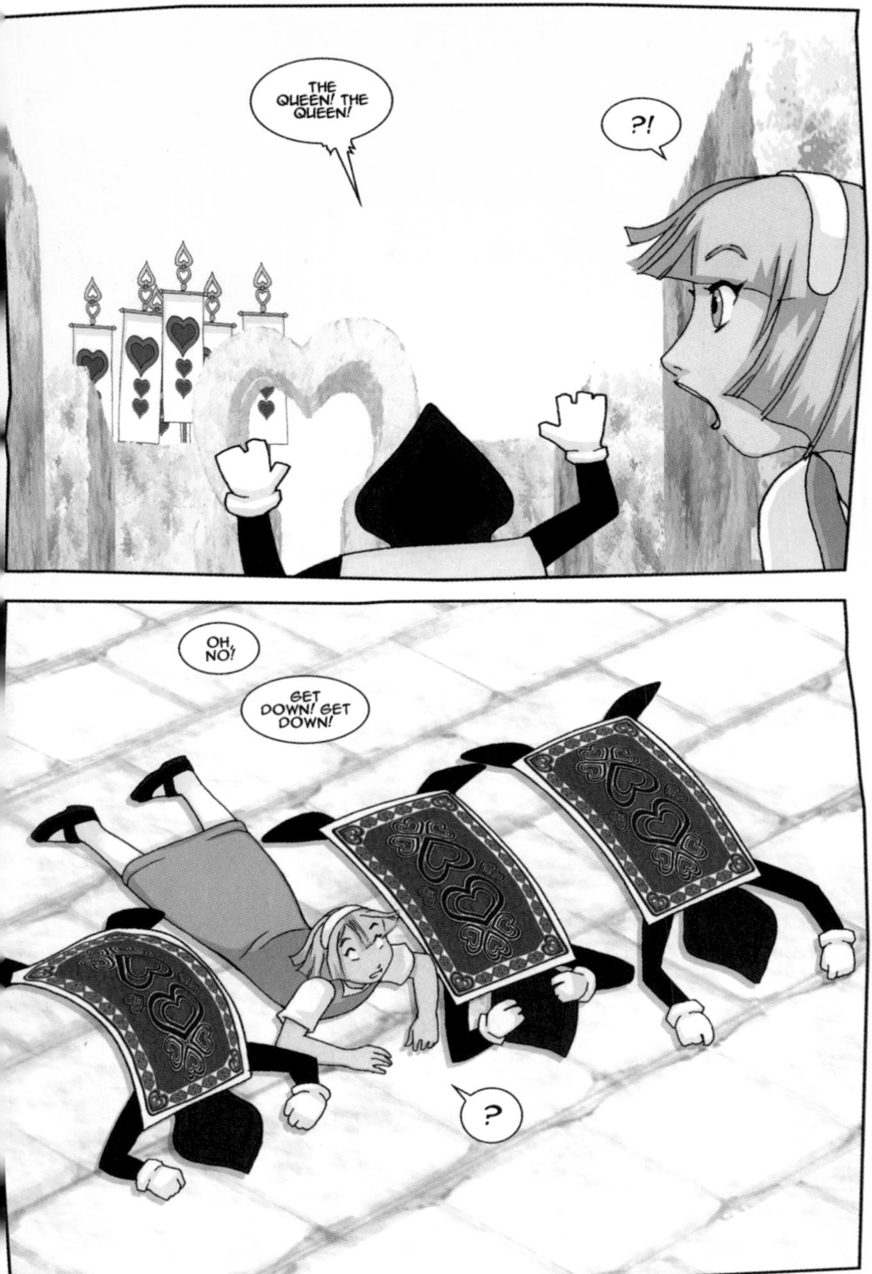
THE QUEEN! THE QUEEN!
?!
OH, NO!
GET DOWN! GET DOWN!
?

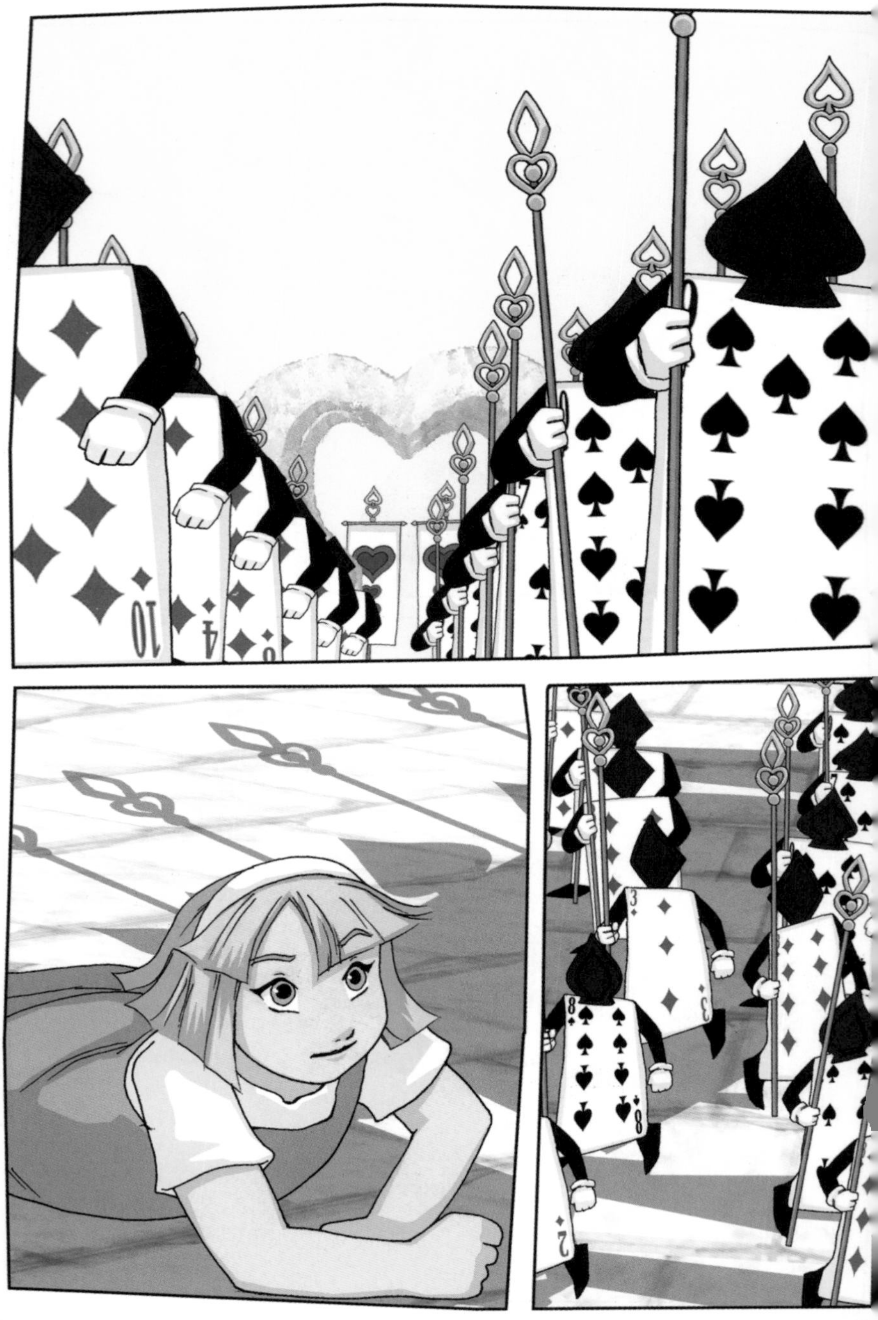

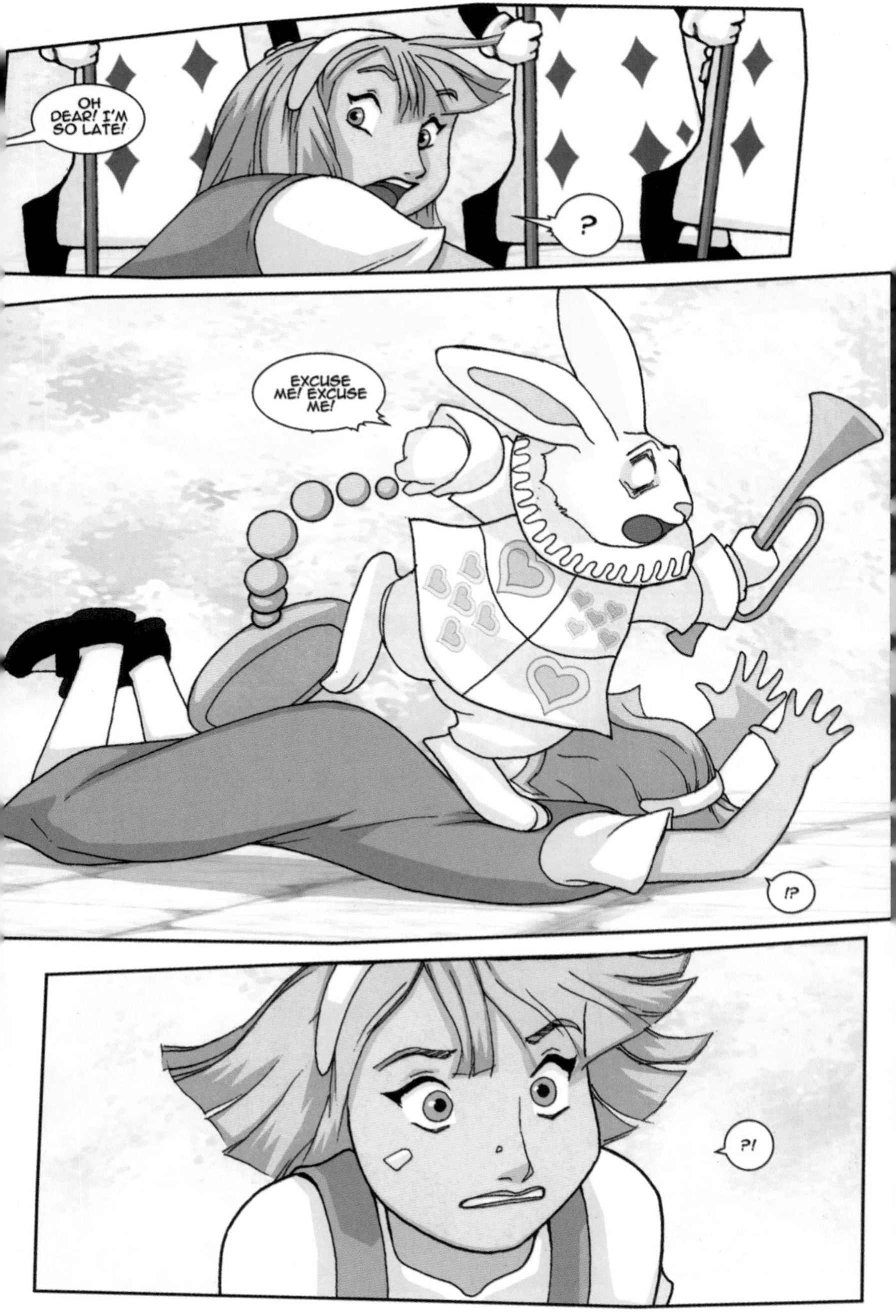
OH DEAR! I'M SO LATE!
?
EXCUSE ME! EXCUSE ME!
!?
?!

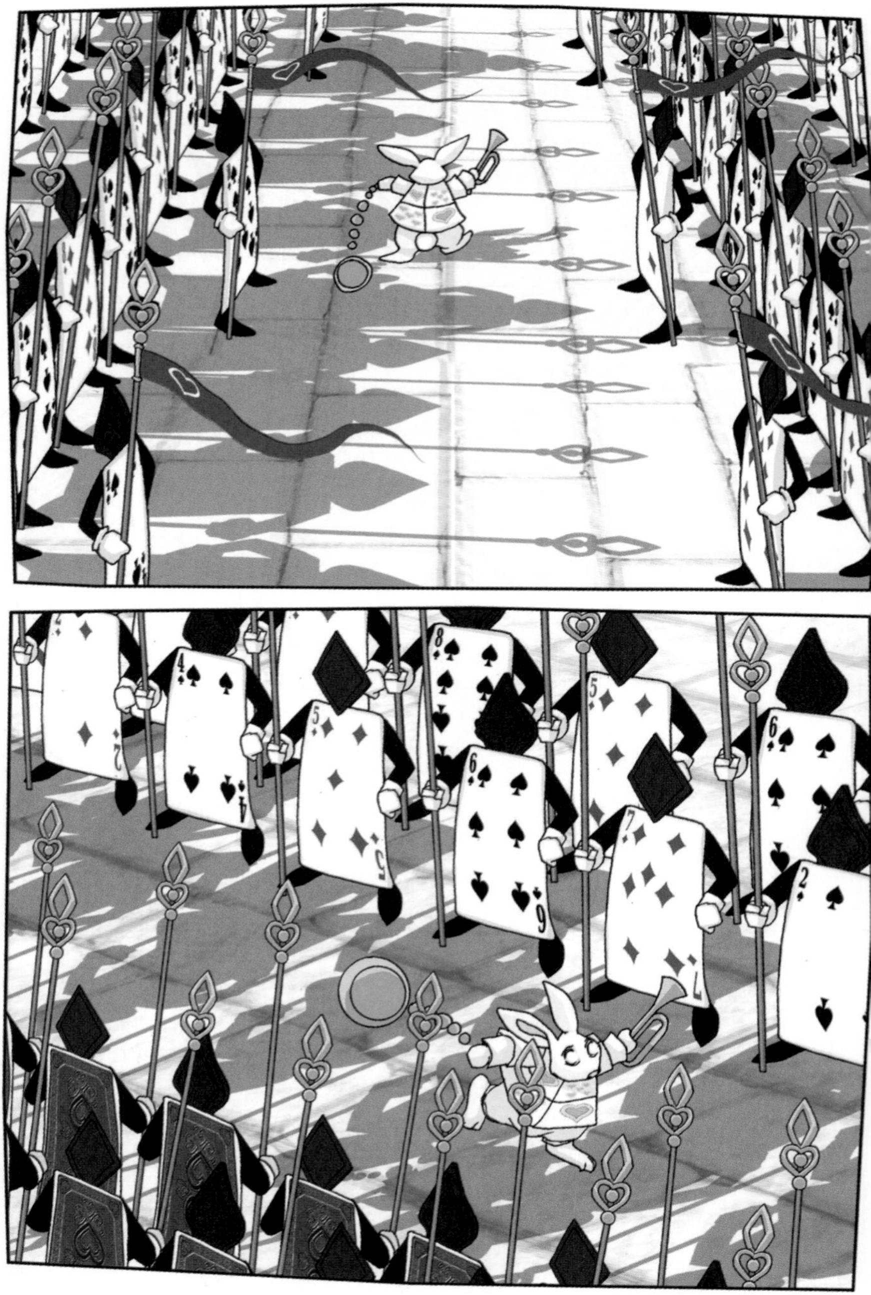

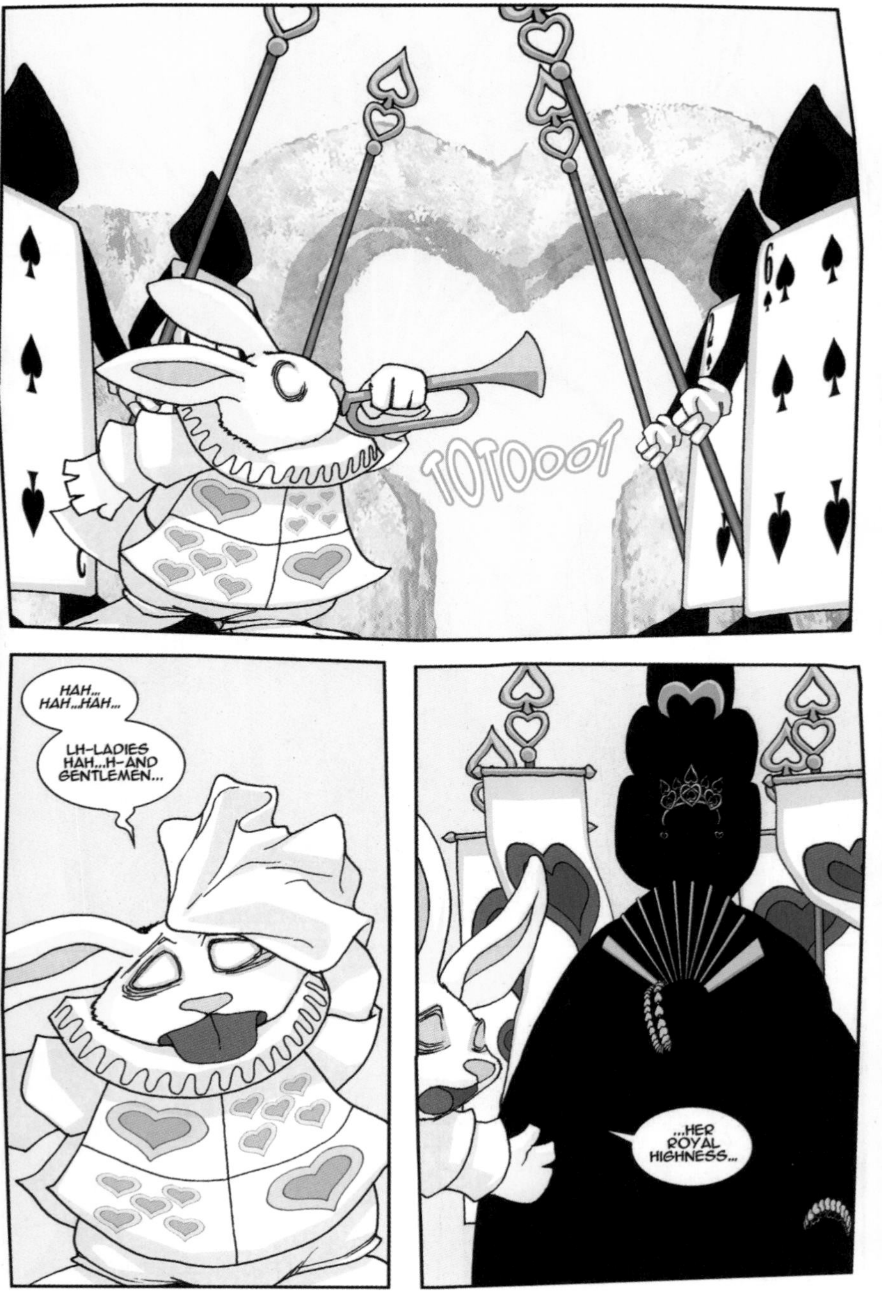
TOTOOOOT
HAH... HAH...HAH...
LH-LADIES HAH...H-AND GENTLEMEN...
...HER ROYAL HIGHNESS...

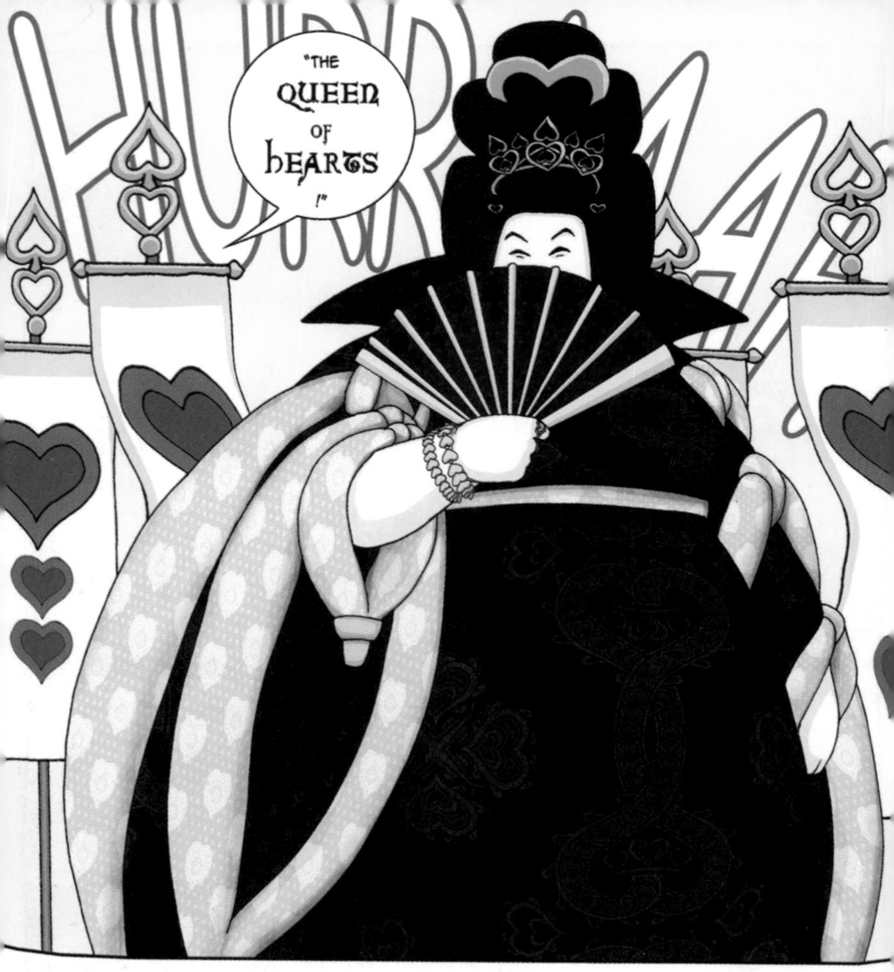
HURRAAAY
"THE QUEEN OF HEARTS!"

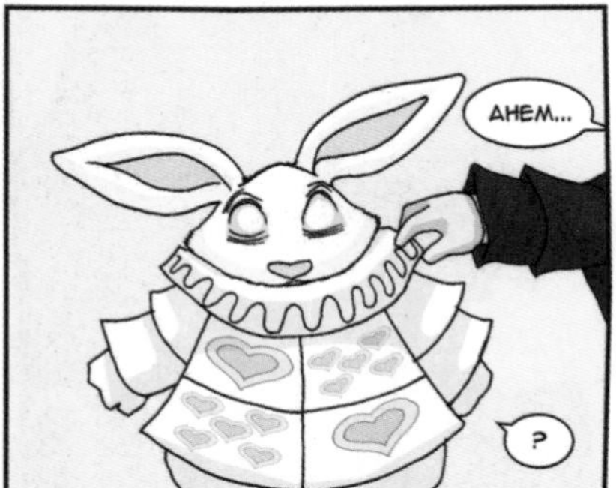
AHEM...
?

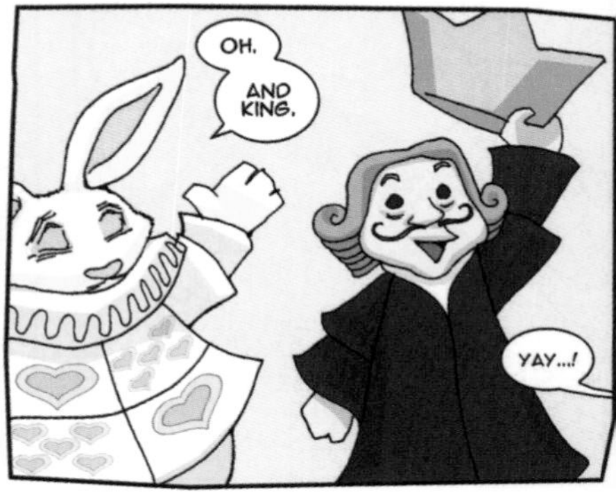
OH.
AND KING.
YAY...!

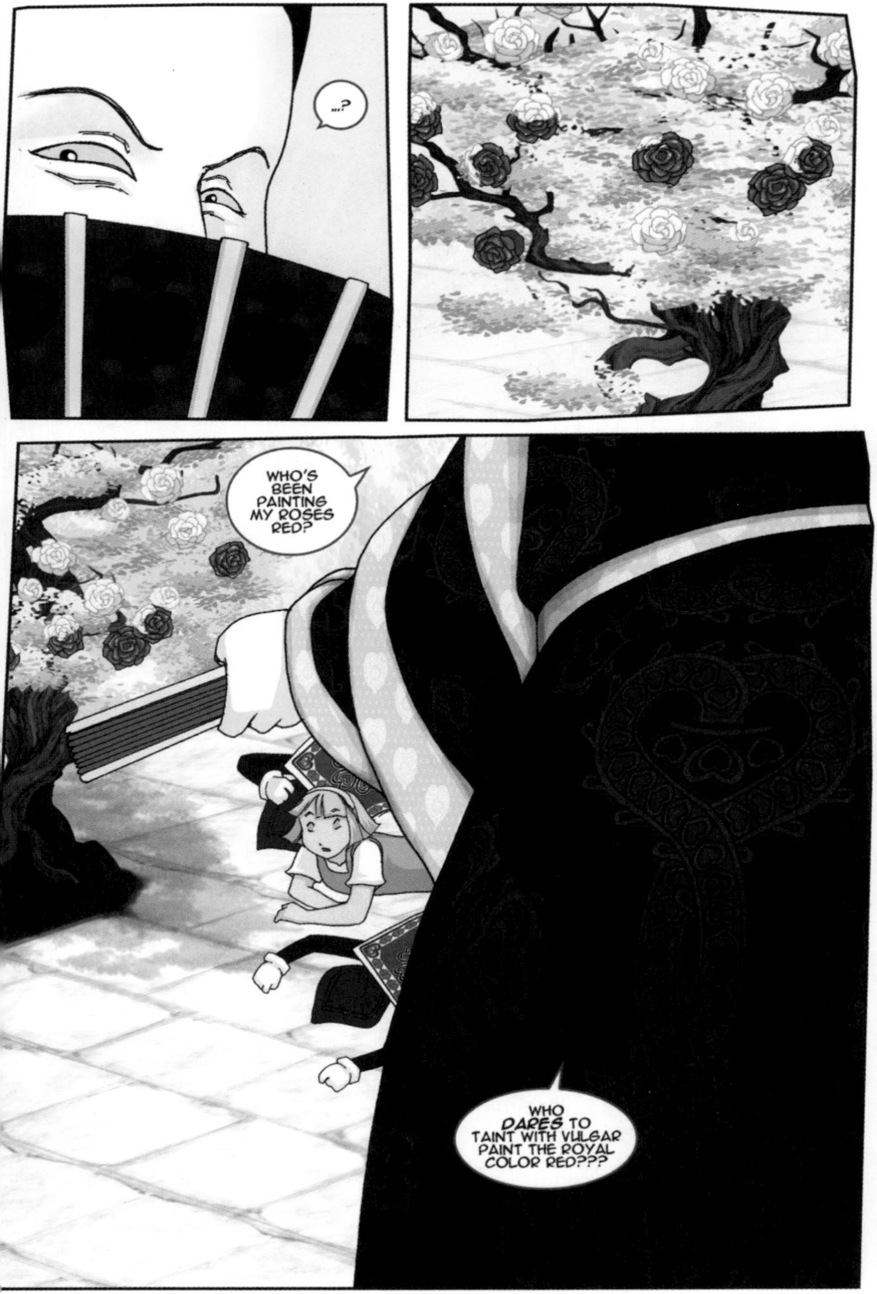
...?
WHO'S BEEN PAINTING MY ROSES RED?
WHO DARES TO TAINT WITH VULGAR PAINT THE ROYAL COLOR RED???

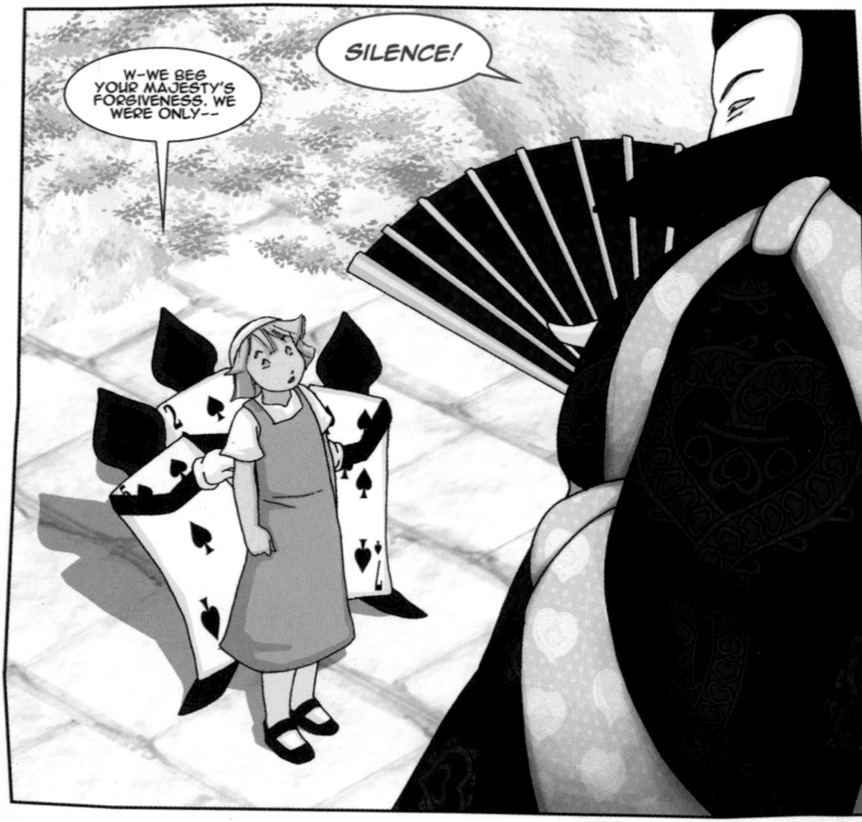
W-WE BEG YOUR MAJESTY'S FORGIVENESS. WE WERE ONLY--
SILENCE!

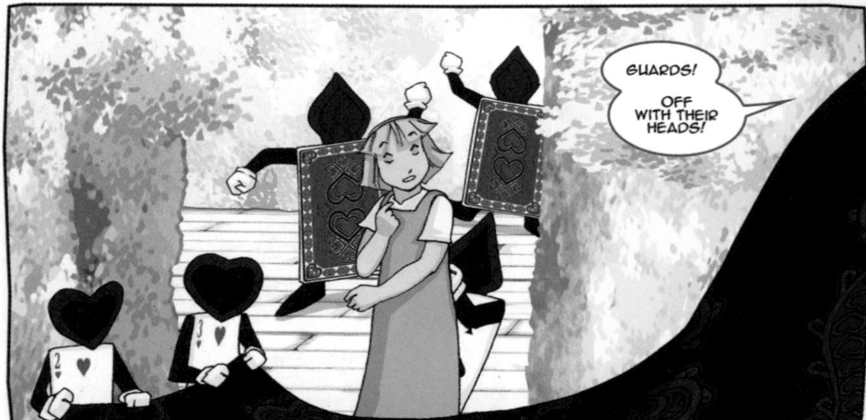
GUARDS!
OFF WITH THEIR HEADS!

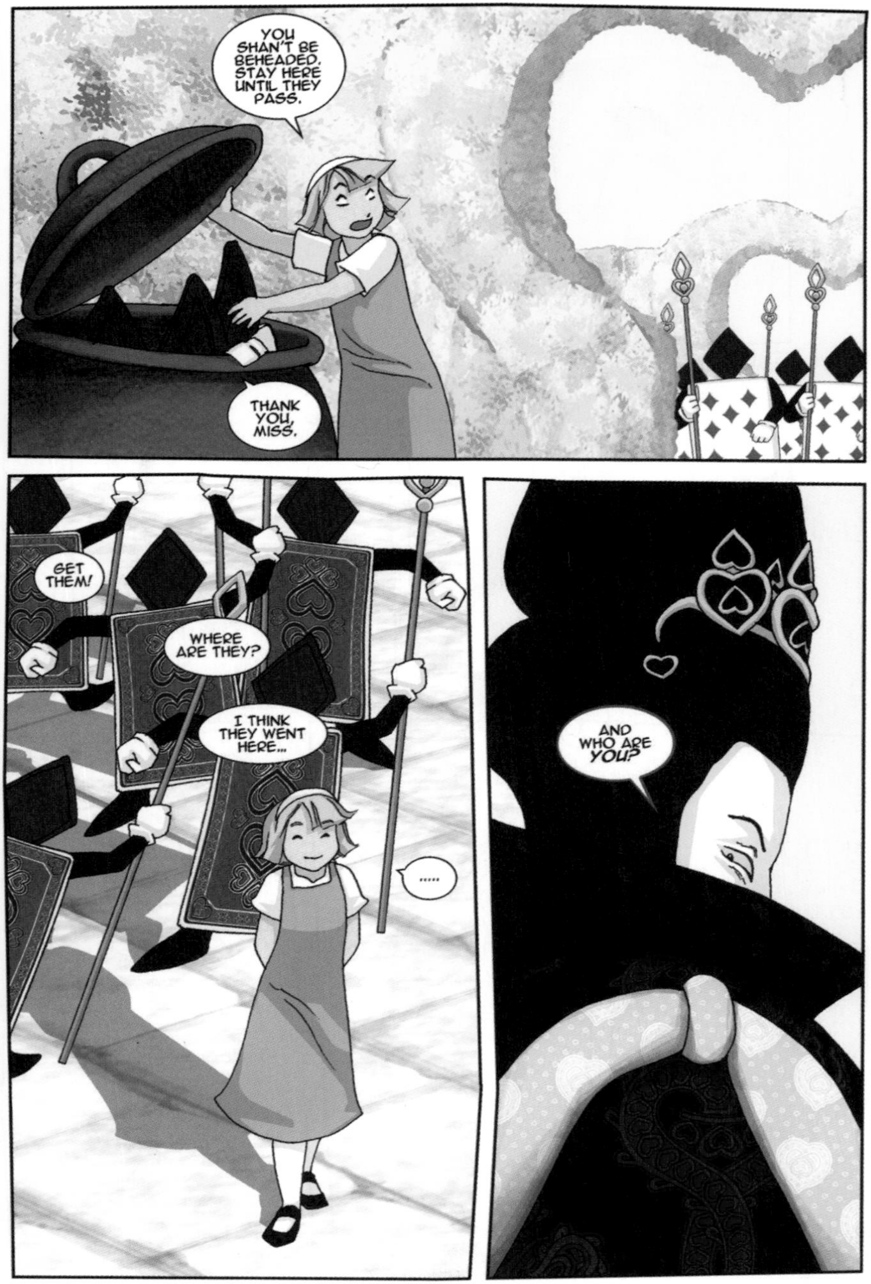
YOU SHAN'T BE BEHEADED. STAY HERE UNTIL THEY PASS.
THANK YOU, MISS.
GET THEM!
WHERE ARE THEY?
I THINK THEY WENT HERE...
.....
AND WHO ARE *YOU?*

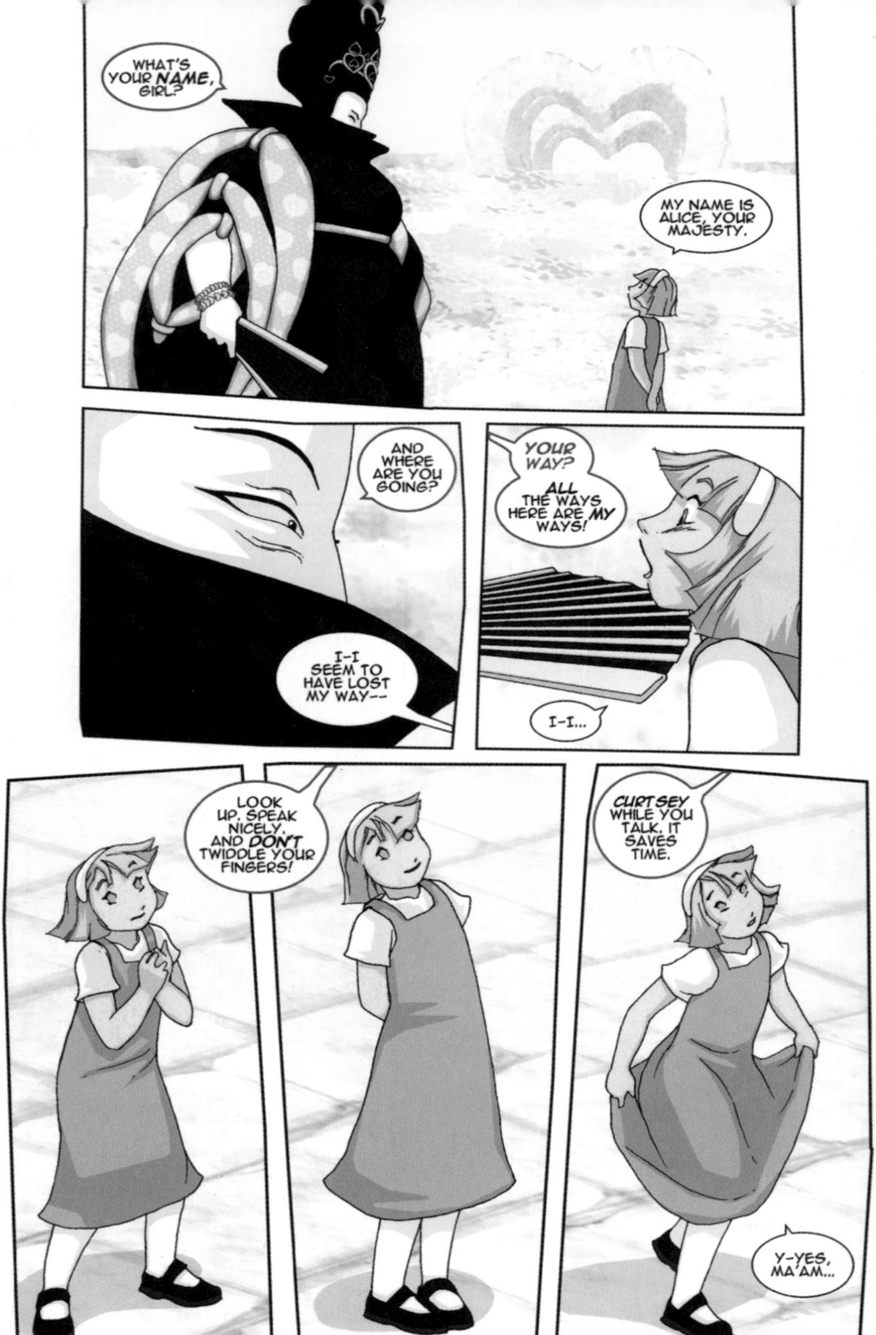
WHAT'S YOUR NAME, GIRL?
MY NAME IS ALICE, YOUR MAJESTY.
AND WHERE ARE YOU GOING?
I-I SEEM TO HAVE LOST MY WAY--
YOUR WAY?
ALL THE WAYS HERE ARE MY WAYS!
I-I...
LOOK UP. SPEAK NICELY. AND DON'T TWIDDLE YOUR FINGERS!
CURTSEY WHILE YOU TALK. IT SAVES TIME.
Y-YES, MA'AM...

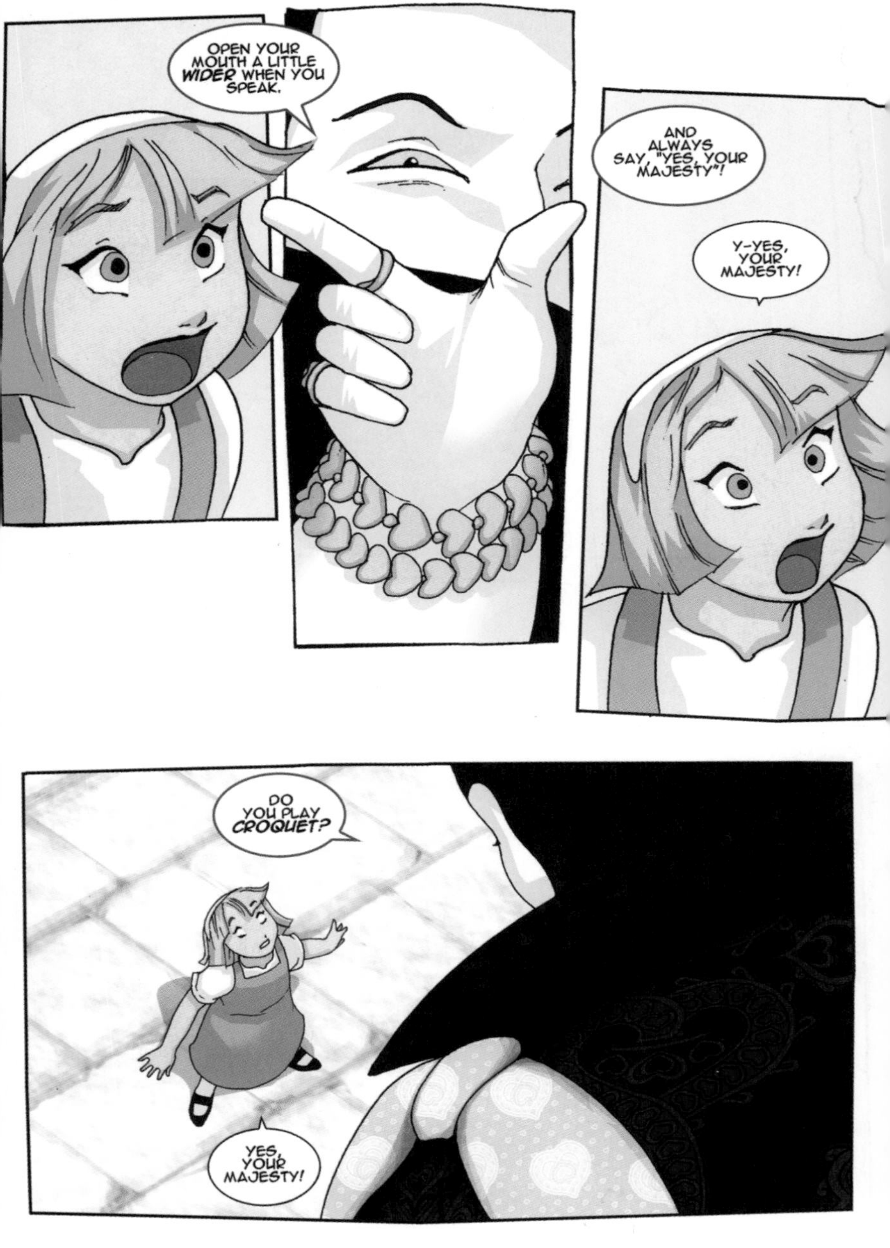
OPEN YOUR MOUTH A LITTLE WIDER WHEN YOU SPEAK.
AND ALWAYS SAY, "YES, YOUR MAJESTY"!
Y-YES, YOUR MAJESTY!
DO YOU PLAY CROQUET?
YES, YOUR MAJESTY!

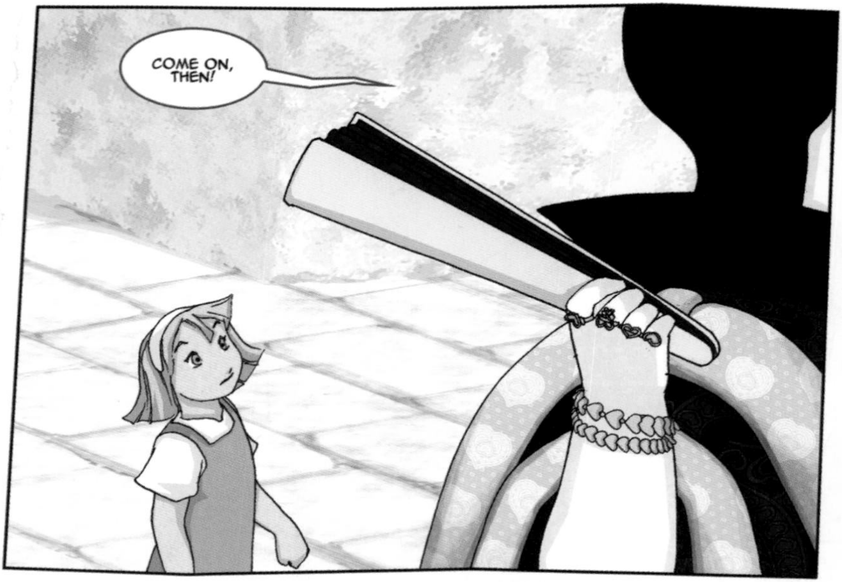
COME ON, THEN!

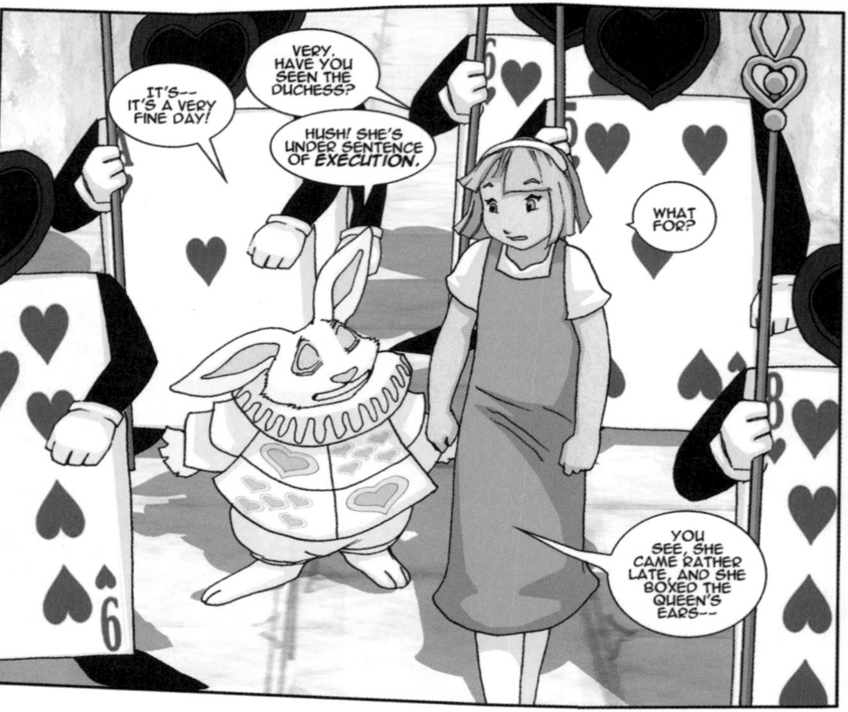
IT'S-- IT'S A VERY FINE DAY!
VERY. HAVE YOU SEEN THE DUCHESS?
HUSH! SHE'S UNDER SENTENCE OF EXECUTION.
WHAT FOR?
YOU SEE, SHE CAME RATHER LATE, AND SHE BOXED THE QUEEN'S EARS--

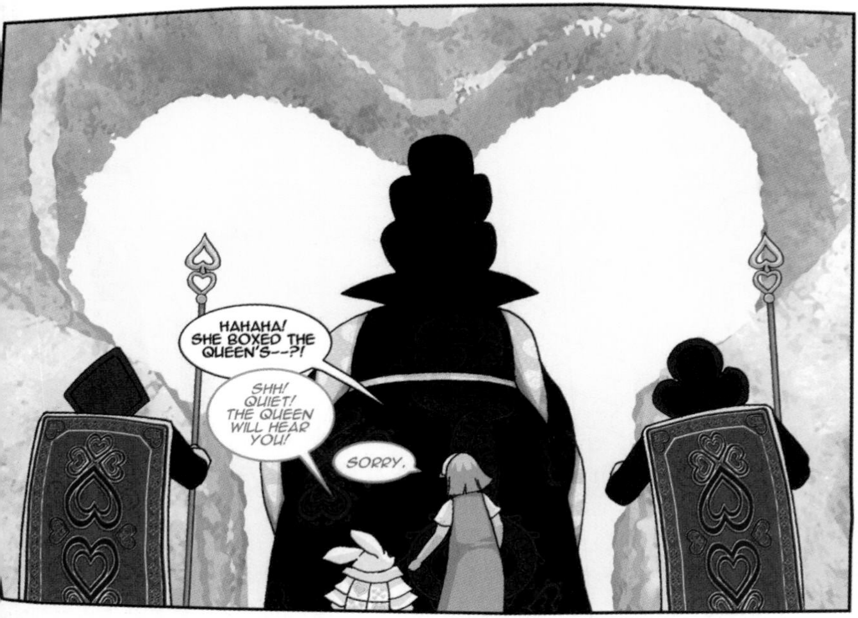
HAHAHA! SHE BOXED THE QUEEN'S--?!
SHH! QUIET! THE QUEEN WILL HEAR YOU!
SORRY.

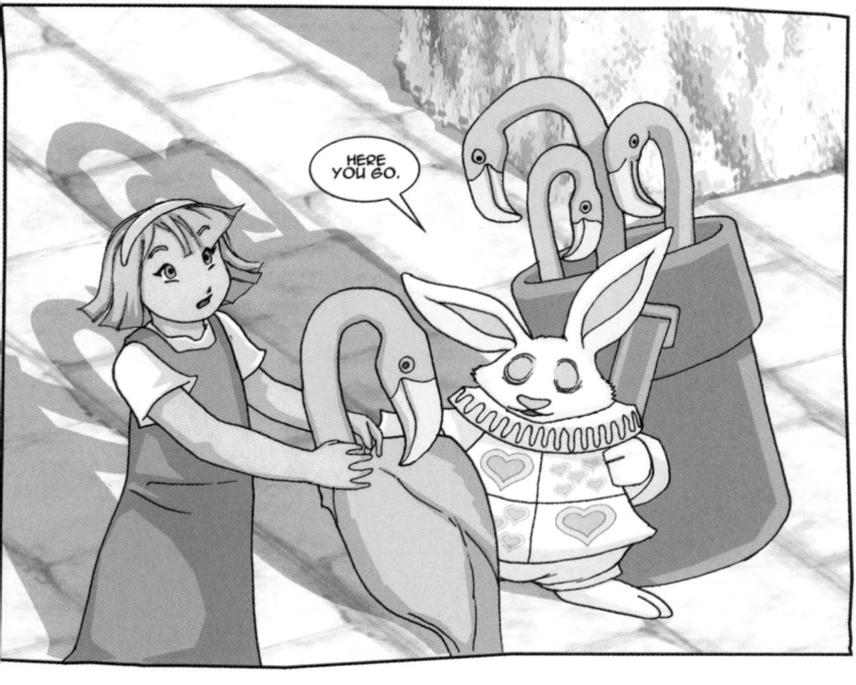
HERE YOU GO.

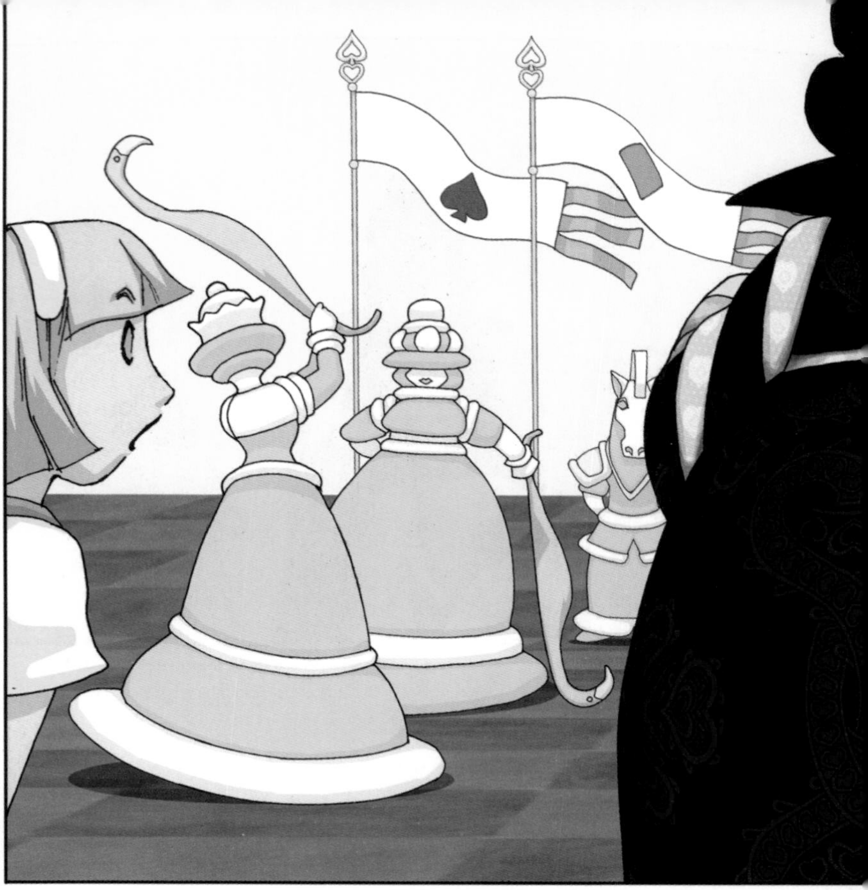

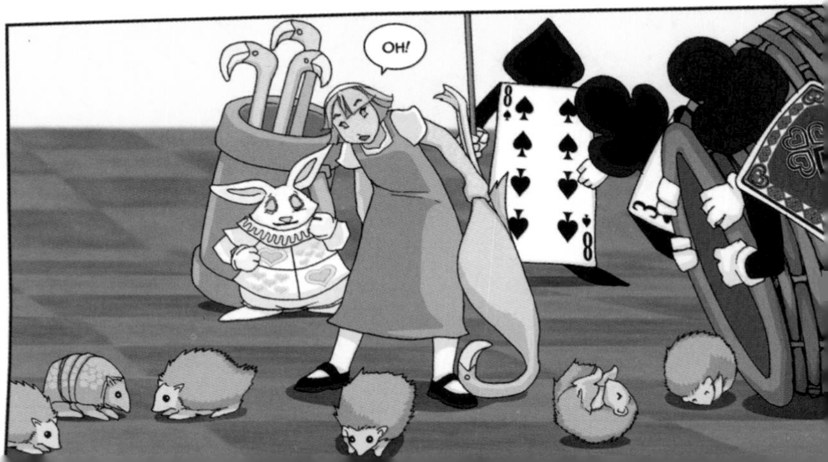
OH!

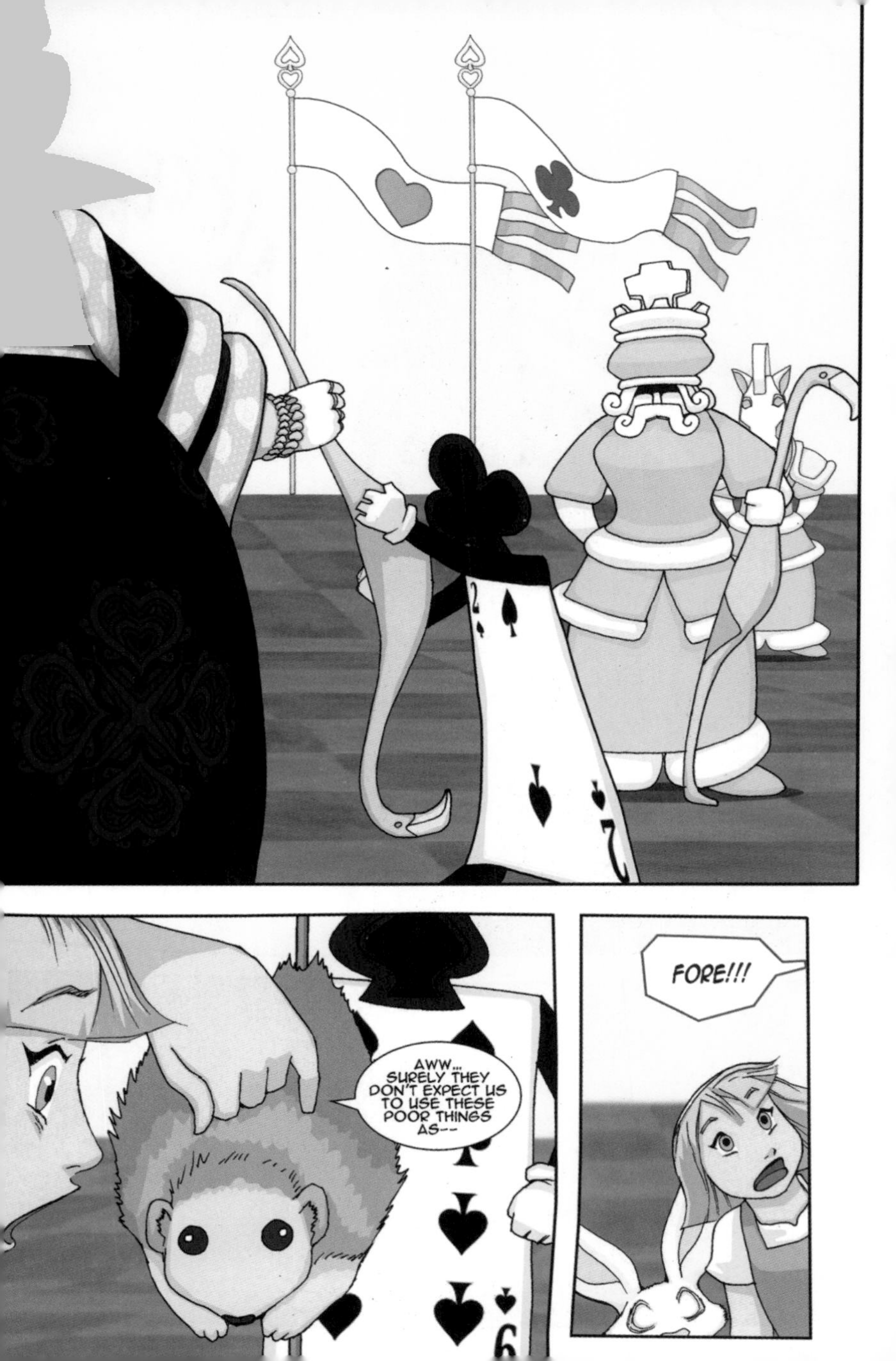
AWW... SURELY THEY DON'T EXPECT US TO USE THESE POOR THINGS AS--
FORE!!!

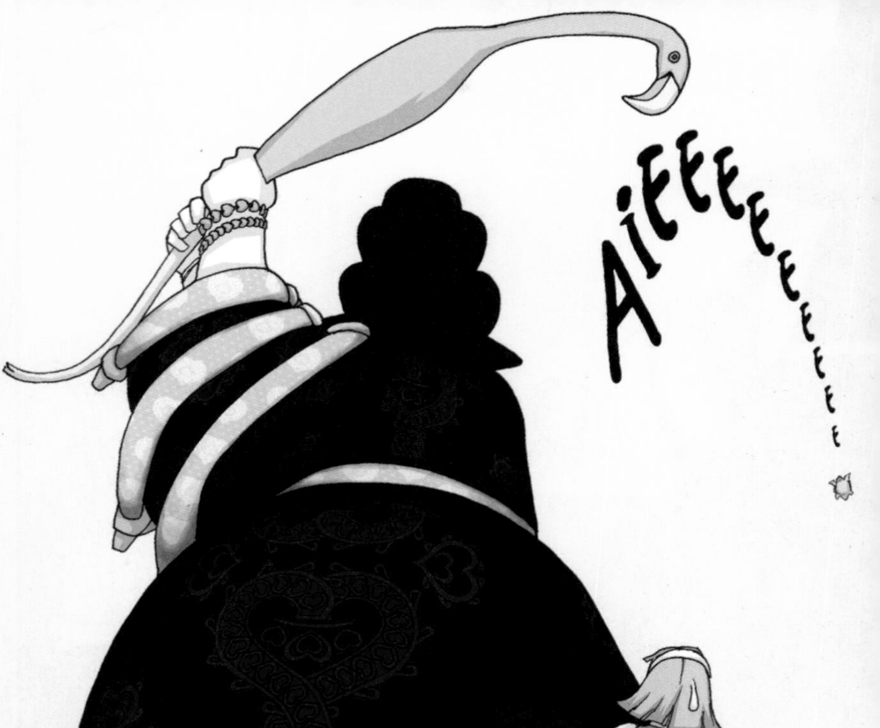
AiEEEEEEEEEE

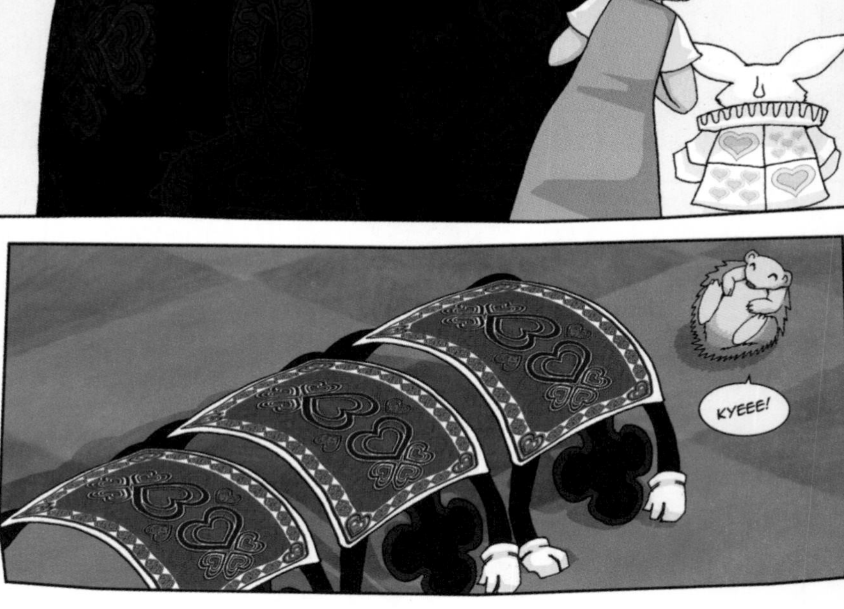
KYEEE!

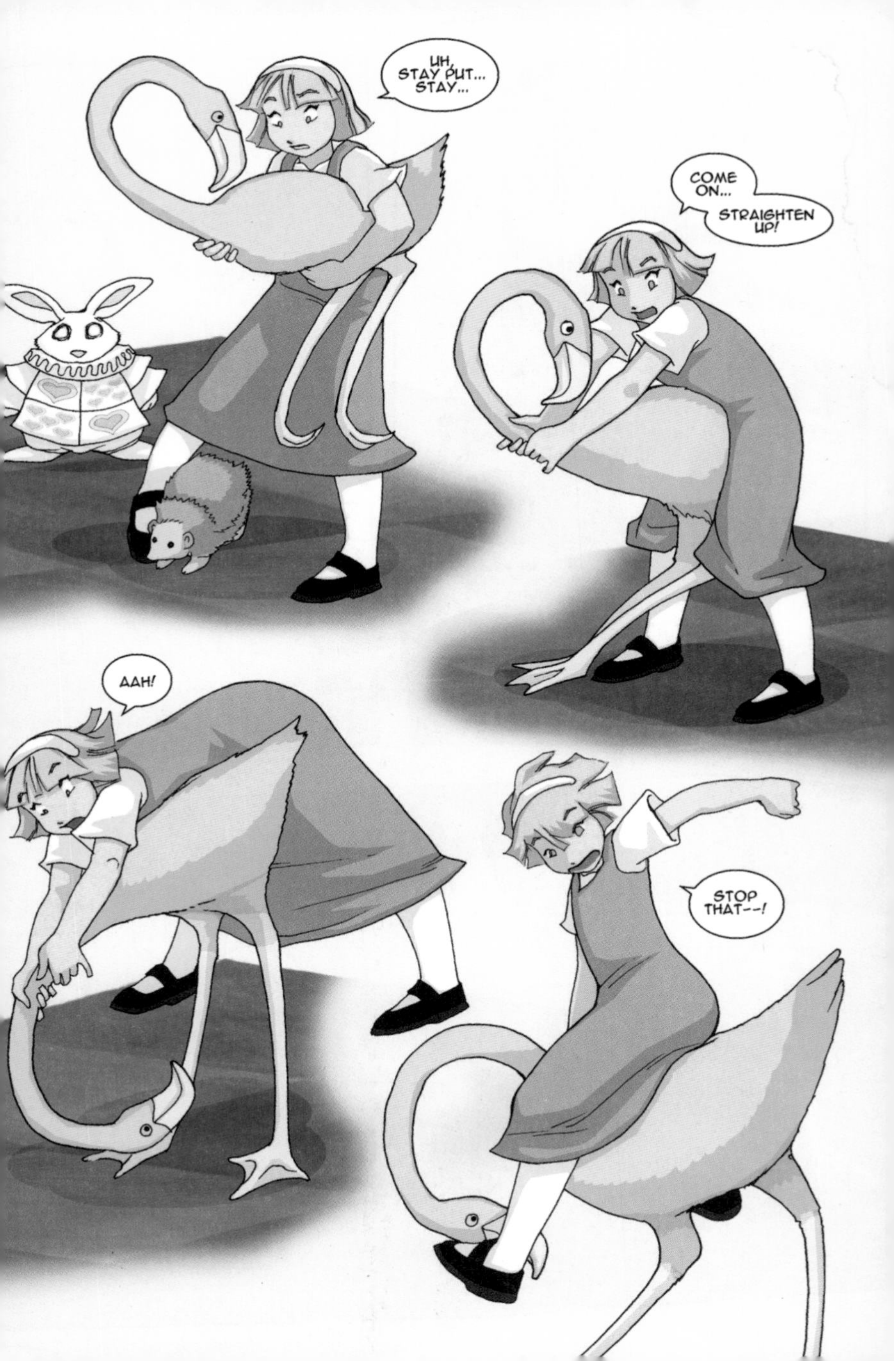
UH, STAY PUT... STAY...
COME ON...
STRAIGHTEN UP!
AAH!
STOP THAT--!

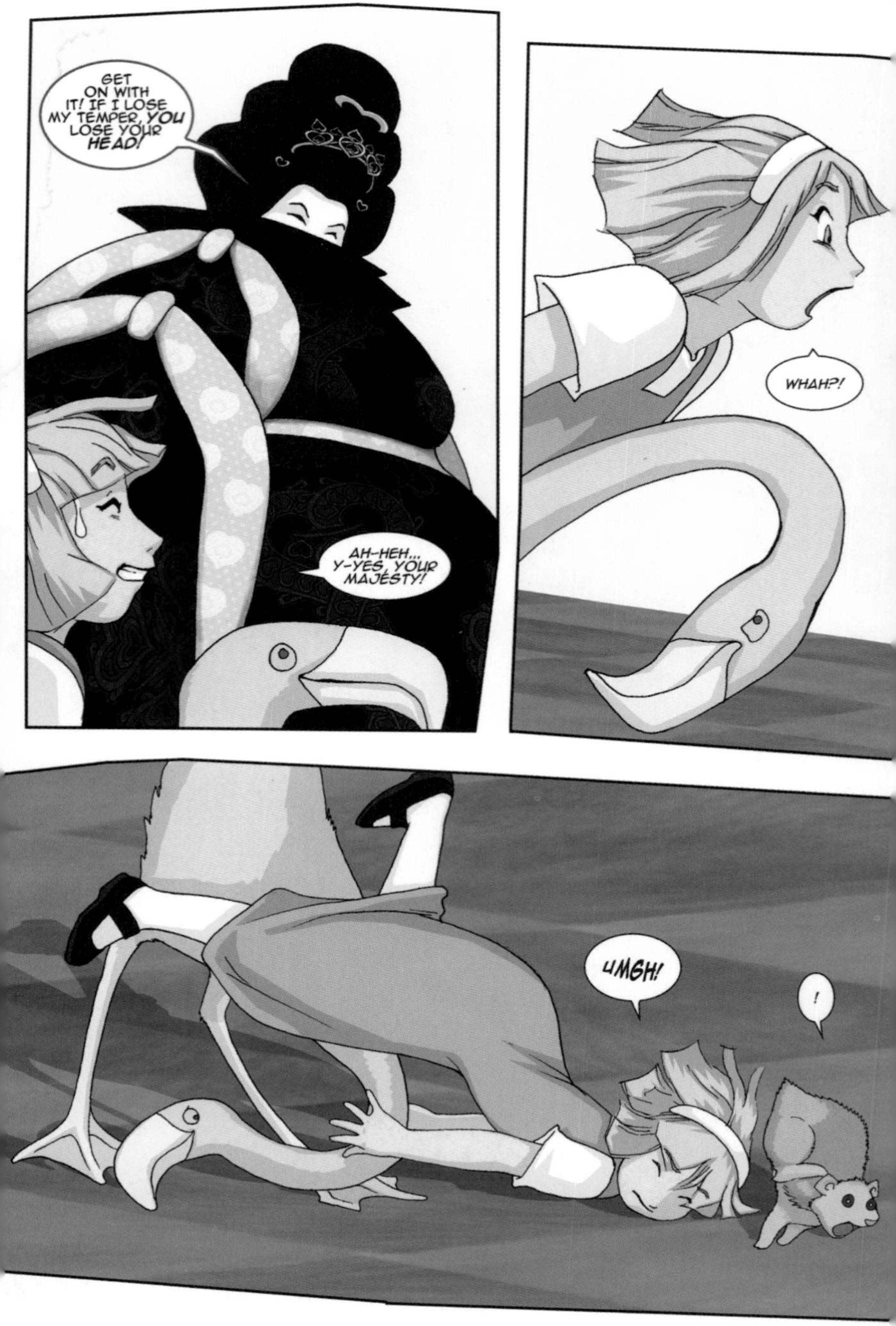
GET ON WITH IT! IF I LOSE MY TEMPER, YOU LOSE YOUR HEAD!
AH-HEH... Y-YES, YOUR MAJESTY!
WHAH?!
UMGH!
!

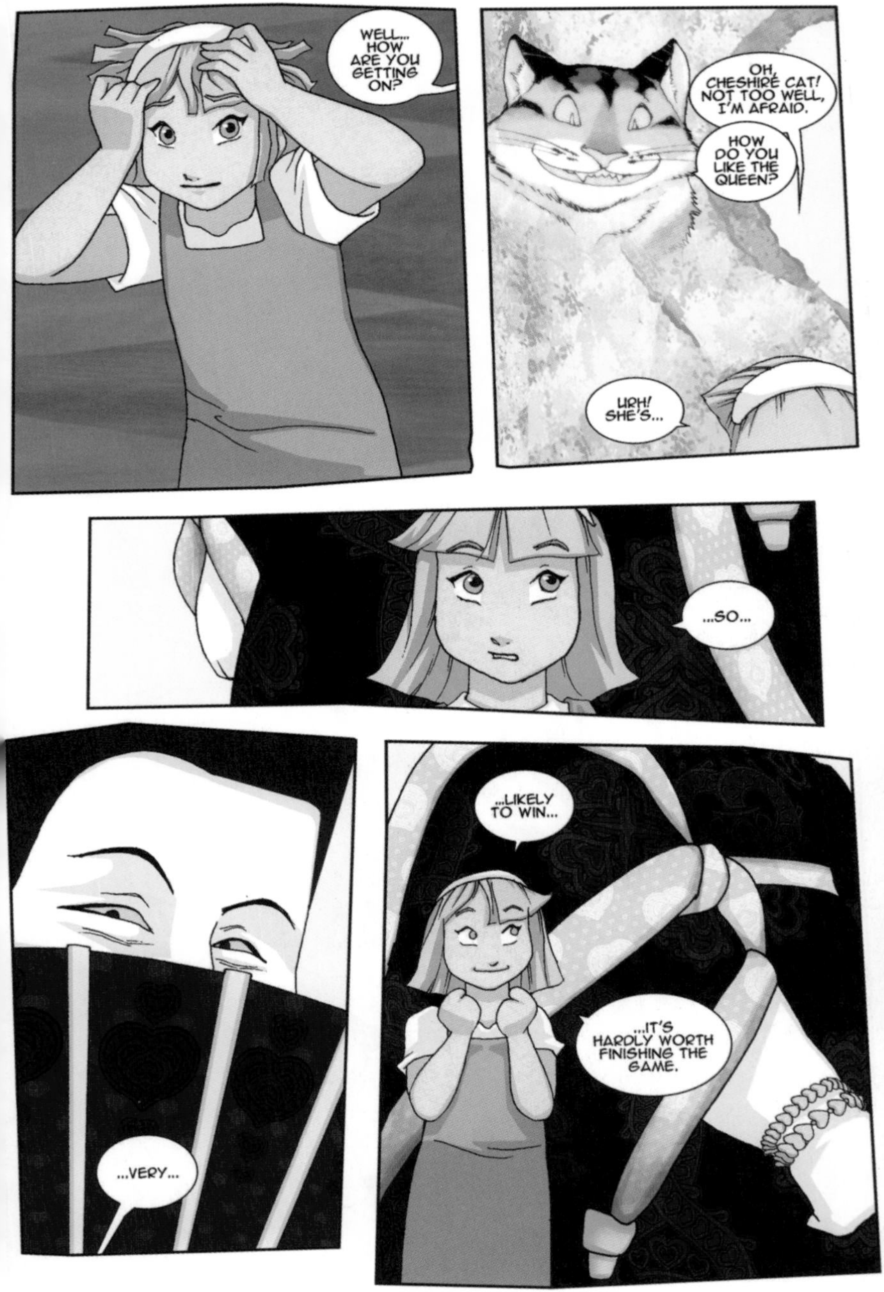

WELL... HOW ARE YOU GETTING ON?
OH, CHESHIRE CAT! NOT TOO WELL, I'M AFRAID.
HOW DO YOU LIKE THE QUEEN?
URH! SHE'S...
...SO...
...VERY...
...LIKELY TO WIN...
...IT'S HARDLY WORTH FINISHING THE GAME.

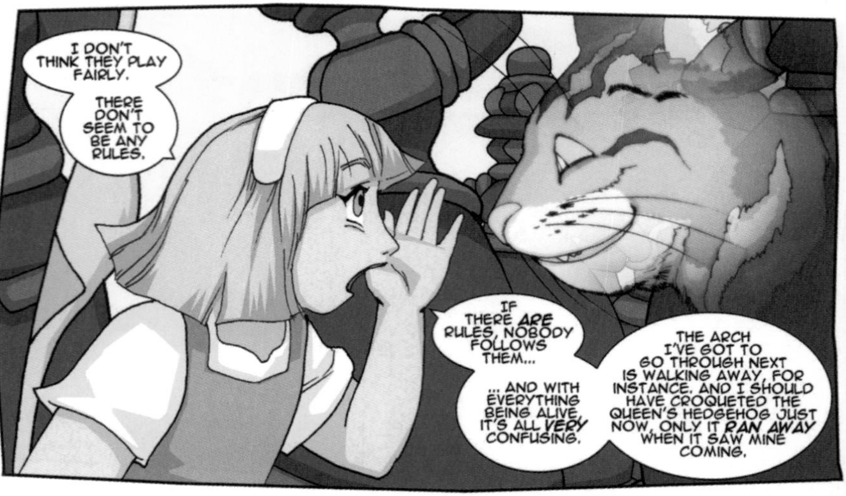
I DON'T THINK THEY PLAY FAIRLY.
THERE DON'T SEEM TO BE ANY RULES.
IF THERE ARE RULES, NOBODY FOLLOWS THEM...
... AND WITH EVERYTHING BEING ALIVE, IT'S ALL VERY CONFUSING.
THE ARCH I'VE GOT TO GO THROUGH NEXT IS WALKING AWAY, FOR INSTANCE. AND I SHOULD HAVE CROQUETED THE QUEEN'S HEDGEHOG JUST NOW, ONLY IT RAN AWAY WHEN IT SAW MINE COMING.

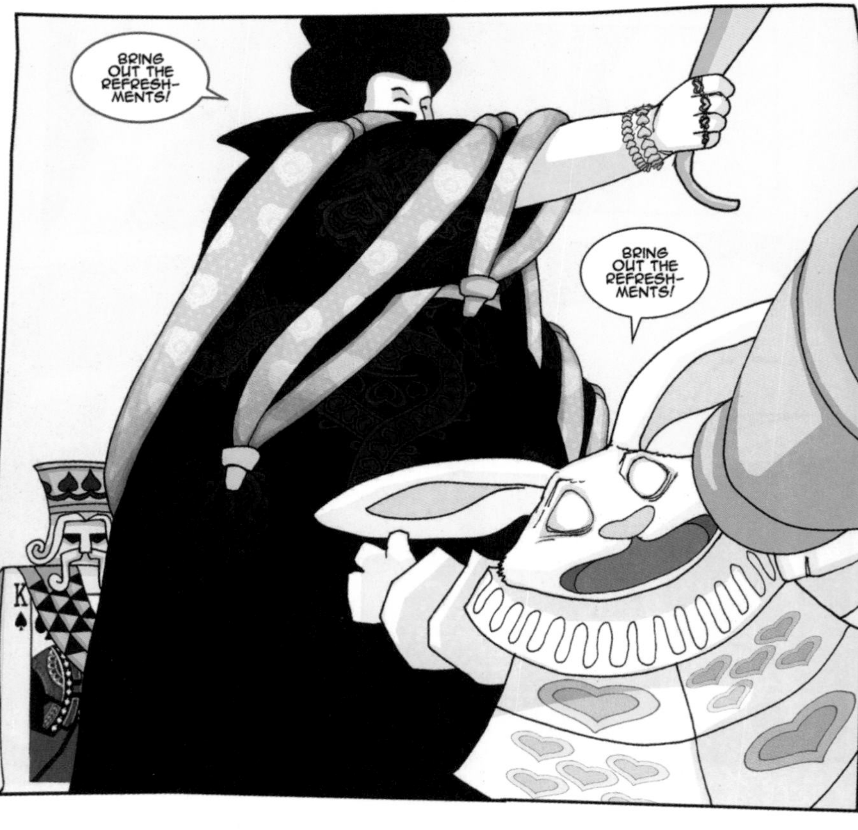
BRING OUT THE REFRESH-MENTS!
BRING OUT THE REFRESH-MENTS!

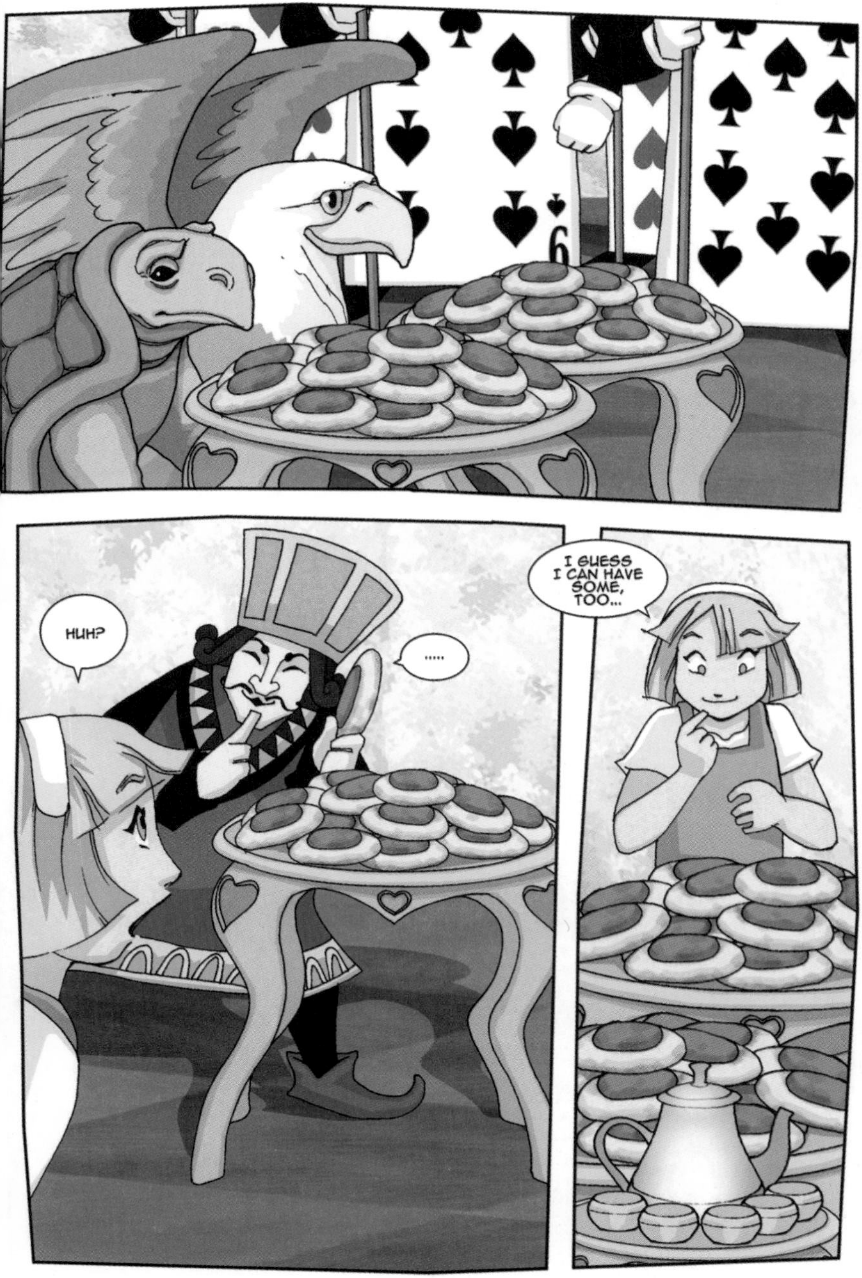
HUH?
.....
I GUESS I CAN HAVE SOME, TOO...

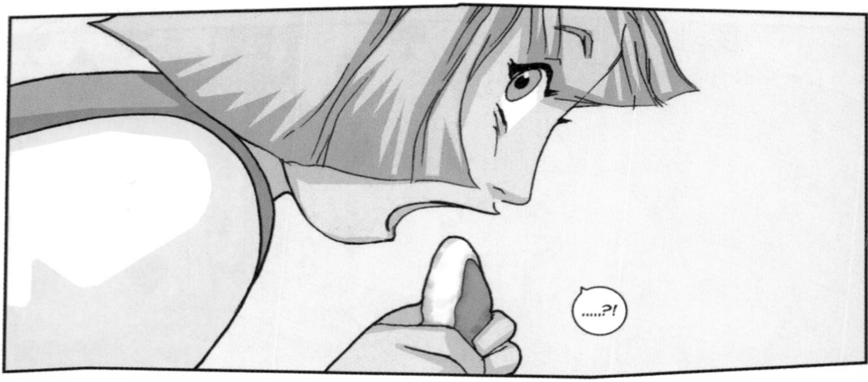
.....?!

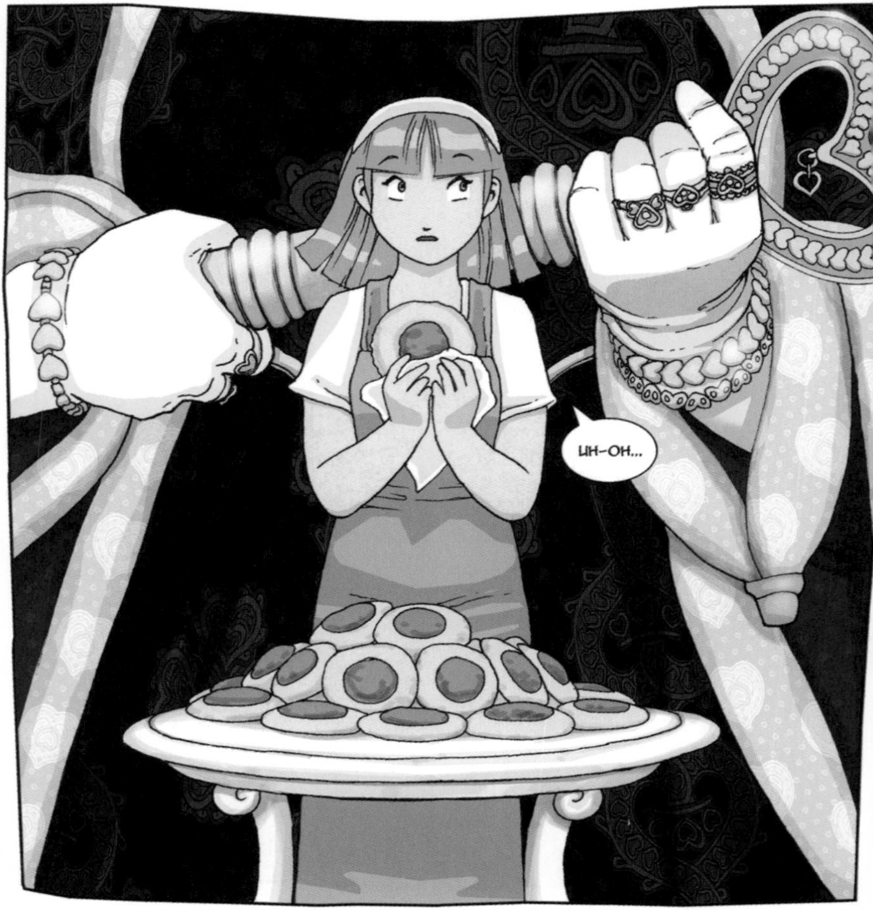
UH-OH...

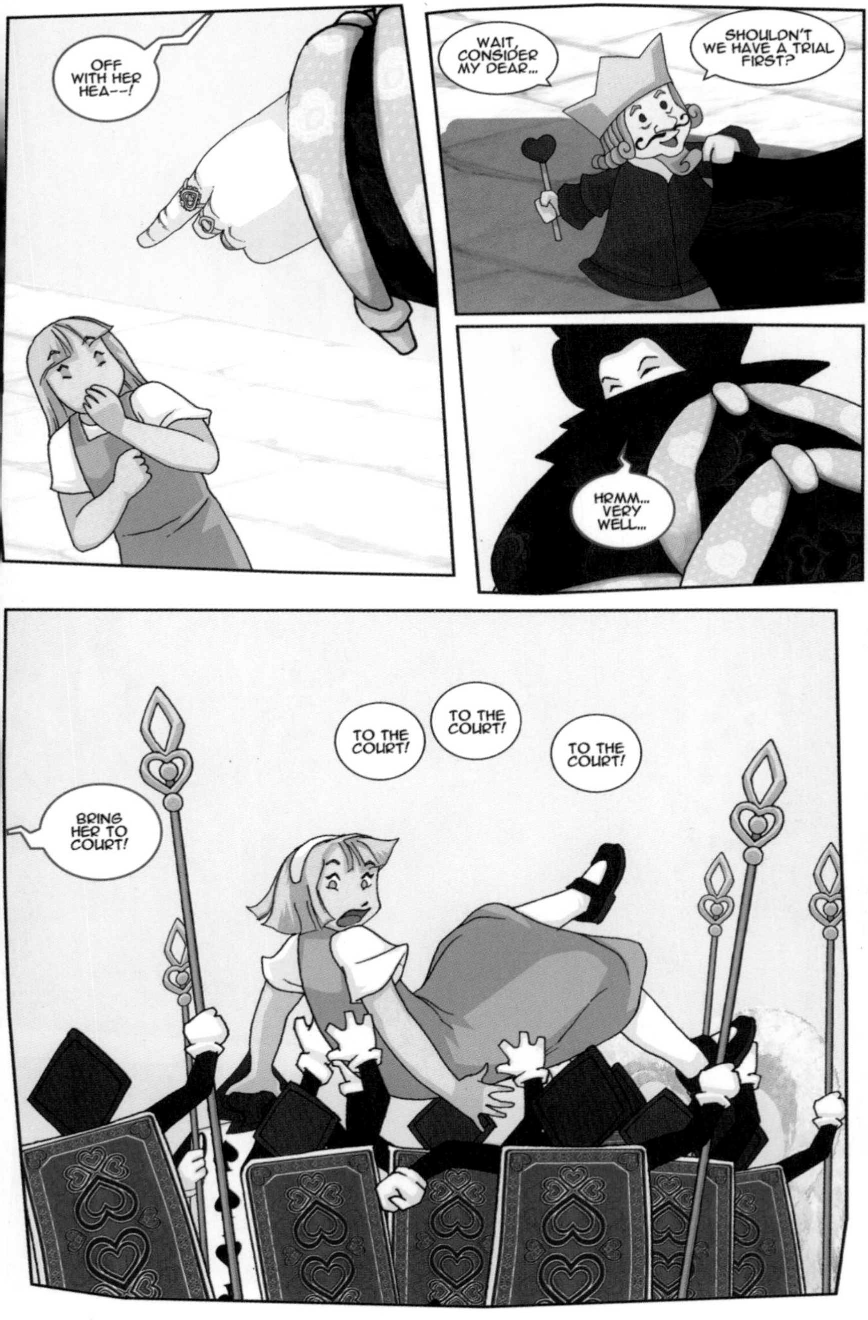
OFF WITH HER HEA--!
WAIT, CONSIDER MY DEAR...
SHOULDN'T WE HAVE A TRIAL FIRST?
HRMM... VERY WELL...
BRING HER TO COURT!
TO THE COURT!
TO THE COURT!
TO THE COURT!

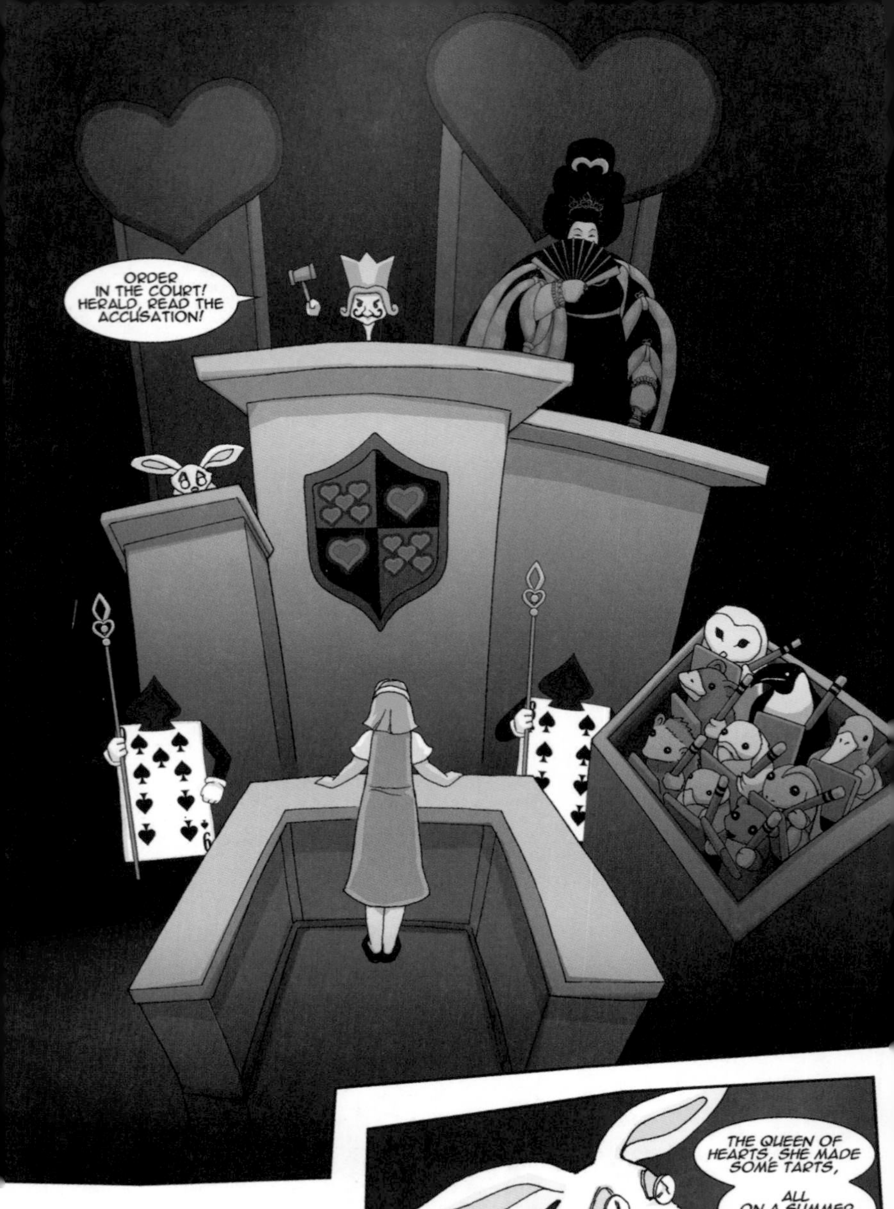
ORDER IN THE COURT! HERALD, READ THE ACCUSATION!

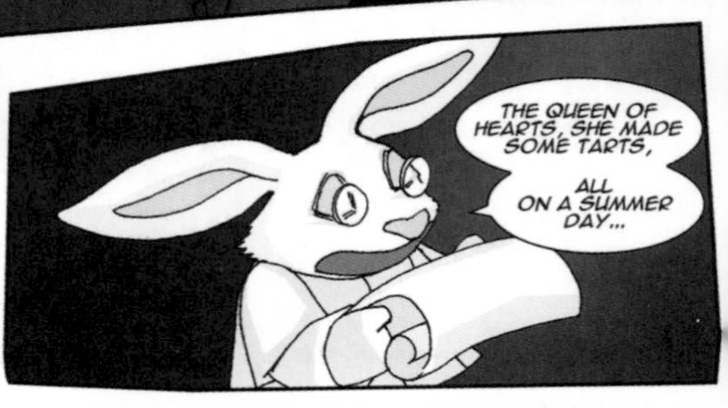
THE QUEEN OF HEARTS, SHE MADE SOME TARTS,
ALL ON A SUMMER DAY...

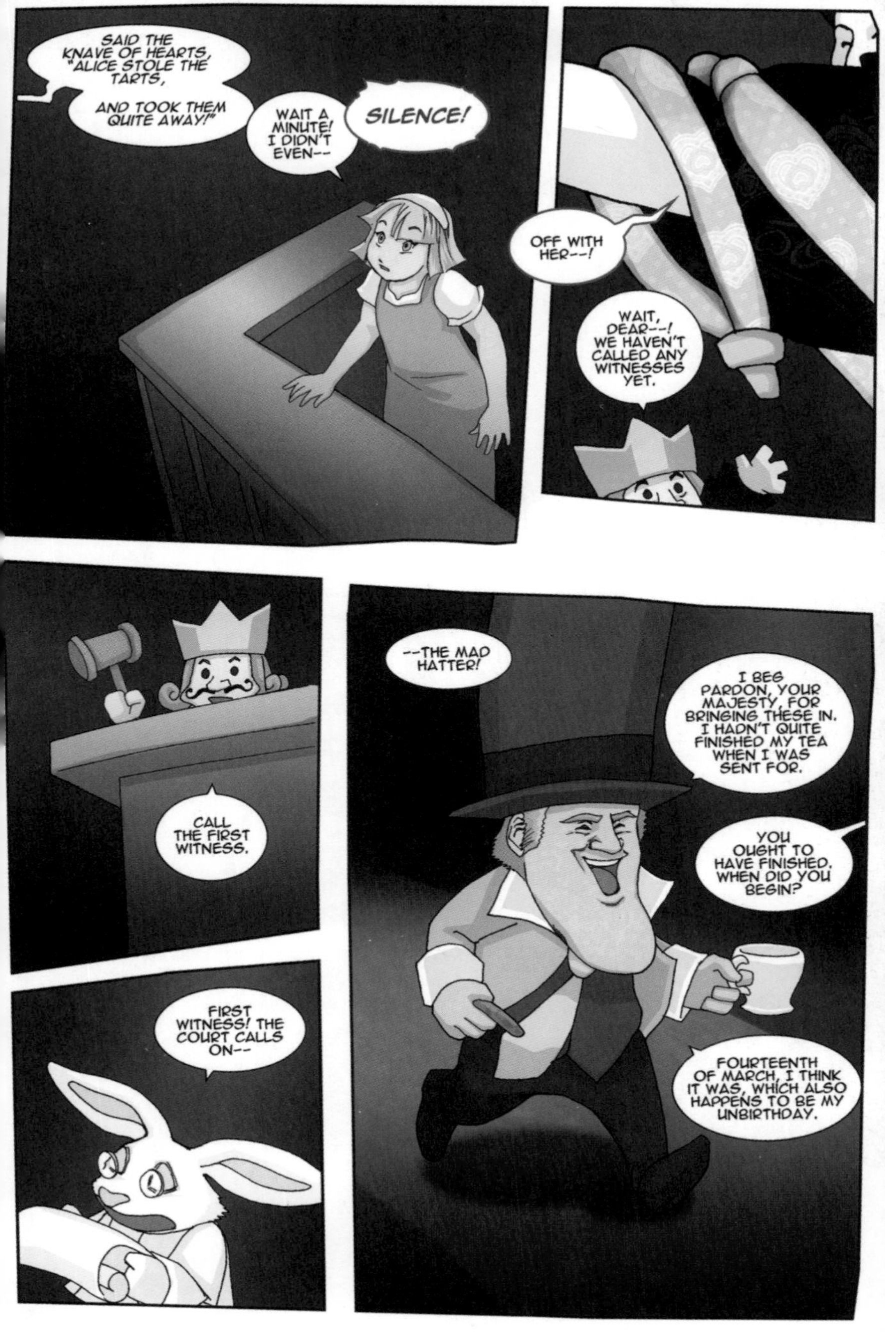
SAID THE KNAVE OF HEARTS, "ALICE STOLE THE TARTS,
AND TOOK THEM QUITE AWAY!"
WAIT A MINUTE! I DIDN'T EVEN--
SILENCE!
OFF WITH HER--!
WAIT, DEAR--! WE HAVEN'T CALLED ANY WITNESSES YET.
CALL THE FIRST WITNESS.
FIRST WITNESS! THE COURT CALLS ON--
--THE MAD HATTER!
I BEG PARDON, YOUR MAJESTY, FOR BRINGING THESE IN. I HADN'T QUITE FINISHED MY TEA WHEN I WAS SENT FOR.
YOU OUGHT TO HAVE FINISHED. WHEN DID YOU BEGIN?
FOURTEENTH OF MARCH, I THINK IT WAS, WHICH ALSO HAPPENS TO BE MY UNBIRTHDAY.

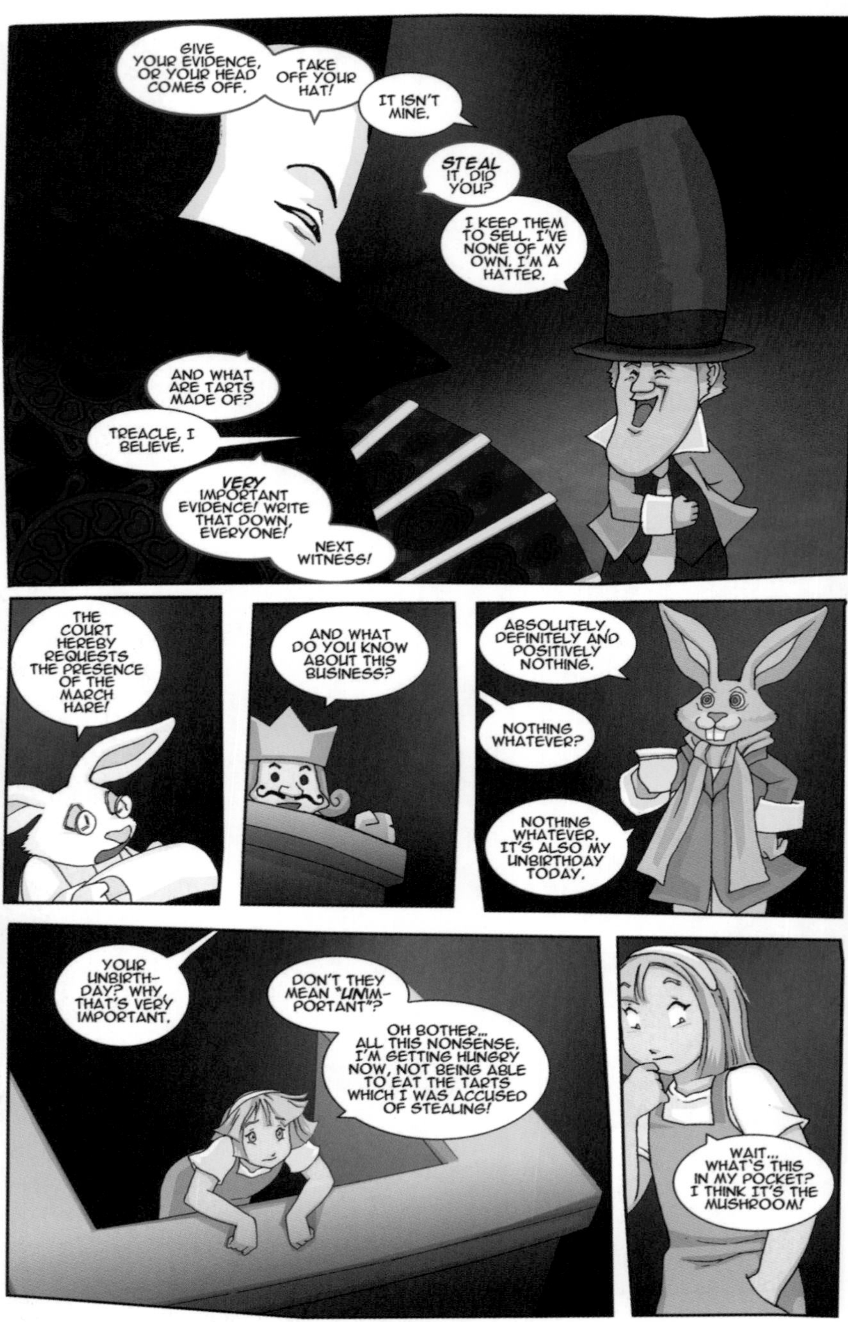
GIVE YOUR EVIDENCE, OR YOUR HEAD COMES OFF.
TAKE OFF YOUR HAT!
IT ISN'T MINE.
STEAL IT, DID YOU?
I KEEP THEM TO SELL. I'VE NONE OF MY OWN. I'M A HATTER.
AND WHAT ARE TARTS MADE OF?
TREACLE, I BELIEVE.
VERY IMPORTANT EVIDENCE! WRITE THAT DOWN, EVERYONE!
NEXT WITNESS!
THE COURT HEREBY REQUESTS THE PRESENCE OF THE MARCH HARE!
AND WHAT DO YOU KNOW ABOUT THIS BUSINESS?
ABSOLUTELY, DEFINITELY AND POSITIVELY NOTHING.
NOTHING WHATEVER?
NOTHING WHATEVER. IT'S ALSO MY UNBIRTHDAY TODAY.
YOUR UNBIRTH-DAY? WHY, THAT'S VERY IMPORTANT.
DON'T THEY MEAN "UNIM-PORTANT"?
OH BOTHER... ALL THIS NONSENSE. I'M GETTING HUNGRY NOW, NOT BEING ABLE TO EAT THE TARTS WHICH I WAS ACCUSED OF STEALING!
WAIT... WHAT'S THIS IN MY POCKET? I THINK IT'S THE MUSHROOM!

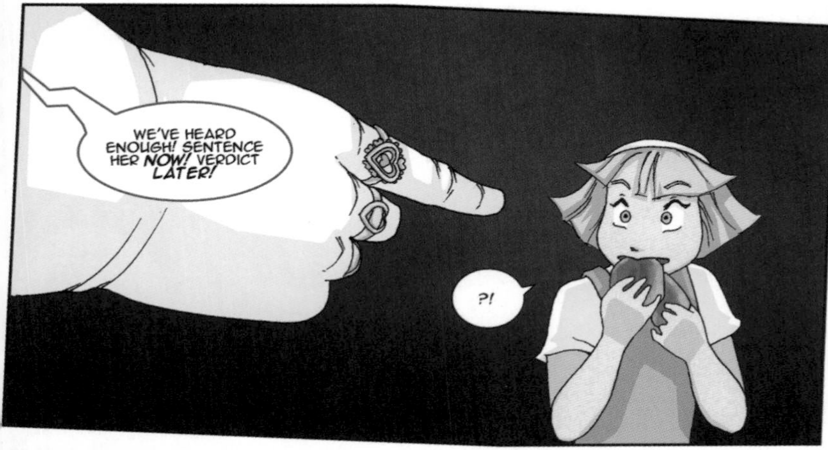
WE'VE HEARD ENOUGH! SENTENCE HER NOW! VERDICT LATER!
?!

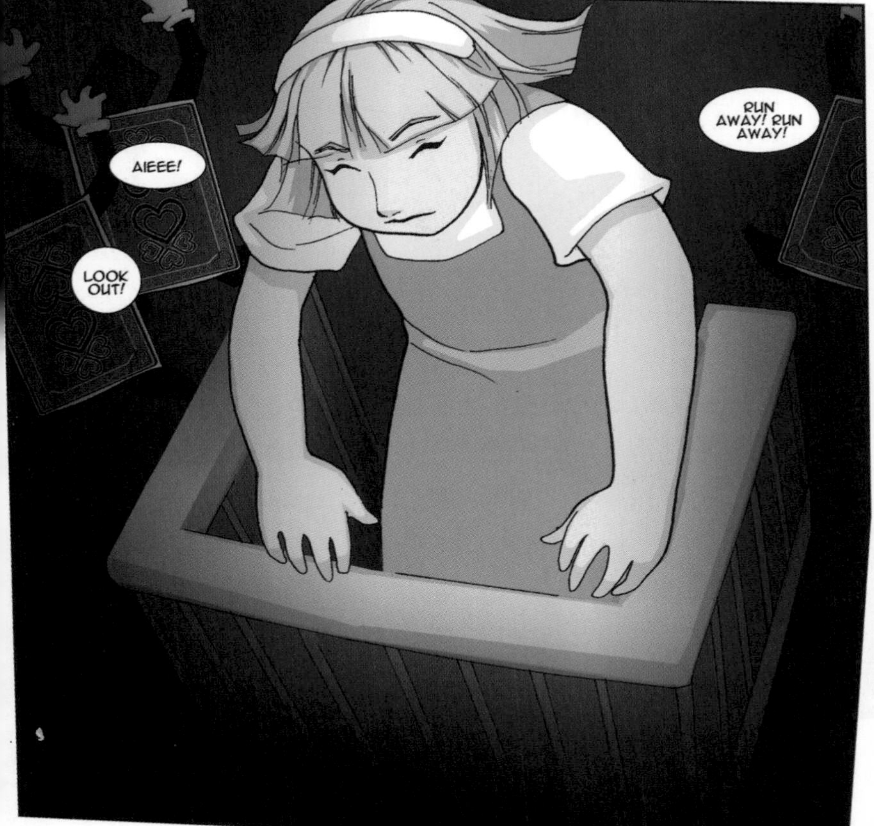
RUN AWAY! RUN AWAY!
AIEEE!
LOOK OUT!

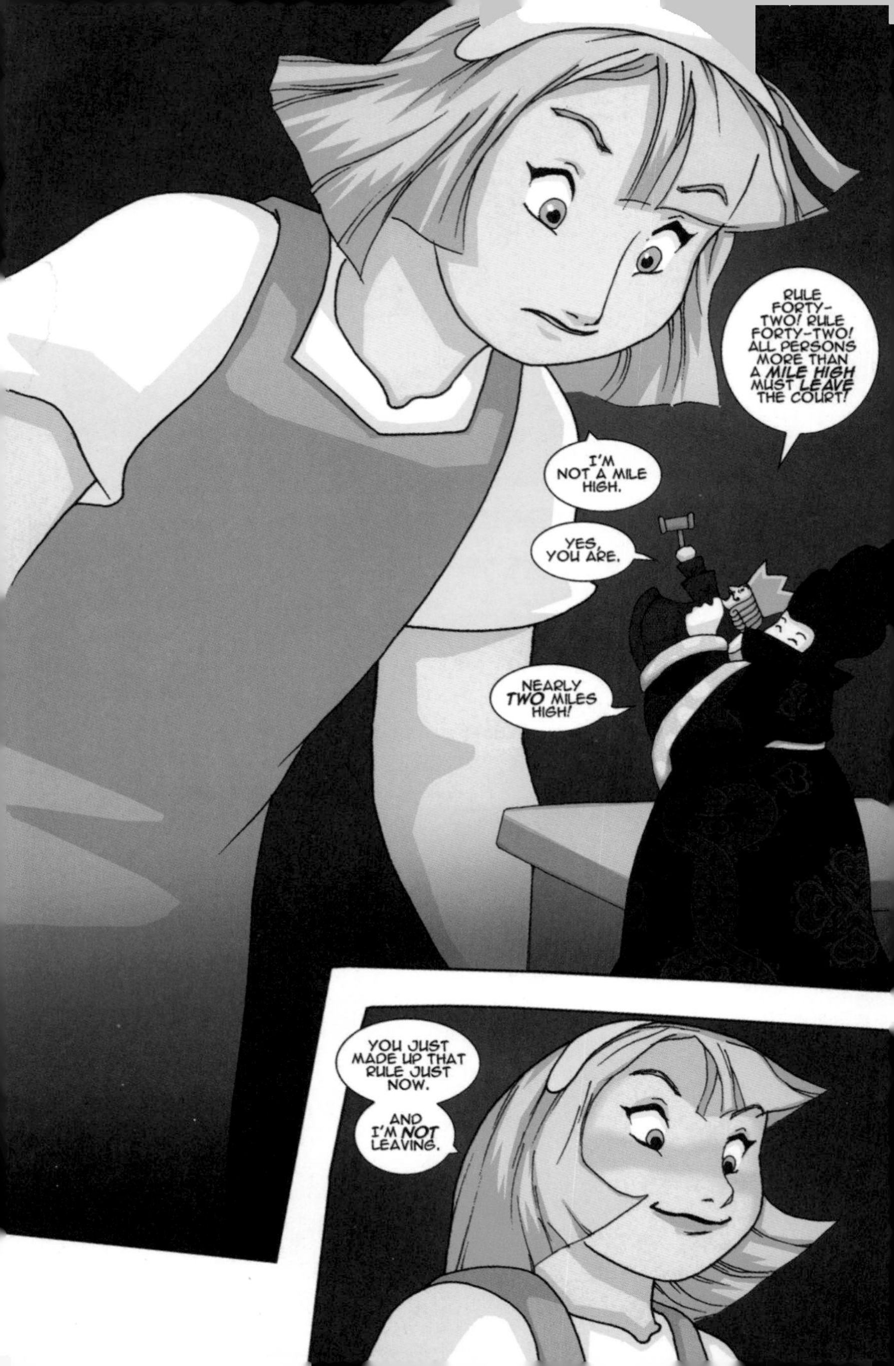
RULE FORTY-TWO! RULE FORTY-TWO! ALL PERSONS MORE THAN A MILE HIGH MUST LEAVE THE COURT!
I'M NOT A MILE HIGH.
YES, YOU ARE.
NEARLY TWO MILES HIGH!
YOU JUST MADE UP THAT RULE JUST NOW.
AND I'M NOT LEAVING.

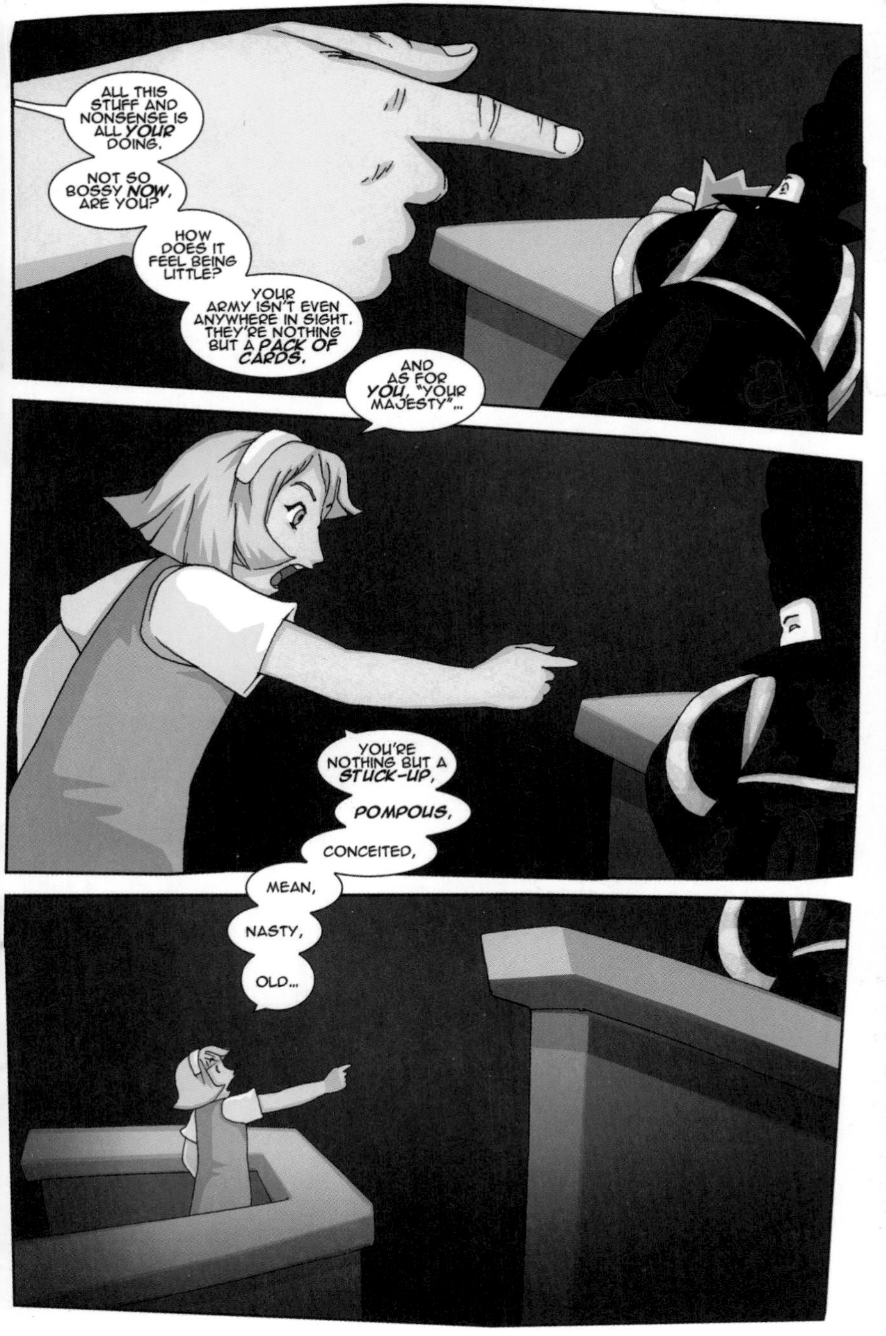
ALL THIS STUFF AND NONSENSE IS ALL *YOUR* DOING.
NOT SO BOSSY *NOW*, ARE YOU?
HOW DOES IT FEEL BEING LITTLE?
YOUR ARMY ISN'T EVEN ANYWHERE IN SIGHT. THEY'RE NOTHING BUT A *PACK OF CARDS*.
AND AS FOR *YOU*, "YOUR MAJESTY"...
YOU'RE NOTHING BUT A *STUCK-UP*,
POMPOUS,
CONCEITED,
MEAN,
NASTY,
OLD...

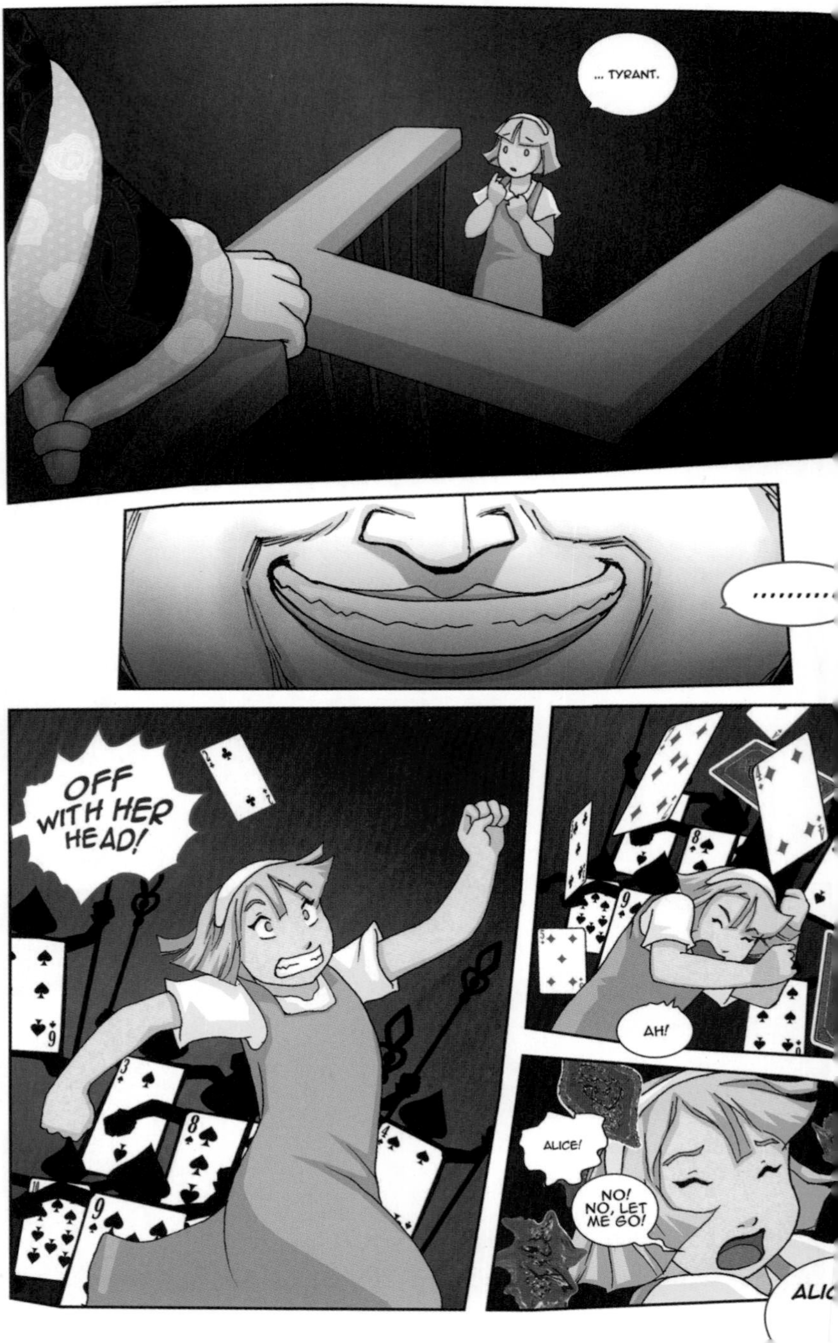

... TYRANT.
....
OFF WITH HER HEAD!
AH!
ALICE!
NO! NO, LET ME GO!

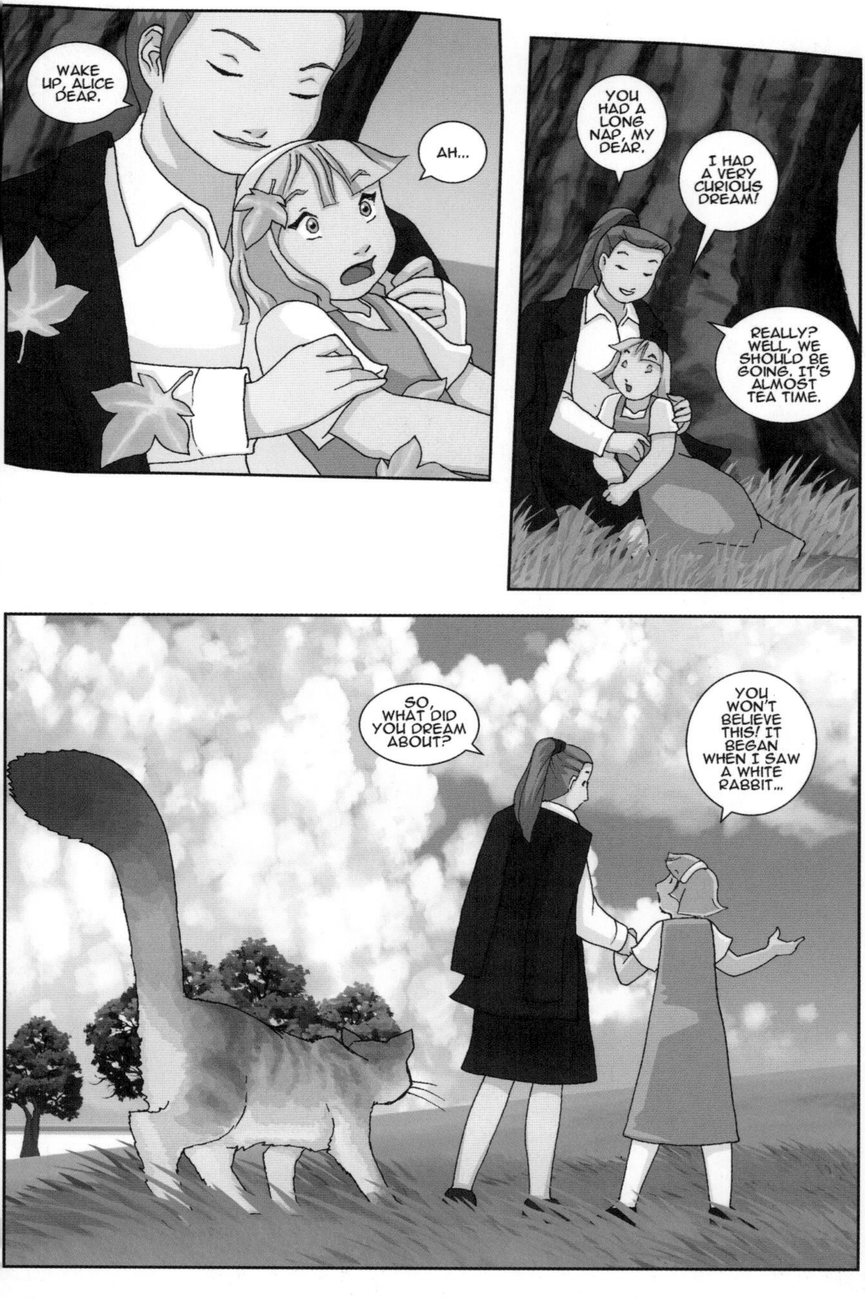
WAKE UP, ALICE DEAR.
AH...
YOU HAD A LONG NAP, MY DEAR.
I HAD A VERY CURIOUS DREAM!
REALLY? WELL, WE SHOULD BE GOING. IT'S ALMOST TEA TIME.
SO, WHAT DID YOU DREAM ABOUT?
YOU WON'T BELIEVE THIS! IT BEGAN WHEN I SAW A WHITE RABBIT...

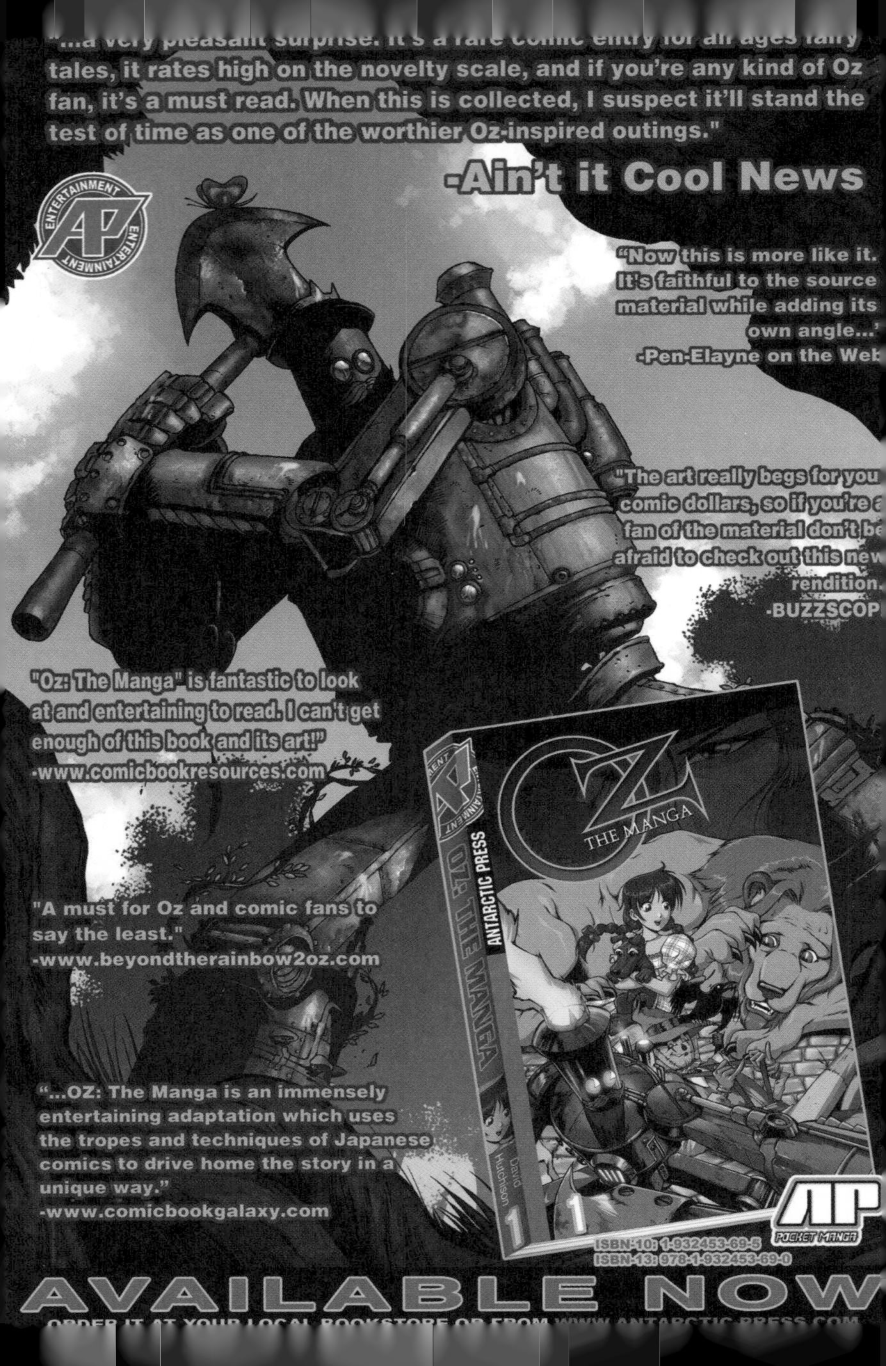
"...a very pleasant surprise. It's a rare comic entry for all ages fairy tales, it rates high on the novelty scale, and if you're any kind of Oz fan, it's a must read. When this is collected, I suspect it'll stand the test of time as one of the worthier Oz-inspired outings."
-Ain't it Cool News
ENTERTAINMENT AP ENTERTAINMENT
"Now this is more like it. It's faithful to the source material while adding its own angle..."
-Pen-Elayne on the Web
"The art really begs for you comic dollars, so if you're a fan of the material don't be afraid to check out this new rendition."
-BUZZSCOPE
"Oz: The Manga" is fantastic to look at and entertaining to read. I can't get enough of this book and its art!"
-www.comicbookresources.com
"A must for Oz and comic fans to say the least."
-www.beyondtherainbow2oz.com
"...OZ: The Manga is an immensely entertaining adaptation which uses the tropes and techniques of Japanese comics to drive home the story in a unique way."
-www.comicbookgalaxy.com
OZ THE MANGA
ANTARCTIC PRESS
OZ: THE MANGA
David Hutchison
1
AP POCKET MANGA
ISBN-10: 1-932453-69-5
ISBN-13: 978-1-932453-69-0
AVAILABLE NOW
ORDER IT AT YOUR LOCAL BOOKSTORE OR FROM WWW.ANTARCTIC-PRESS.COM